FIREFIGHTER EXAM

LEARNINGEXPRESS

NEW YORK

Library of Congress Cataloging-in-Publication Data

Firefighter exam.

    p.   cm.

    ISBN 1-57685-294-6 (pbk.)

    1. Fire extinction—Examinations—Study guides.   2. Fire extinction—United States—Examinations, questions, etc.   3. Fire extinction—Vocational guidance.

    TH9157 F525 2000

    628.9'25'086—dc21

00-027484

Printed in the United States of America

9 8 7 6 5 4 3 2

First Edition

ISBN 1-57685-294-6

Regarding the Information in this Book

We attempt to verify the information presented in our books prior to publication. It is always a good idea, however, to double-check such important information as minimum requirements, application and testing procedures, and deadlines with your local firefighting agency, as such information can change from time to time.

For Further Information

For information on LearningExpress, other LearningExpress products, or bulk sales, please write to us at:

    LearningExpress®

    900 Broadway

    Suite 604

    New York, NY 10003

    www.LearnX.com

CONTENTS

LIST OF CONTRIBUTORS

The following individuals contributed to the content of this book.

American Fire Services is a Connecticut-based research organization focused on public fire protection in the United States and Canada.

Elizabeth Chesla is an adult educator and curriculum developer at Polytechnic University in New York who has also taught reading and writing at New York University School of Continuing Education and New York Institute of Technology in New York City.

Edcon Associates, based in New York City and New Jersey, has been conducting workshops and seminars to prepare candidates for entry-level and promotional exams in fire service for over 20 years.

Judith N. Meyers is director of the Two Together Tutorial Program of the Jewish Child Care Association in New York City and formerly Adult Basic Education Practitioner at City University New York.

Judith F. Olson, M.A., is chairperson of the language arts department at Valley High School in West Des Moines, Iowa, where she also conducts test preparation workshops.

Judith Robinovitz is an independent educational consultant and director of Score At the Top, a comprehensive test preparation program in Vero Beach, Florida.

Steven M. Truitt, P.E., is a civil engineer and technical writer specializing in environmental engineering and pollution control in Golden, Colorado.

HOW TO USE
THIS BOOK

So you want to be a firefighter! It's no wonder—the job pays well, you get good benefits, and the work is certainly interesting. But the road to fulfilling your dream isn't lined with gold; you have a rigorous selection process ahead of you. Competition is tough, and you'll need a top score on the written exam to be an attractive candidate. This book is here to help. Through numerous practice exams and instructional chapters, it will give you the practice and review you need to pass with flying colors. You'll also learn all about the different stages of the selection process.

You'll want to begin your preparation by reading Chapter 1, "What Firefighters Really Do." This chapter gives a summary of the duties and responsibilities of a firefighter. You'll have the opportunity to evaluate your own interests and abilities as you learn about getting hired, trained, paid, and promoted. It's important to read this chapter carefully so that you understand how to prepare yourself to become a part of this vital and challenging career.

Next, in Chapter 2, "How Firefighters Are Selected," you'll read a summary of the selection process, from the initial application to the training academy. By learning the exact steps you'll need to take in order to become a firefighter, you'll have an edge over those applicants coming in cold.

Chapter 3, "The LearningExpress Test Preparation System," will give you invaluable advice on how to organize your time before and during the written exam. If you've had trouble with written exams in the past (anxiety, bad study habits, running out of time), you definitely don't want to skip this chapter—it even gives you great tips on how to choose the right multiple-choice answer when you're unsure. Even if written exams aren't that hard for you, be sure to take advantage of the sample study plans in this chapter. The best insurance for acing your exam is good preparation, and these study schedules will help you organize your time.

After devising a study plan for yourself, you'll want to jump right in and take a practice exam. Note that not all of the exams test the same skills. Because fire departments around the country use different types of exams, we included a variety in this book—four different exams.

In order to use your study time most efficiently, you should find out what skills the department you want to apply to will be testing. (Chapter 3 shows you how.) Then you can concentrate on the practice exams in this book that correspond to the one you'll be taking. At the beginning of each exam, you'll find a description of what skills are tested.

Once you've taken one or two exams and know what areas need the most work, you can begin studying the different subjects covered in Chapters 6–12. After substantial review of your problem subjects, move on

to another practice exam to see if your score improves. From there, you can determine how much more preparation you need and whether you want to seek help from a friend, a book on the subject, or a tutor.

And don't forget to read Chapters 15 and 16, which cover the ins and outs of the Physical Ability Test and the Oral Interview.

In short, this book is here to help. It covers all the basics of what fire departments across the country are looking for in a candidate, and it gives you examples of what typical firefighter exams are like. You've given yourself a big advantage by choosing to use this book. However, one essential ingredient that this book doesn't provide is *specific* requirements for the fire department in your city of interest. It's important for you to get all the information your fire department provides and make a few phone calls to clarify exactly what steps you need to take. Your success in becoming a firefighter depends largely on your desire to become one and the amount of work you're willing to do to achieve your goals.

GOOD LUCK!

C·H·A·P·T·E·R

WHAT FIREFIGHTERS REALLY DO

1

CHAPTER SUMMARY

If you're looking for a vital and challenging career, you're on the right track. Firefighters are true champions of the public good—with hefty doses of bravery and skill mixed in. This chapter describes the duties and demands of the job. You'll learn about getting hired, trained, paid and promoted. Plus you'll find information on how this profession is changing and how you can prepare yourself to become a part of it.

ou see flames. You smell smoke. An alarm goes off. Someone yells "fire." For most people, this would be the time to evacuate the premises. But if you happen to be a firefighter, it's time to go to work.

Describing firefighters without using the word "hero" would be tough. After all, their ultimate goal is to prevent or relieve human suffering and loss. They regularly put their own lives on the line to save other lives and protect property. Much of their work is physically exhausting, mentally demanding and highly dangerous. When a fire or other emergency strikes, they're on the scene battling flames, smoke, collapsing walls, chemical explosions and numerous other threats. Unlike "civilians," they can't evacuate the premises. They are smack-dab ON the premises until the crisis has passed.

Behind every heroic moment, of course, are countless hours of preparation. Career firefighters are highly trained professionals. Their services are essential to every community and every stretch of land across this country. If you make this your number-one career choice, rest assured that the need for firefighters is constant and the job prospects are promising. But this is a competitive field. Wherever you apply, you'll need to show that you've got what it takes to meet the demands of the job—and the hiring process.

WHERE THE JOBS ARE

Roughly 300,000 career firefighters are employed nationwide as paid, full-time professionals. So who hires all these career firefighters? Well, if you're in the majority—9 out of 10, according to the Bureau of Labor Statistics (BLS)—you'll be employed by a municipal or county fire department, typically serving a community with a population of 50,000 or more. Not surprisingly, large cities are the largest employers.

JUST THE FACTS
"The Fire Triangle" refers to the three elements—fuel, heat and air—that must be present for a fire to occur. If you remove any one of these elements, the fire will go out.

Full-time firefighters are also hired by federal and state government agencies to protect government-owned property and special facilities. For example, the U.S. Forest Service, Bureau of Land Management and Park Service offer both year-round and seasonal fire service jobs to protect the country's national parks, forests and other lands.

In the private sector, many large industrial companies have their own firefighting forces, especially companies in the oil, chemical, aircraft and aerospace industries. Other employers include airports, ship-

yards and military bases. Also, a growing number of companies are in the business of providing fire protection services—including on-call or on-site firefighting teams—to other businesses and institutions.

In addition to career firefighters, there are still large numbers of volunteer or "paid-call" reserve firefighters nationwide. These individuals work mostly in rural or small communities and may receive compensation only when they are called to duty.

On the Job

The foremost duty of a firefighter is exactly what the job title says—to fight fires. Whether a fire breaks out at a 2-story home, a 700-room hotel or a 10,000-acre farm, the next sound you'll hear is the familiar wail of those massive red trucks barreling their way to the scene, loaded with firefighters in oversized suits, big heavy boots and odd-shaped hats.

But firefighters today do a lot more than put out fires. Natural disasters, bombing incidents, gas pipe explosions and hazardous waste spills are just a few of the situations where firefighters often are called on to provide emergency services. Sometimes these circumstances pose the threat of fire. Other times a rescue operation may be the main order of business. Whatever the crisis at hand, something else that firefighters are trained to do is to administer and/or coordinate basic medical care to any injured persons there may be.

Fire departments also provide many non-emergency services. One highly important task is to inspect buildings and facilities for compliance with fire codes and safety regulations. Another is to educate the public about fire prevention and safety procedures. This could include giving presentations to local schools and community groups, or sponsoring campaigns aimed at making people more aware of fire hazards—sort of a local version of Smokey the Bear's "Only you can prevent forest fires" campaign! Firefighters often participate in public education efforts, but building inspection more often is handled by higher-ranked fire service personnel who have had special training.

What the average person may not be aware of is simply how much mental knowledge goes into firefighting. We see them driving the red truck, attaching a hose to a hydrant, dousing flames, busting out windows with a pickax, climbing tall ladders. These activities alone require a high level of technical skill and a great deal of physical stamina and strength. Firefighters also face serious physical risks from being exposed to flames, smoke, fumes and explosive or toxic materials, as well as from walls and buildings caving in or collapsing.

To reduce those risks, it's critical that they stay in top physical condition and master the use of various equipment and tools. But it's equally critical that they have a knowledge bank filled with scientific and technical information about combustible materials, building construction, ventilation systems, sprinkler systems, electrical circuitry, chemical reactions and a host of other subjects. Firefighters are educated, trained and drilled again and again in each of these critical areas.

Much of this preparation and learning goes on back at the station house. At departments with full-time personnel, on-duty firefighters usually eat, sleep and make a home away from home at the station. Although most rotate between day and night shifts, the length of their tour of duty and their shifts varies from department to department. For example, they may work four days on, then four days off, putting in anywhere from 10- to 16-hour shifts. Or they may work a 24-hour shift, followed by 48 hours off, then the cycle repeats. Whatever the work schedule, it's not the corporate nine-to-five routine.

Clearly it's not every day that a firefighter rescues a child from a burning building. It's always a case of the fewer sirens the better because nobody hopes for disaster to strike. But since there's no predicting when it will, a firefighting force must be on the alert 24 hours a day, 365 days a year. Between sirens, their on-duty time is devoted to practice drills, training and education programs, equipment maintenance and other routine activities.

JUST THE FACTS

Everybody knows that firehouse dogs traditionally are dalmatians. But did you know that firehouse dogs, past and present, have nearly all been named Sparky? That's why the National Fire Protection Association (NFPA) chose this name for its fire prevention symbol.

THE PAYBACK: SALARY AND BENEFITS

As with nearly every job, firefighters earn different salaries depending on where they work and who they work for. The size and location of the department or agency makes a difference. So does a firefighter's level of experience and time on the job. Salary data for several municipal departments in your state are provided in later chapters. The statistics that follow will give you a sense of the "big picture" nationwide.

Salary data reported by the International City Management Association (ICMA) cites $26,899 as the minimum annual base salary paid to sworn full-time firefighters, and $35,206 as the maximum salary. These figures are an average based on all geographical locations and departments of every size.

If you work in a small city, you can expect a smaller annual salary than in large cities. Geographically speaking, salaries tend to be lowest in the southern region of the U.S. and highest out west.

Typical working hours for full-time firefighters range from 40 to 56 hours a week. They are entitled by law to overtime pay, which kicks in at an average of 53 or more hours a week during a work period. Many departments also offer longevity pay to career firefighters, usually around $1,000 a year. This extra pay generally is separate from any salary increase that comes with a promotion.

Employee benefit packages for firefighters also vary from department to department, but they tend to be substantial. Common benefits include medical, disability and life insurance; sick leave, vacation and holiday pay; educational incentives; and a generous pension plan. Departments also supply uniforms and personal equipment you use on the job.

Unions play a large role in negotiating and protecting the salaries and benefits that firefighters earn. The BLS notes that most firefighters in medium to large departments are members of the International Association of Fire Fighters (IAFF), which maintains a national office and local chapters. The IAFF and other professional organizations also work to resolve labor disputes and sponsor governmental legislation on behalf of their members.

HIRING TRENDS

Employment of firefighters is expected to increase 5% to 14% over the next decade, according to the BLS. Some new jobs will be created in suburban communities where populations are on the rise. Other new jobs will come in small communities and rural areas where departments are in transition from a volunteer to a paid force. Employment at large, urban departments will be stable—not producing many new jobs, but holding steady on the large numbers they already employ. Overall, the majority of job openings will come about simply to replace firefighters who retire or leave the job for other reasons.

Firefighting certainly can be called "a steady job." Since fires can happen anywhere and at any time, no department that maintains a paid force is going to go out of business! On the whole, turnover is low and layoffs are rare in this profession. Even when local governments call for budget cuts, communities generally rally to keep or grow the number of firefighters their tax dollars support. For the most part, too, the job market is not subject to seasonal fluctuations. One exception is forestry firefighting, which is mostly seasonal employment and almost exclusively available through state and federal agencies.

Along with job security, you've got other pluses described earlier: relatively high wages, good benefits, a generous pension and the chance to do challenging, exciting and important work. All these pluses add up to steep competition for these jobs. Most fire departments—especially large, urban departments—have many more applicants than they do job openings.

JUST THE FACTS
Firefighters have been sliding down the firehouse pole ever since April 21, 1878, when Captain David B. Kenyon installed the first pole at Engine Company No. 21 in New York City.

APPLYING FOR THE JOB

Because municipal and county fire departments operate independently, no one set of qualifications and hiring procedures is used by each and every department nationwide. However, though the particulars may vary, certain standards are likely wherever you plan to apply. For example, most departments:

- Have a minimum age requirement between 18 and 21
- Require a high school education or a General Equivalency Degree (GED); some departments have a higher education requirement
- run a background check on your employment and education and a criminal record check

HELPFUL RESOURCES

Listed below are several major professional organizations and publications in the fire service field. You may want to take advantage of the information and assistance that these organizations have to offer regarding fire service opportunities, training and education, union activities, and other career-related matters. You can also learn more and keep up on the latest fire-service news by reading dedicated magazines and journals, which you may be able to find at a local library or can get by subscription.

Organizations

International Association of Fire Chiefs
1329 18th Street, N.W.
Washington, DC 20036
(703) 273-0911

International Association of Fire Fighters
1750 New York Avenue, N.W. #300
Washington, DC 20006
(202) 737-8484
www.iaff.org

International Fire Service Training Association
Oklahoma State University
1723 Tyler St. West
Stillwater, OK 74078
1 (800) 304-5727
www.ifsta.org

National Fire Protection Association
1 Batterymarch Park
PO Box 9101
Quincy, MA 02269-9101
(617) 770-3000
www.nfpa.org

Publications

American Fire Journal
9072 East Artesia Blvd., Suite 7
Bellflower, CA 90706
(562) 866-1664

Fire Chief Magazine
307 North Michigan Avenue
Chicago, IL 60604
(312) 726-7277
www.firechief.com

Fire Command Magazine, Fire Technology and NFPA Journal, published by the National Fire Protection Association (listed above)

Fire Engineering Magazine
875 Third Avenue
New York, NY 10022
(201) 845-0800
www.fire-eng.com

FireHouse Magazine
82 Firehouse Lane, Box 2433
Boulder, CO 80321
(516) 845-2700
www.firehouse.com

International Fire Fighter, published by the International Association of Fire Fighters (listed above)

■ require that you pass a series of tests, including a written examination, physical ability test, medical exam (often with drug screening), an oral interview and possibly psychological testing

Departments often have residency requirements stating that you must live in the city or county in which you apply. Experience as an Emergency Medical Technician (EMT) or paramedic is always a plus and sometimes a requirement for employment, either at the time you apply and test for the job or to be satisfied before you begin active duty. Affirmative Action or other minority hiring requirements also can factor into the selection process.

In general, previous work experience looks good on the application form. Jobs in construction, mechanics, landscaping, masonry and plumbing are some that demonstrate the physical strength and dexterity needed to be a firefighter. But the basic idea is to show that you have held a responsible job, followed a boss' orders and are a team player. Also, whether it's required or not, departments tend to look favorably on applicants who have attended college. Even better is having taken courses in fire science. Keep in mind how much competition you're apt to have for a firefighting job. Any advantage you have or can give yourself—which includes preparing yourself for the written exam—really can make the difference in getting hired.

Both the National Fire Protection Association and the International Society of Fire Service Instructors have set certain hiring and training standards that many departments use, though often with their own local "spin" on the process. Also, some states require applicants to pass state certification tests, over and above meeting requirements and passing tests at the local (city or county) level.

As for federal and state firefighter jobs, you can expect similar requirements and testing procedures.

Application procedures for these jobs are handled by the individual hiring agencies, state civil service commissions, local branches of the Office of Personnel Management (OPM) or other government organizations. In the private sector, you'll find more variation in the employment procedures. Basically, it's like looking for a job in any private business: companies make their choices based on an applicant's education, experience and ability to handle the responsibilities and physical demands of the job.

> **JUST THE FACTS**
> Benjamin Franklin founded this country's first volunteer fire department in 1736 in Philadelphia, Pennsylvania. He also became its first volunteer fire chief.

STARTING OUT AND MOVING UP

Once you're hired as a firefighter, your department will make sure you get all the training you need to do the job. Many large, urban departments run their own on-site formal training programs or fire academy. Smaller departments may send new recruits to a fire academy in their region. Some stick mostly to on-the-job training supervised by experienced fire service personnel.

Academy training generally lasts several weeks, with part of the time spent on classroom instruction and part on practical training. You'll cover areas such as firefighting and prevention techniques, hazardous and combustible materials, local building codes and emergency medical procedures. You'll also learn how to use various kinds of firefighting and rescue equipment.

As you continue on the job, you'll regularly receive training to learn new skills and keep you up to date on the latest equipment and firefighting techniques. This ongoing training is aimed at improving your overall performance as a firefighter. If, down the road, you want to move up the ranks, you'll have to meet a different set of training, education and testing requirements.

For any rank promotion, factors such as your on-the-job performance, a recommendation from your supervisor and how long you've been on the job are taken into account. But there's more. You'll also need to pass a written exam for most promotions, for example, to become a driver operator, lieutenant, captain, battalion chief, assistant chief, deputy chief or chief. You'll probably have to "show your stuff" in a physical performance test where you demonstrate techniques or use equipment relative to the position you want. You might have to become certified in specialized areas, usually through a combination of skills training and knowledge-based education programs, followed by a written certification exam.

Higher education is another requirement you may face for promotion. If you haven't done so already, you may need to take certain college classes or earn a college degree. For example, many departments require an associate's degree to become a lieutenant or captain. The BLS reports that generally a master's degree in public administration, business administration or a related field is required for any rank at or above battalion chief. Advanced education and training programs are available through a variety of sources, including community colleges and universities, professional organizations and state-sponsored fire academies.

JUST THE FACTS
Supposedly the Great Chicago Fire of 1871 started when Mrs. Catherine O'Leary's cow kicked over a kerosene lamp in her barn. Whether it was the cow's fault or not, the anniversary of that fire marks the date of National Fire Prevention Week, the annual event which began in 1925 by proclamation of President Calvin Coolidge.

THE FUTURE

The days of fighting fires by bucket brigade are long gone. Professional firefighters are here to stay, a permanent fixture in every community. Meanwhile, their job is becoming more sophisticated all the time.

You can see this happening even with the tools of the job. It's true that there may be no substitutes for basic firefighting equipment like hoses, pumps and ladders. Yet even the most basic equipment continues to be improved—for example, made more lightweight or built to operate electronically instead of manually. The same thing applies to developing better materials for uniforms, ones that are more lightweight, heat-resistant and flame-retardant.

When it comes to the job itself, experts in the field are constantly at work developing new methods both to prevent and to control fires. They're coming up with chemical solutions to quench fires and computerized ways of simulating and solving fire-related problems. They're also perfecting devices such as smoke detectors and indoor sprinkler systems, which are much more widely used these days and can help to avoid full-scale destruction by fire.

Not all changes in society work to the firefighter's advantage, however. For one thing, take modern architecture. The size, design, construction and high-tech elements of buildings today can make the firefighter's job a whole lot tougher. You've probably seen "The Towering Inferno." You probably know about the fire that leveled the huge MGM Grand Hotel in Las Vegas a few years back. One's a movie, one's sadly real, but both are perfect examples of how modern structures can raise new difficulties for firefighters. We've also got chemical spills. Terrorist bombings. Large aircraft crashes. Firefighters play a big role in handling these and many other kinds of crises. After the Oklahoma City bombing in 1995, for instance, firefighters were a significant force in the search and rescue operation.

As a firefighter, it's important to stay aware of changes and advancements in society that affect your profession. Any number of hot items in the news—from anti-government groups and toxic waste dumping to the latest greatest pesticide or home security system—may pose new job-related challenges for you. To keep up with these challenges, you can expect to see fire departments boosting their standards for hiring, training and educating firefighters. That's why it's so important for you to show, right from the start, your willingness and ability to constantly develop new skills and knowledge.

> **JUST THE FACTS**
> St. Florian, born in 256 A.D., is considered to be the patron saint of the fire service in countries around the world. Legend has it that a person can be saved from fire by invoking his name.

MAKING THE COMMITMENT

What would we do without firefighters? Somebody has to snuff out major fires. Somebody has to make a dedicated effort to prevent them in the first place. Somebody has to be there to lend an expert hand during all types of emergencies. These "somebodies" are the fire service professionals who have the knowledge, training and courage to do the job.

If that's the kind of somebody you want to be, there's no time like the present to begin preparing for the application and selection process. Along with all the tips and practical guidance you'll find in this book, here are five next steps to head you in that direction.

1. Get fit. Make a physical fitness program part of your daily routine. You'll need to be in top shape to pass the physical performance test in the hiring process and to do the job once you're part of the force. The usual activities will do the trick—recreational sports, weightlifting, jogging. You also might want to try the martial arts. Karate, judo and the like are great to build up your endurance and strength, but also for developing a "mind/body connection" that can help you stay in control and focused under stressful circumstances. (For some specific training tips, see the later chapter in this book on the firefighter's Physical Ability Test.)

2. Do some networking. The best resources for "telling it like it is" are people now working in the field. Start with your family and friends and then move on from there —you're bound to find someone who knows or can lead you to fire service professionals. Ask them questions. Get some pointers. Find out what it's really like to be a firefighter from people who have first-hand knowledge.

3. Do some research. Spend some time at local and college libraries or on the World Wide Web reading whatever information they have about the fire service profession. Contact professional organizations for any newsletters, articles and papers they publish. Subscribe to magazines in the field. Also don't forget to scan the daily newspaper with an eye toward articles about firefighting and on topics that affect the profession.

4. Prepare for the written exam. Your test score on the written exam really counts. It's not just a matter of passing the exam. Your goal is to wind up with a score that puts you in a good position with the competition. So give yourself plenty of time to get ready—in other words, start studying and taking the practice exams in

this book as far in advance of the exam as you can.

5. Prepare for the oral interview. Naturally you want to feel confident and comfortable when you're interviewed for this job. To help your cause, put in some practice time. Think about why you want to become a firefighter. Think about the abilities, knowledge and experience you can bring to the force. Think about your long-term goals. Then have a friend or family member run you through a practice interview. The point isn't to memorize what you plan to say. It's to get a good sense of your talents and goals and to help you feel comfortable talking about yourself. (You'll find out more about what's involved in the oral interview, and how to prepare for it, in a later chapter that covers this part of the selection process.)

If you really want to be a firefighter, it's up to you to make the commitment. So take these next steps. Get yourself ready. Take charge of your future. A career in firefighting promises many challenges and rewards. All of them could be yours.

THE FIREFIGHTER'S CREED

When I'm called to duty, God,
wherever flames may rage,
give me strength to save a life,
whatever be its age.

Help me to embrace a little child
before it is too late
or save an older person from
the horror of that fate.

Enable me to be alert
to hear the weakest shout
and quickly and efficiently
to put the fire out.

I want to fill my calling and
to give the best in me;
to guard my neighbor and
protect his property.

And if, according to your will,
I have to lose my life,
bless with your protecting hand
my children and my wife.

—Anonymous

C·H·A·P·T·E·R

HOW FIREFIGHTERS ARE SELECTED

CHAPTER SUMMARY

Throughout the country, fire departments use a number of different ways to assess firefighter candidates. This chapter provides a summary of the process of selecting recruits, from the initial application to the training academy.

Firefighting is demanding, sometimes dangerous, work. It's also a position of public trust. People's lives depend on what firefighters do, particularly at the scene of an emergency but also during more routine tasks. That's why fire departments put job applicants through a rigorous selection process that can take from several months to a year or more. Firefighters have to be smart enough to learn the chemistry, physics, and biology of emergency services; strong enough to carry a person out of a burning building; fit enough to respond to several emergencies in a day, sometimes without sleep; honest enough to be trusted inside every home and business in town; and compassionate and polite enough to interact with the public daily.

In most large cities, more people apply for firefighting positions than can ever be accepted. A large percentage of people who apply fail one or another part of the selection process: the written exam, the physical ability test, the oral interview or board, or one of the other steps in the process. You don't want to be one of those people.

That's one reason you're reading this book: it will tell you what to expect, so you'll know exactly what the steps are in becoming a firefighter. Knowing those steps, you'll have an edge over applicants coming in cold. Knowing those steps, you can make a realistic assessment of your skills and abilities.

During this assessment, you might find things that make becoming a firefighter unrealistic for you. However, you might instead find weaknesses that *you can correct*—and you can address them *now*, before you get involved in the selection process.

THE ELIGIBILITY LIST

Most fire departments, or the city personnel departments that handle the selection process for them, establish a list of eligible candidates; many such lists rank candidates from highest to lowest. How ranks are determined varies from place to place; sometimes the rank is based solely on the written exam score, sometimes on the physical ability test, and sometimes on a combination of factors. The point is, even if you make it through the entire selection process, the likelihood that you will be hired as a firefighter often depends on *the quality of your performance* in one or more parts of the selection process.

Make a commitment now: you need to work hard, in advance, to do well on the written exam, the physical ability test, and the oral interview (if there is one), so that your name will stand out at the top of your agency's eligibility list.

First, though, you need information. You need to know about the selection process for firefighters. This chapter outlines the basic process in its many steps. Not every fire department includes all of the steps discussed. The particulars of the process in the city you're applying to are usually available from the city personnel department or fire department itself.

BASIC QUALIFICATIONS

The basic qualifications you need in order to even think about becoming a firefighter vary from city to city. It's worthwhile to find out what those qualifications are in the agency you want to serve. Some qualifications are pretty standard:

- A minimum age—sometimes 18, more often 20 or 21—and, in some departments, a maximum age, which can range from 30 to 45
- A high school diploma or its equivalent and, increasingly, some college
- A clean criminal record
- Excellent physical and mental health
- A valid driver's license and a satisfactory driving record

Many jurisdictions, but not all, require that you live in the jurisdiction or nearby. Many fire departments give preference to otherwise qualified veterans over civilians. This may take the form of a policy, sometimes called a "Veteran's Preference" policy, whereby points are automatically added to the written exam. Is this unfair? No. Fire companies are a lot like military units. They follow a strict chain of command, and firefighters on the line work as a team, knowing that their lives are in each other's hands. Military personnel have learned the discipline and teamwork that are vital to firefighting and emergency services. Veterans are simply better qualified than most other people.

Increasingly, fire departments are also giving preference to certified Emergency Medical Technicians (EMTs) or paramedics. As the work of fire departments becomes less involved strictly with fighting fires and more with other kinds of emergency services, many departments require qualified EMTs.

THE EXAM OR POSITION ANNOUNCEMENT

Applying to be a firefighter differs from applying for most other jobs. The differences begin with the exam or position announcement. You rarely see fire department openings advertised in the Help Wanteds. Instead, the city usually starts looking for potential firefighters by means of a special announcement. This announcement will outline the basic qualifications for the position as well as the steps you will have to go through in the selection process. It often tells you some of the duties you will be expected to perform. It may give the date and place of the written exam, which is usually the first step in the selection process.

Get a copy of this announcement. Often your public library will have a copy. Or you can get one directly from the fire department or city personnel department. If exams are held irregularly, the fire or personnel department may maintain a mailing list, so that you can receive an exam announcement the next time an exam is scheduled. If exams are held frequently, you will sometimes be told to simply show up at the exam site on a given day of the week or month. In those cases you usually get more information about the job and the selection process if you pass the written exam. *Study the exam announcement,* as well as any other material, such as brochures, that the department sends you. You need to be prepared for the whole selection process in order to be successful.

THE APPLICATION

Often the first step in the process of becoming a firefighter is filling out an application. Sometimes this is a real application, asking about your education, employment experience, personal data, and so on. Sometimes there's just an application to take the written or physical test, with a fuller application coming later. In any case, at some point you will probably be asked some questions you wouldn't expect to see on a regular job application. You might be asked things like whether you've ever gotten any speeding tickets or been in trouble with the law, whether you've used illegal drugs, even whether any relatives work for the city or for the fire department. Your answers to these, as well as the more

Application Tips

- Neatness and accuracy count. Filling in your apartment number in the blank labeled "city" reflects poorly on your ability to follow directions.
- Most agencies *don't want your resume.* It goes straight into the circular file. Save your time and energy for filling out the application form the agency gives you.
- Verify all information you put on the form. Don't guess or estimate; if you're not sure of, for instance, the exact address of the company you used to work for, look it up.
- If you're mailing your application, take care to submit it to the proper address. It might go to the personnel department rather than to the fire department. Follow the directions on the exam announcement.

conventional questions, will serve as the starting point if the department conducts an investigation of your background, so it's important to answer all questions accurately and honestly. If you don't remember what year you worked for XYZ Company or your exact address your sophomore year of high school, don't fudge; look it up instead.

THE WRITTEN EXAM

In most jurisdictions, taking a written exam is the next step in the application process, though in some cases the physical ability test comes first.

The written exam is your first opportunity to show that you have what it takes to be a firefighter. As such, it's extremely important. People who don't pass the written exam don't go any farther in the selection process. Furthermore, the written exam score often figures into applicants' rank on the eligibility list; in some cases, this score by itself determines your rank, while in others it is combined with other scores, such as physical ability or oral board scores. In those places, a person who merely passes the exam with a score of, say, 70, is unlikely to be hired when there are plenty of applicants with scores in the 90s. The exam bulletin may specify what your rank will be based on.

What the Written Exam Is Like

Most written exams simply test basic skills and aptitudes: how well you understand what you read, your ability to follow directions, your judgment and reasoning skills, your ability to read and understand maps and floor plans, and sometimes your memory or your math. In this preliminary written exam, *you will not be tested on your knowledge of fire behavior, firefighting procedures, or any other specific body of knowledge.* This test is designed *only* to see if you can read, reason, and do basic math.

In some places, taking the exam involves studying written materials in advance and then answering questions about them on the exam. These written materials generally have to do with fire and firefighting—but all you have to do is study the guide you're given. You're still being tested just on your reading skills and memory, and there are good reasons for this.

Firefighters have to be able to read, understand and act on complex written materials—not only fire law and fire procedures, but also scientific materials about fire, combustible materials, chemicals, and so forth. They have to be able to think clearly and independently, because lives depend on decisions they make in a split second. They have to be able to do enough math to read and understand pressure gauges or estimate the height of a building and the amount of hose needed to reach to the third floor. They have to be able to read maps so they can get to the emergency site quickly and floor plans so that they can find their way to an exit even in a smoke-filled building.

Most exams are multiple-choice tests of the sort you've often encountered in school. You get an exam book and an answer sheet where you have to fill in little circles (bubbles) or squares with a number 2 pencil.

How to Prepare for the Written Exam

Pay close attention to any material the fire department or city personnel department puts out about the exam. If there's a study guide, study it. Pay close attention to what you're going to be tested on, and then practice with similar materials.

That's where this book comes in. There are four practice exams here that include the skills most commonly tested. There are also chapters on each kind of question you're most likely to encounter. Each chapter includes not only sample questions but also tips and hints on how to prepare for that kind of question and how to do well in the exam itself. You should also check out the chapter "The LearningExpress Test Preparation

System," which tells you all you need to know about preparing for and taking standardized tests.

Finding Out How You Did

Applicants are generally notified in writing about their performance on the exam. The notification may simply say whether or not you passed, but it may tell you what your score was. It may also say when you should show up for the next step in the process, which is often a physical ability test.

THE PHYSICAL ABILITY TEST

The physical ability test is the next step in the process for many fire departments; some put this step first. You may have to bring a note from your doctor saying that you are in good enough shape to undertake this test before you will be allowed to participate. The fire department wants to make sure that no one has a heart attack in the middle of the test. This is a clue: expect the test to be tough.

Firefighting is, after all, physically demanding work. Once again, lives depend on whether your strength, stamina, and overall fitness allow you to carry out the necessary tasks during an emergency. If you make it to the academy and later into a fire company, you can expect to continue physical training and exer-

cises throughout your career. In fact, in some cities all firefighters are required to retake the physical ability test every year.

What the Physical Ability Test Is Like

The exact events that make up the physical ability test vary from place to place, but the tasks you have to perform are almost always job-related—they're a lot like the physical tasks you will actually have to perform as a firefighter. Many times the test is set up like an obstacle course, and usually the test is timed, with a cutoff time for passing. Often you have to wear full (heavy) protective gear, including an air pack, throughout these events. Here's an example of the events in a test that you would typically have five to seven minutes to complete:

- Dummy drag
- Hose drag
- Climb stairs
- Climb through tunnel
- Raise and climb ladder
- Jump over wall

In an obstacle-course setup like this one, you might be given the opportunity to walk the course before you actually have to take the test. In the test itself, you would be timed as you went through the events, and you would have to complete the events within a set

---

Written Exam Tips

- Ask for and *use* any material the fire department or personnel department puts out about the written test. Some agencies have study guides; some even conduct study sessions. Why let others get a vital advantage while you don't?
- Practice, practice, practice. And then practice some more.
- Try to find some people who have taken the exam recently, and ask them about what was on the exam. Their hindsight—"I wish I had studied . . ."—can be your foresight.

time to pass. In departments where the physical ability test figures into your rank on the eligibility list, merely meeting the maximum time to pass isn't good enough; people who have lower times will be hired before you are.

Different departments have different policies on retesting if you fail. Some allow you to retest on the same day after a rest period. Some allow you to come back another time and try again, usually up to a set maximum number of tries. And in some departments, your first try is the only chance you get; if you fail, you're out, at least until the next testing period. Few departments will allow you to retest, if you have already passed, simply to better your time.

You can usually find out just what tasks are included in the physical ability test from the exam announcement or related materials.

How to Prepare for the Physical Ability Test

Many urban fire departments report that the physical ability test is the one step of the process in which the most applicants fail. People come in unprepared, they're simply not strong enough or fast enough to do all the events, while wearing heavy gear, in the time allotted.

Female applicants, in particular, have high failure rates on physical ability tests because some of the events require a lot of upper-body strength.

But don't despair. The physical ability test is one area where advance preparation is almost guaranteed to pay off. No matter how good a shape you're in, start an exercise program *now*. You can design your program around the requirements listed in the exam announcement if you want, but any exercise that will increase your strength and stamina will help. Because sheer brute force is required to drag a 150-pound dummy or to lift a 50-foot ladder, exercises that increase your strength are particularly important. But you'll also want to include some aerobic exercise such as running or swimming to improve your stamina and overall fitness as well.

If you're *not* in great shape, consult a doctor before you begin. Start slow and easy and increase your activity as you go. As you gain strength, start wearing weights on your ankles and wrists, and later add a backpack stuffed with dictionaries or rocks. And remember that you don't have to do all this work alone. Working out with a friend not only is more fun, it also helps guard against the temptation to cheat by skipping a day or doing fewer "reps."

Physical Ability Tips

- Take advantage of any training sessions or test-course walk-throughs the fire department offers. The whole purpose of such sessions is to help you pass the physical test.
- Start exercising *now*. Yes, today. Work up to a 45-minute workout at least five times a week.
- Exercises that increase your upper-body strength are particularly useful. Consider pumping iron several times a week.
- If you smoke, stop.
- If you're overweight, diet along with your exercise.
- Exercise with a friend. Listen to tunes while you work out. Give yourself rewards for reaching milestones like shaving a minute off your mile-run time or bench pressing ten more pounds. Find out what will motivate you to work hard, and do it.

Many fire departments conduct training sessions for would-be applicants, to help them get up to the required level of fitness. Some allow you to walk through the course ahead of time. If any of these opportunities are available to you, be sure to use them.

For more information on the physical ability test and how to prepare for it, see the chapter entitled "The Physical Ability Test" later in this book.

The Background Investigation

Most fire departments conduct background investigations of applicants who pass the written and physical tests. Firefighters have to be honest, upright citizens who can get along with both their company and the people they serve, so the fire department conducts a background investigation to make sure you're the right kind of person. You may not even know such an investigation is going on—until someone at the oral interview asks you why you wrote on your application that you never used drugs when your high school friends all say you regularly smoked marijuana on weekends. (That's why it's important to answer honestly on your application.)

What the Background Investigation Is Like

The rigorousness with which your background will be checked depends on the policies of your department. Some conduct a fairly superficial check, calling your former employers and schools simply to verify that you were there when you say you were there and didn't cause any problems during that time.

Other departments will investigate you in a great deal more depth, asking their contacts how long and how well they knew you and what kind of person they found you to be. Did you meet your obligations? How did you deal with problems? Did they find you to be an honest person? Do they know of anything that might affect your fitness to be a firefighter? The references you provided will lead the investigator to other people who knew you, and when the investigator is finished, he or she will have a pretty complete picture of what kind of person you are.

A few fire departments include a polygraph, or "lie detector" test, as part of the background investigation. As long as you've been honest in what you've said when your stress reactions weren't being monitored by a polygraph machine, a lie detector test is nothing to worry about.

How to Prepare for the Background Investigation

The best way you can improve your chances of getting through a background investigation with flying colors is by working on any problems in your background. You can't change the past, exactly, but you can use the present to improve your chances in the future. You can address problems that might give a background investigator pause: pay your old traffic tickets, get that juvenile offense that the lawyer said wouldn't "count" officially expunged from your record, document your full recovery from a serious illness or your drug-free status since high school.

You can also take steps to make yourself a more attractive candidate by getting related experience. You can, for instance, do volunteer work in the fire department or enroll in a fire cadet program. If you have enough time, you can take an Emergency Medical Technician course; if there's not much time before this step, at least enroll in a first-aid course.

ORAL INTERVIEWS AND BOARDS

The selection process in your fire department is likely to include one or more oral interviews. There may be an individual interview with the chief or deputy chief, or there may be an oral board, in which you would meet with several people. Or you may face both. Whether it's an individual interview or an oral board, the interviewers are interested in your interpersonal skills—how well you communicate *with them*—as well as in your qualifications to be a firefighter.

What the Oral Interview Is Like

In some cities, applicants who get this far in the process meet with the chief or deputy chief, who may conduct something like a typical job interview. The chief or deputy chief might describe in detail what the job is like, ask you how well you think you can do a job like that, and ask you why you want to be a firefighter in the first place. In the process, the chief will also be assessing your interpersonal skills, whether you seem honest and (relatively) comfortable in talking to him or her. You may also be asked questions about your background and experience.

This interview can be a make-or-break part of the process, with the chief turning thumbs up or down to your candidacy, or the chief may rank you against other applicants, in which case the chief's assessment of you is likely to figure into your place on the eligibility list.

The chief's interview may also include situational questions like those typically asked by an oral board. Or you may be facing an oral board in addition to your interview with the chief.

What the Oral Board Is Like

The oral board typically assesses such qualities as interpersonal skills, communication skills, judgment and decision-making abilities, respect for diversity, and adaptability. The board itself consists of two to five people, who may be firefighters or civilian personnel or interview specialists. There's usually some variety in the makeup of the board: officers of various ranks and/or civilians from the personnel department or from the community.

The way the interview is conducted depends on the practices of the individual department. You may be asked a few questions similar to those you would be asked at a normal employment interview: Why do you want to be a firefighter? What qualities do you have that would make you good at this job? You may be asked questions about your background, especially if your application or background investigation raised any questions in the board members' minds. Have answers prepared for such questions in case they come.

Instead of or in addition to such questions, you may be presented with hypothetical situations that you will be asked to respond to. A board member may say something like this: "After a dwelling fire is under control, you're walking through the building checking its structural soundness. When you walk into the bedroom, you see a fellow firefighter sticking a jewelry box into the pocket of his coat. What would you do?" You would then have to come up with an appropriate response to this situation.

Increasingly, cities have standardized the oral board questions. The same questions are asked of every candidate, and when the interview is over the board rates each candidate on a standard scale. This procedure helps the interviewers reach a somewhat more objective conclusion about the candidates they have interviewed and may result in a score that is included in the factors used to rank candidates in the eligibility list.

How to Prepare for the Oral Board or Interview

If the agency you're applying to puts out any material about the oral board, study it carefully. It may tell you what the board is looking for. It may even give you some sample questions you can practice with.

Whether you're facing an oral board or an individual interview, think about your answers to questions you might be asked. You might even try to write your own oral board questions and situations. Write down your answers if you want. Practice saying them in front of a mirror until you feel comfortable, but don't memorize them. You don't want to sound like you're reciting from a book. Your answers should sound conversational even though you've prepared in advance.

Then enlist friends or family to serve as a mock oral board or interviewer. If you know a speech teacher, get him or her to help. Give them your questions, tell them about what you've learned, and then have a practice oral board or interview. Start from the moment you walk into the room. Go through the entire session as if it were the real thing, and then ask your mock board or interviewer for their feedback on your performance. It may even help to videotape your mock board session. The camera can reveal things about your body language or habits that you don't even know about.

For more information about the oral board or interview and how to prepare for it, see Chapter 16, entitled "The Oral Interview," later in this book.

THE PSYCHOLOGICAL EVALUATION

Some cities, though not all, include a psychological evaluation as part of the firefighter selection process. The fire department wants to make sure that you are emotionally and mentally stable before putting you in a high-stress job in which you have to interact with peers, superiors, and the public. Don't worry, though; the psychological evaluation is not designed to uncover your deep dark secrets. Its only purpose is to make sure you have the mental and emotional health to do the job.

What the Psychological Evaluation Is Like

If your fire department has a psychological evaluation, most likely that means you'll be taking one or two written tests. A few cities have candidates interviewed by a psychologist or psychiatrist.

If you have to take a written psychological test, it is likely to be a standardized multiple-choice or true-false test licensed from a psychological testing company. The Minnesota Multiphasic Personality Inventory (MMPI) is one commonly used test. Such tests typically

---

Oral Board or Interview Tips

- Dress neatly and conservatively, as you would for a business interview.
- Be polite; say "please" and "thank you," "sir" and "ma'am."
- Remember, one-half of communication is listening. Look at board members or interviewers as they speak to you, and listen carefully to what they say.
- Think before you speak. Nod or say "OK" to indicate that you understand the question, and then pause a moment to collect your thoughts before speaking.
- If you start to feel nervous, take a deep breath, relax and just do your best.

ask you about your interests, attitudes, and background. They may take one hour or several; the hiring agency will let you know approximately how much time to allot.

If your process includes an oral psychological assessment, you'll meet with a psychologist or psychiatrist, who may be either on the hiring agency's staff or an independent contractor. The psychologist may ask you questions about your schooling and jobs, your relationships with family and friends, your habits, your hobbies. The psychologist may be as interested in the way you answer—whether you come across as open, forthright, and honest—as in the answers themselves.

How to Prepare for the Psychological Evaluation

There's only one piece of advice we can offer you for dealing with a psychological evaluation, whether written or oral: *Don't try to psych out the assessment.* The psychologists who designed the written test know more about psyching out tests than you do. They designed the test so that one answer checks against another to find out whether test-takers are lying. Just answer honestly, and don't worry about whether your answers to some of the questions seem to you to indicate that you might be nuts after all. They probably don't.

Similarly, if you are having an oral interview, there's no point in playing psychological games with someone who's better trained at it than you are. Just answer openly and honestly, and try to relax. The psychologist isn't really interested in your feelings about your mother, unless they're so extreme that they're likely to make you unfit to be a firefighter.

THE MEDICAL EXAMINATION

Before passage of the Americans With Disabilities Act (ADA), many fire departments conducted a medical examination early in the process, before the physical ability test. Now, the ADA says it's illegal to do any examinations or ask any questions that could reveal an applicant's disability until after a conditional offer of employment has been made. That means that in most jurisdictions you will get such a conditional offer before you are asked to submit to a medical exam.

You should know, however, that almost any disability is grounds for disqualification as a firefighter, even under the protections provided by ADA. Firefighting requires a high level of physical and mental fitness, and a host of disabilities that would not prevent a candidate from doing some other job would prevent a firefighter from fulfilling essential job functions. Even, for instance, a skin condition that requires a man to wear facial hair would disqualify that man from being a firefighter, because facial hair interferes with proper operation of the breathing apparatus.

Drug Testing

Note, however, that a test for use of illegal drugs *can* be administered before a conditional offer of employment. Because firefighters have to be in tiptop physical shape, and because they are in a position of public trust, the fire department expects you to be drug-free. You may have to undergo drug testing periodically throughout your career as a firefighter.

What the Medical Exam Is Like

The medical exam itself is nothing to be afraid of. It will be just like any other thorough physical exam. The doctor may be on the staff of the hiring agency or someone outside the department with his or her own practice, just like your own doctor. Your blood pressure, temperature, weight, and so on will be measured; your heart and lungs will be listened to and your limbs examined. The doctor will peer into your eyes, ears, nose, and mouth, and maybe some other body cavities . . . but it won't be that painful. You'll also have to donate some blood and some urine. Because of those tests, you won't know the results of the physical exam right away. You'll probably be notified in writing in a few weeks, after the test results come in.

IF AT FIRST YOU DON'T SUCCEED, PART ONE

The selection process for firefighters is a rigorous one. If you fail one of the steps, take time for some serious self-evaluation.

If you fail the written test, look at the reasons you didn't do well. Was it just that the format was unfamiliar? Well, now you know what to expect.

Do you need to brush up on some of the skills tested? There are lots of books out there to help people with basic skills. You might start with the Learning-Express Skill Builders, a set of four books that help improve your practical math, writing, vocabulary and spelling, and reading comprehension. Enlist a teacher or a friend to help you, or check out the inexpensive courses offered by local high schools and community colleges.

Some fire departments allow you to retest after a waiting period—a period you should use to improve your skills. If the exam isn't being offered again for years, consider trying some other jurisdiction.

If you fail the physical ability test, your course of action is clear. Increase your daily physical exercise until you *know* you can do what is required, and then retest or try another jurisdiction.

If you fail the oral board or interview, try to figure out what the problem was. Do you think your answers were good but perhaps you didn't express them well? Then you need some practice in oral communication. You can take courses or enlist your friends to help you practice.

Did the questions and situations throw you for a loop, so you made what now seem like inappropriate answers? Then try to bone up for the next time. Talk to candidates who were successful and ask them what they said. Talk with firefighters you know about what might have been good answers for the questions you were asked. Even if your department doesn't allow you to redo the oral board, you can use what you learn in applying to another department.

If the medical exam eliminates you, you will usually be notified as to what condition caused the problem. Is the condition one that can be corrected? See your doctor for advice.

If you don't make the list and aren't told why, the problem might have been the oral board or, more likely, the psychological evaluation or the background investigation. Now you really have to do some hard thinking.

Can you think of *anything* in your past that might lead to questions about your fitness to be a firefighter? Could any of your personal traits or attitudes raise such questions? And then the hard question: is there anything you can do to change these aspects of your past or your personality? If so, you might have a chance when you reapply or apply to another department. If not, it's time to think about another field.

If you feel you were wrongly excluded on the basis of a psychological evaluation or background check, most departments have appeals procedures. However, that word *wrongly* is very important. The psychologist or background investigator almost certainly had to supply a rationale in recommending against you. Do you have solid factual evidence that you can use in an administrative hearing to counter such a rationale? If not, you'd be wasting your time and money, as well as the hiring agency's, by making an appeal. Move carefully and get legal advice before you take such a step.

The Waiting Game

You went through the whole long process, passed all the tests, did the best you could, made the eligibility list—and now you wait. You *could* just sit on your hands. Or you could decide to *do* something with this time to prepare for what you hope is your new career. Do some networking. Talk to firefighters about what the job is really like. Find out if your fire department offers volunteer opportunities or a cadet program. Take a course in first aid or enroll in an Emergency Medical Technician program. Even if you don't get called, even if your rank on the score doesn't get you a job this time, you'll be better qualified for the next try.

Here's one thing you *don't* want to do while you're waiting: Don't call to find out what your chances are or how far down on the list they've gotten or when they might call you. You probably won't get to talk to the people making those decisions, so you'll just annoy some poor receptionist. If you did get through to the decision-makers, you'd be in even worse shape: you'd be annoying *them*.

IF AT FIRST YOU DON'T SUCCEED, PART TWO

If you make the list, go through the waiting game and finally aren't selected, don't despair. Think through all the steps of the selection process, and use them to do a critical self-evaluation.

Maybe your written, physical, or oral board score was high enough to pass but not high enough to put you near the top of the list. At the next testing, make sure you're better prepared.

Maybe you had an excellent score that should have put you at the top of the list, and you suspect that you were passed over for someone lower down. That means

someone less well qualified was selected while you were not, right? Maybe, maybe not.

There were probably a lot of people on the list, and a lot of them may have scored high. One more point on the test might have made the difference, or maybe the department had the freedom to pick and choose on the basis of other qualifications. Maybe, in comparison with you, a lot of people on your list had more education or experience. Maybe there were plenty of certified Emergency Medical Technicians on the list, and they got first crack at the available jobs. And yes, members of minority groups may have been given preference in hiring. Whether or not you think that's fair, you can be assured that it was a conscious decision on the part of the hiring agency; it may even have been mandated from above.

What can you do? You've heard or read about suits being brought against cities by people who thought their selection process was unfair. That's a last resort, a step you would take only after getting excellent legal advice and thinking through the costs of time, money, and energy. You'd also have to think about whether you'd want to occupy a position you got as the result of a lawsuit and whether you'd be hurting your chances of being hired somewhere else.

Most people are better off simply trying again. And don't limit your options. There are lots of fire departments all over the country; there are volunteer and part-time positions available, particularly in smaller towns; and there are a growing number of private fire protection service agencies. Do your research. This book is a good start. Find out what's available. Find out who's hiring. Being turned down by one department need not be the end of your firefighting career.

AND WHEN YOU DO SUCCEED . . .

Congratulations! The end of the waiting game for you is notification to attend the fire service academy. You're on the road to your career as a firefighter.

The road is hardly over, though. First, you have to make it through the academy, where you can expect physical training as well as training in fire and emergency services. You'll also have a lot of learning to do in your first year or so on the job. Throughout your career, you'll need to keep up with new techniques, new equipment, and new procedures. And if you decide to go for a promotion, there will be more steps, more tests, more evaluations. But you can do it, if you're determined and committed. You've already made a good start.

C·H·A·P·T·E·R 3

THE LEARNINGEXPRESS TEST PREPARATION SYSTEM

CHAPTER SUMMARY

Taking the firefighter written exam can be tough. It demands a lot of preparation if you want to achieve a top score. Your rank on the eligibility list is often determined largely by this score. The LearningExpress Test Preparation System, developed exclusively for LearningExpress by leading test experts, gives you the discipline and attitude you need to be a winner.

First, the bad news: Taking the firefighter written exam is no picnic, and neither is getting ready for it. Your future career in fire fighting depends on your getting a high score on the various parts of the test, but there are all sorts of pitfalls that can keep you from doing your best on this all-important exam. Here are some of the obstacles that can stand in the way of your success:

- Being unfamiliar with the format of the exam
- Being paralyzed by test anxiety
- Leaving your preparation to the last minute
- Not preparing at all!
- Not knowing vital test-taking skills: how to pace yourself through the exam, how to use the process of elimination, and when to guess
- Not being in tip-top mental and physical shape

■ Messing up on test day by having to work on an empty stomach or shivering through the exam because the room is cold

What's the common denominator in all these test-taking pitfalls? One word: *control*. Who's in control, you or the exam?

Now the good news: The LearningExpress Test Preparation System puts *you* in control. In just nine easy-to-follow steps, you will learn everything you need to know to make sure that *you* are in charge of your preparation and your performance on the exam. *Other* test-takers may let the test get the better of them; *other* test-takers may be unprepared or out of shape, but not *you*. *You* will have taken all the steps you need to take to get a high score on the firefighter exam.

Here's how the LearningExpress Test Preparation System works: Nine easy steps lead you through everything you need to know and do to get ready to master your exam. Each of the steps listed below includes both reading about the step and one or more activities. It's important that you do the activities along with the reading, or you won't be getting the full benefit of the system. Each step tells you approximately how much time that step will take you to complete.

Step 1. Get Information	30 minutes
Step 2. Conquer Test Anxiety	20 minutes
Step 3. Make a Plan	50 minutes
Step 4. Learn to Manage Your Time	10 minutes
Step 5. Learn to Use the Process of Elimination	20 minutes
Step 6. Know When to Guess	20 minutes
Step 7. Reach Your Peak Performance Zone	10 minutes
Step 8. Get Your Act Together	10 minutes
Step 9. Do It!	10 minutes
Total	**3 hours**

We estimate that working through the entire system will take you approximately three hours, though it's perfectly OK if you work faster or slower than the time estimates assume. If you can take a whole afternoon or evening, you can work through the whole LearningExpress Test Preparation System in one sitting. Otherwise, you can break it up, and do just one or two steps a day for the next several days. It's up to you—remember, *you're* in control.

STEP 1: GET INFORMATION

Time to complete: 30 minutes
Activities: Read Chapter 2, "How Firefighters Are Selected"

Knowledge is power. The first step in the LearningExpress Test Preparation System is finding out everything you can about your firefighter exam. Contact the fire department you want to apply to and ask who you should speak to about applying to be a firefighter. In larger cities, you'll be referred to a recruiting unit or to the personnel department. In smaller towns, you may speak to someone right there in the department. Request a position announcement or exam bulletin and ask when the next exam is scheduled. The exam bulletin usually gives a brief outline of what skills will be tested on the written exam.

What You Should Find Out

The more details you can find out about the exam, either from the bulletin or from speaking with a recruiter, the more efficiently you'll be able to study. Here's a list of some things you might want to find out about your exam:

- What skills are tested
- How many sections are on the exam
- How many questions each section has
- Whether the questions are ordered from easy to hard, or if the sequence is random
- How much time is allotted for each section
- If there are breaks between sections
- What the passing score is and how many questions you have to answer right in order to get that score
- Whether a higher score gives you any advantages, like a better rank on the eligibility list
- How the test is scored: is there a penalty for wrong answers?
- Whether you're permitted to go back to a prior section or move on to the next section if you finish early
- Whether you can write in the test booklet or will be given scratch paper
- What you should bring with you on exam day

What's on Most Firefighter Exams

The skills that the firefighter written exam tests vary from city to city. That's why it's important to contact the recruiting office or fire department to find out what skills are covered. Below are the most commonly tested subjects:

- Reading Comprehension
- Verbal Expression
- Spatial Relations
- Judgment and Reasoning
- Map Reading
- Memory and Observation
- Mechanical Aptitude
- Math

If you haven't already done so, stop here and read Chapter 2 of this book, which gives you an overview of the entire selection process. Then move on to the next step and get rid of that test anxiety!

STEP 2: CONQUER TEST ANXIETY

Time to complete: 20 minutes
Activity: Take the Test Stress Test

Having complete information about the exam is the first step in getting control of the exam. Next, you have to overcome one of the biggest obstacles to test success: test anxiety. Test anxiety can not only impair your performance on the exam itself; it can even keep you from preparing! In Step 2, you'll learn stress management techniques that will help you succeed on your exam. Learn these strategies now, and practice them as you work through the exams in this book, so they'll be second nature to you by exam day.

COMBATING TEST ANXIETY

The first thing you need to know is that a little test anxiety is a good thing. Everyone gets nervous before a big exam—and if that nervousness motivates you to prepare thoroughly, so much the better. It's said that Sir Laurence Olivier, one of the foremost British actors of this century, threw up before every performance. His stage fright didn't impair his performance; in fact, it probably gave him a little extra edge—just the kind of edge you need to do well, whether on a stage or in an examination room.

On the next page is the Test Stress Test. Stop here and answer the questions on that page, to find out whether your level of test anxiety is something you should worry about.

Stress Management Before the Test

If you feel your level of anxiety getting the best of you in the weeks before the test, here is what you need to do to bring the level down again:

- **Get prepared.** There's nothing like knowing what to expect and being prepared for it to put you in control of test anxiety. That's why you're reading this book. Use it faithfully, and remind yourself that you're better prepared than most of the people taking the test.
- **Practice self-confidence.** A positive attitude is a great way to combat test anxiety. This is no time to be humble or shy. Stand in front of the mirror and say to your reflection, "I'm prepared. I'm full of self-confidence. I'm going to ace this test. I know I can do it." Say it into a tape recorder and play it back once a day. If you hear it often enough, you'll believe it.
- **Fight negative messages.** Every time someone starts telling you how hard the exam is or how it's almost impossible to get a high score, start telling them your self-confidence messages above. If the someone with

(continued on page 6)

Test Stress Test

You only need to worry about test anxiety if it is extreme enough to impair your performance. The following questionnaire will provide a diagnosis of your level of test anxiety. In the blank before each statement, write the number that most accurately describes your experience.

0 = Never   1 = Once or twice   2 = Sometimes   3 = Often

_____ I have gotten so nervous before an exam that I simply put down the books and didn't study for it.

_____ I have experienced disabling physical symptoms such as vomiting and severe headaches because I was nervous about an exam.

_____ I have simply not showed up for an exam because I was scared to take it.

_____ I have experienced dizziness and disorientation while taking an exam.

_____ I have had trouble filling in the little circles because my hands were shaking too hard.

_____ I have failed an exam because I was too nervous to complete it.

_____ **Total: Add up the numbers in the blanks above.**

Your Test Stress Score

Here are the steps you should take, depending on your score. If you scored:
- **Below 3,** your level of test anxiety is nothing to worry about; it's probably just enough to give you that little extra edge.
- **Between 3 and 6,** your test anxiety may be enough to impair your performance, and you should practice the stress management techniques listed in this section to try to bring your test anxiety down to manageable levels.
- **Above 6,** your level of test anxiety is a serious concern. In addition to practicing the stress management techniques listed in this section, you may want to seek additional, personal help. Call your local high school or community college and ask for the academic counselor. Tell the counselor that you have a level of test anxiety that sometimes keeps you from being able to take the exam. The counselor may be willing to help you or may suggest someone else you should talk to.

the negative messages is *you*, telling yourself *you don't do well on exams, you just can't do this,* don't listen. Turn on your tape recorder and listen to your self-confidence messages.

- **Visualize.** Imagine yourself reporting for duty on your first day of firefighter training. Think of yourself wearing your uniform with pride and learning skills you will use for the rest of your life. Visualizing success can help make it happen—and it reminds you of why you're doing all this work in preparing for the exam.
- **Exercise.** Physical activity helps calm your body down and focus your mind. Besides, being in good physical shape can actually help you do well on the exam. Go for a run, lift weights, go swimming—and do it regularly.

Stress Management on Test Day

There are several ways you can bring down your level of test anxiety on test day. They'll work best if you practice them in the weeks before the test, so you know which ones work best for you.

- **Deep breathing.** Take a deep breath while you count to five. Hold it for a count of one, then let it out on a count of five. Repeat several times.
- **Move your body.** Try rolling your head in a circle. Rotate your shoulders. Shake your hands from the wrist. Many people find these movements very relaxing.
- **Visualize again.** Think of the place where you are most relaxed: lying on the beach in the sun, walking through the park, or whatever. Now close your eyes and imagine you're actually there. If you practice in advance, you'll find that you only need a few seconds of this exercise to experience a significant increase in your sense of well-being.

When anxiety threatens to overwhelm you right there during the exam, there are still things you can do to manage the stress level:

- **Repeat your self-confidence messages.** You should have them memorized by now. Say them quietly to yourself, and believe them!
- **Visualize one more time.** This time, visualize yourself moving smoothly and quickly through the test answering every question right and finishing just before time is up. Like most visualization techniques, this one works best if you've practiced it ahead of time.
- **Find an easy question.** Skim over the test until you find an easy question, and answer it. Getting even one circle filled in gets you into the test-taking groove.
- **Take a mental break.** Everyone loses concentration once in a while during a long test. It's normal, so you shouldn't worry about it. Instead, accept what has happened. Say to yourself, "Hey, I lost it there for a minute. My brain is taking a break." Put down your pencil, close your eyes, and do some deep breathing for a few seconds. Then you're ready to go back to work.

Try these techniques ahead of time, and see if they don't work for you!

STEP 3: MAKE A PLAN

Time to complete: 50 minutes

Activity: Construct a study plan

Maybe the most important thing you can do to get control of yourself and your exam is to make a study plan. Too many people fail to prepare simply because they fail to plan. Spending hours on the day before the exam poring over sample test questions not only raises your level of test anxiety, it also is simply no substitute for careful preparation and practice over time.

Don't fall into the cram trap. Take control of your preparation time by mapping out a study schedule. There are four sample schedules on the following pages, based on the amount of time you have before the exam. If you're the kind of person who needs deadlines and assignments to motivate you for a project, here they are. If you're the kind of person who doesn't like to follow other people's plans, you can use the suggested schedules here to construct your own.

In constructing your plan, you should take into account how much work you need to do. If your score on the sample test wasn't what you had hoped, consider taking some of the steps from Schedule A and getting them into Schedule D somehow, even if you do have only three weeks before the exam.

You can also customize your plan according to the information you gathered in Step 1. If the exam you have to take doesn't include verbal expression questions, for instance, you can skip Chapter 12 and concentrate instead on some other area that *is* covered. Below is a table that lists all the chapters you need to study for each exam.

Even more important than making a plan is making a commitment. You can't improve your skills in reading, writing, and judgment overnight. You have to set aside some time every day for study and practice. Try for at least 20 minutes a day. Twenty minutes daily will do you much more good than two hours on Saturday.

If you have months before the exam, you're lucky. Don't put off your study until the week before the exam! Start now. Even ten minutes a day, with half an hour or more on weekends, can make a big difference in your score—and in your chances of making the force!

Exams	Study Chapters
Exam 1, Chapter 4 Exam 3, Chapter 13	6, "Reading Comprehension" 7, "Memory and Observation" 9, "Judgment and Reasoning" 11, "Spatial Relations" 12, "Verbal Expression"
Exam 2, Chapter 5 Exam 4, Chapter 14	6, "Reading Comprehension" 8, "Math" 9, "Judgment and Reasoning" 10, "Mechanical Aptitude" 12, "Verbal Expression"

SCHEDULE A: THE LEISURE PLAN

If no test is announced in your city, you may have a year or more in which to get ready. This schedule gives you six months to sharpen your skills. If an exam is announced in the middle of your preparation, you can use one of the later schedules to help you compress your study program. Only study the chapters that are relevant to the type of exam you'll be taking.

Time	Preparation
Exam minus 6 months	Take one of the exams from Chapters 4 or 5. Then study the explanations for the answers until you know you could answer all the questions right.
Exam minus 5 months	Read Chapter 6 and work through the exercises. Start going to the library once every two weeks to read books or magazines about firefighting. Find other people who are preparing for the test and form a study group.
Exam minus 4 months	Read Chapters 7 and 8 and work through the exercises. Use at least one of the additional resources for each chapter. Start practicing your math by making up problems out of everyday events. Exercise your memory by making note of the buildings and rooms you see each day.
Exam minus 3 months	Read Chapters 9 and 10 and work through the exercises. Visit your local auto mechanic and familiarize yourself with the tools you see there. You're still doing your reading, aren't you?
Exam minus 2 months	Read Chapters 11 and 12 and work through the exercises. Practice your map-reading skills by drawing a map of your neighborhood and finding the most direct routes to the places you frequent.
Exam minus 1 month	Take one of the sample tests in either Chapter 13 or 14. Use your score to help you decide where to concentrate your efforts this month. Go back to the relevant chapters and use the additional resources listed there, or get the help of a friend or teacher.
Exam minus 1 week	Review the sample tests. See how much you've learned in the past months. Concentrate on what you've done well and decide not to let any areas where you still feel uncertain bother you.
Exam minus 1 day	Relax. Do something unrelated to firefighter exams. Eat a good meal and go to bed at your usual time.

SCHEDULE B: THE JUST-ENOUGH-TIME PLAN

If you have three to six months before the exam, that should be enough time to prepare for the written test, especially if you score above 70 on the first sample test you take. This schedule assumes four months; stretch it out or compress it if you have more or less time, and only study the chapters that are relevant to the type of exam you'll be taking.

Time	Preparation
Exam minus 4 months	Take one practice exam from Chapters 4 or 5 to determine where you need most work. Read Chapters 6, 7, and 8 and work through the exercises. Use at least one of the additional resources listed in each chapter. Start going to the library once every two weeks to read books about firefighting. Exercise your memory by making note of the buildings and rooms you see each day. Practice your math by making up problems out of everyday events.
Exam minus 3 months	Read Chapters 9 and 10 and work through the exercises. Use at least one of the additional resources for each chapter. Visit your local auto mechanic and familiarize yourself with the tools you see there.
Exam minus 2 months	Read Chapters 11 and 12 and work through the exercises. Practice your map reading skills by drawing a map of your neighborhood and finding the most direct routes to the places you frequent. You're still doing your reading, aren't you?
Exam minus 1 month	Take one of the sample tests in either Chapter 13 or 14. Use your score to help you decide where to concentrate your efforts this month. Go back to the relevant chapters and use the extra resources listed there, or get the help of a friend or teacher.
Exam minus 1 week	Review the sample tests. See how much you've learned in the past months. Concentrate on what you've done well, and decide not to let any areas where you still feel uncertain bother you.
Exam minus 1 day	Relax. Do something unrelated to firefighter exams. Eat a good meal and go to bed at your usual time.

SCHEDULE C: MORE STUDY IN LESS TIME

If you have one to three months before the exam, you still have enough time for some concentrated study that will help you improve your score. This schedule is built around a two-month time frame. If you have only one month, spend an extra couple of hours a week to get all these steps in. If you have three months, take some of the steps from Schedule B and fit them in. Only study the chapters that are relevant to the type of exam you'll be taking.

Time	Preparation
Exam minus 8 weeks	Take one sample test from Chapters 4 or 5 to find one or two areas you're weakest in. Choose the appropriate chapter(s) from among Chapters 6–12 to read in these two weeks. Use some of the additional resources listed there. When you get to those chapters in this plan, review them.
Exam minus 6 weeks	Read Chapters 6–9 and work through the exercises.
Exam minus 4 weeks	Read Chapters 10–12 and work through the exercises.
Exam minus 2 weeks	Take one of the second sample tests in either Chapter 13 or 14. Then score it and read the answer explanations until you're sure you understand them. Review the areas where your score is lowest.
Exam minus 1 week	Review the sample tests, concentrating on the areas where a little work can help the most.
Exam minus 1 day	Relax. Do something unrelated to firefighter exams. Eat a good meal and go to bed at your usual time.

SCHEDULE D: THE CRAM PLAN

If you have three weeks or less before the exam, you really have your work cut out for you. Carve half an hour out of your day, *every day*, for study. This schedule assumes you have the whole three weeks to prepare in; if you have less time, you'll have to compress the schedule accordingly. Only study the chapters that are relevant to the type of exam you'll be taking.

Time	Preparation
Exam minus 3 weeks	Take one practice exam from Chapter 4 or 5. Then read the material in Chapters 6–9 and work through the exercises.
Exam minus 2 weeks	Read the material in Chapters 10–12 and work through the exercises. Take one of the sample tests in either Chapter 13 or 14.
Exam minus 1 week	Evaluate your performance on the second sample test. Review the parts of Chapters 6–12 that you had the most trouble with. Get a friend or teacher to help you with the section you had the most difficulty with.
Exam minus 2 days	Review the sample tests. Make sure you understand the answer explanations.
Exam minus 1 day	Relax. Do something unrelated to firefighter exams. Eat a good meal and go to bed at your usual time.

STEP 4: LEARN TO MANAGE YOUR TIME

Time to complete: 10 minutes to read, many hours of practice!

Activities: Practice these strategies as you take the sample tests in this book

Steps 4, 5, and 6 of the LearningExpress Test Preparation System put you in charge of your exam by showing you test-taking strategies that work. Practice these strategies as you take the sample tests in this book, and then you'll be ready to use them on test day.

First, you'll take control of your time on the exam. The first step in achieving this control is to find out the format of the exam you're going to take. Some firefighter exams have different sections that are each timed separately. If this is true of the exam you'll be taking, you'll want to practice using your time wisely on the practice exams and trying to avoid mistakes while working quickly. Other types of exams don't have separately timed sections. If this is the case, just practice pacing yourself on the practice exams so you don't spend too much time on difficult questions.

- **Listen carefully to directions.** By the time you get to the exam, you should know how the test works, but listen just in case something has changed.
- **Pace yourself.** Glance at your watch every few minutes, and compare the time to how far you've gotten in the section. When one-quarter of the time has elapsed, you should be a quarter of the way through the section, and so on. If you're falling behind, pick up the pace a bit.
- **Keep moving.** Don't dither around on one question. If you don't know the answer, skip the question and move on. Circle the number of the question in your test booklet in case you have time to come back to it later.
- **Keep track of your place on the answer sheet.** If you skip a question, make sure you skip on the answer sheet too. Check yourself every 5–10 questions to make sure the question number and the answer sheet number are still the same.
- **Don't rush.** Though you should keep moving, rushing won't help. Try to keep calm and work methodically and quickly.

STEP 5: LEARN TO USE THE PROCESS OF ELIMINATION

Time to complete: 20 minutes

Activity: Complete worksheet on Using the Process of Elimination

After time management, your next most important tool for taking control of your exam is using the process of elimination wisely. It's standard test-taking wisdom that you should always read all the answer choices before choosing your answer. This helps you find the right answer by eliminating wrong answer choices. And, sure enough, that standard wisdom applies to your exam, too.

Let's say you're facing a vocabulary question that goes like this:

13. "Biology uses a <u>binomial</u> system of classification." In this sentence, the word <u>binomial</u> most nearly means
   a. understanding the law
   b. having two names
   c. scientifically sound
   d. having a double meaning

If you happen to know what *binomial* means, of course, you don't need to use the process of elimination, but let's assume that, like most people, you don't. So you look at the answer choices. "Understanding the law" sure doesn't sound very likely for something having to do with biology. So you eliminate choice **a**—and now you only have three answer choices to deal with. Mark an X next to choice **a** so you never have to read it again.

On to the other answer choices. If you know that the prefix *bi-* means *two*, as in *bicycle*, you'll flag answer **b** as a possible answer. Mark a check mark beside it, meaning "good answer, I might use this one."

Choice **c**, "scientifically sound," is a possibility. At least it's about science, not law. It could work here, though, when you think about it, having a "scientifically sound" classification system in a scientific field is kind of redundant. You remember the *bi* thing in *binomial*, and probably continue to like answer **b** better. But you're not sure, so you put a question mark next to **c**, meaning "well, maybe."

Now, choice **d**, "having a double meaning." You're still keeping in mind that *bi-* means *two*, so this one looks possible at first. But then you look again at the sentence the word belongs in, and you think, "Why would biology want a system of classification that has two meanings? That wouldn't work very well!" If you're really taken with the idea that *bi* means *two*, you might put a question mark here. But if you're feeling a little more confident, you'll put an X. You've already got a better answer picked out.

Now your question looks like this:

13. "Biology uses a <u>binomial</u> system of classification." In this sentence, the word <u>binomial</u> most nearly means
   ✕ **a.** understanding the law
   ✔ **b.** having two names
   ? **c.** scientifically sound
   ? **d.** having a double meaning

You've got just one check mark, for a good answer. If you're pressed for time, you should simply mark answer **b** on your answer sheet. If you've got the time to be extra careful, you could compare your check-mark answer to your question-mark answers to make sure that it's better. (It is: the *binomial* system in biology is the one that gives a two-part genus and species name like *homo sapiens*.)

It's good to have a system for marking good, bad, and maybe answers. We're recommending this one:

   ✕ = bad
   ✔ = good
   ? = maybe

If you don't like these marks, devise your own system. Just make sure you do it long before test day—while you're working through the practice exams in this book—so you won't have to worry about it during the test.

Even when you think you're absolutely clueless about a question, you can often use process of elimination to get rid of one answer choice. If so, you're better prepared to make an educated guess, as you'll see in Step 6. More often, the process of elimination allows you to get down to only *two* possibly right answers. Then you're in a strong position to guess. And sometimes, even though you don't know the right answer, you find it simply by getting rid of the wrong ones, as you did in the example above.

Try using your powers of elimination on the questions in the worksheet Using the Process of Elimination beginning on this page. The answer explanations there show one possible way you might use the process to arrive at the right answer.

The process of elimination is your tool for the next step, which is knowing when to guess.

Using the Process of Elimination

Use the process of elimination to answer the following questions.

1. Ilsa is as old as Meghan will be in five years. The difference between Ed's age and Meghan's age is twice the difference between Ilsa's age and Meghan's age. Ed is 29. How old is Ilsa?
   a. 4
   b. 10
   c. 19
   d. 24

2. "All drivers of commercial vehicles must carry a valid commercial driver's license whenever operating a commercial vehicle." According to this sentence, which of the following people need NOT carry a commercial driver's license?
   a. a truck driver idling his engine while waiting to be directed to a loading dock
   b. a bus operator backing her bus out of the way of another bus in the bus lot
   c. a taxi driver driving his personal car to the grocery store
   d. a limousine driver taking the limousine to her home after dropping off her last passenger of the evening

3. Smoking tobacco has been linked to
   a. increased risk of stroke and heart attack
   b. all forms of respiratory disease
   c. increasing mortality rates over the past ten years
   d. juvenile delinquency

4. Which of the following words is spelled correctly?
    a. incorrigible
    b. outragous
    c. domestickated
    d. understandible

Answers

Here are the answers, as well as some suggestions as to how you might have used the process of elimination to find them.

1. **d.** You should have eliminated answer **a** off the bat. Ilsa can't be four years old if Meghan is going to be Ilsa's age in five years. The best way to eliminate other answer choices is to try plugging them in to the information given in the problem. For instance, for answer **b,** if Ilsa is 10, then Meghan must be 5. The difference in their ages is 5. The difference between Ed's age, 29, and Meghan's age, 5, is 24. Is 24 two times 5? No. Then answer **b** is wrong. You could eliminate answer **c** in the same way and be left with answer **d.**

2. **c.** Note the word *not* in the question, and go through the answers one by one. Is the truck driver in choice **a** "operating a commericial vehicle"? Yes, idling counts as "operating," so he needs to have a commercial driver's license. Likewise, the bus operator in answer **b** is operating a commercial vehicle; the question doesn't say the operator has to be on the street. The limo driver in **d** is operating a commercial vehicle, even if it doesn't have passenger in it. However, the cabbie in answer **c** is *not* operating a commercial vehicle, but his own private car.

3. **a.** You could eliminate answer **b** simply because of the presence of the word *all.* Such absolutes hardly ever appear in correct answer choices. Choice **c** looks attractive until you think a little about what you know—aren't *fewer* people smoking these days, rather than more? So how could smoking be responsible for a higher mortality rate? (If you didn't know that *mortality rate* means the rate at which people die, you might keep this choice as a possibility, but you'd still be able to eliminate two answers and have only two to choose from.) And choice **d** is plain silly, so you could eliminate that one, too. And you're left with the correct choice, **a.**

4. **a.** How you used the process of elimination here depends on which words you recognized as being spelled incorrectly. If you knew that the correct spellings were *outrageous, domesticated,* and *understandable,* then you were home free. Surely you knew that at least one of those words was wrong!

STEP 6: KNOW WHEN TO GUESS

Time to complete: 20 minutes

Activity: Complete worksheet on Your Guessing Ability

Armed with the process of elimination, you're ready to take control of one of the big questions in test-taking: Should I guess? The first and main answer is Yes. Unless the exam has a so-called "guessing penalty," you have nothing to lose and everything to gain from guessing. The more complicated answer depends both on the exam and on you—your personality and your "guessing intuition."

Most firefighter exams don't use a guessing penalty. The number of questions you answer correctly yields your score, and there's no penalty for wrong answers. So most of the time, you don't have to worry—simply go ahead and guess. But if you find that your exam does have a "guessing penalty," you should read the section below to find out what that means to you.

How the "Guessing Penalty" Works

A "guessing penalty" really only works against *random* guessing—filling in the little circles to make a nice pattern on your answer sheet. If you can eliminate one or more answer choices, as outlined above, you're better off taking a guess than leaving the answer blank, even on the sections that have a penalty.

Here's how a "guessing penalty" works: Depending on the number of answer choices in a given exam, some proportion of the number of questions you get wrong is subtracted from the total number of questions you got right. For instance, if there are four answer choices, typically the "guessing penalty" is one-third of your wrong answers. Suppose you took a test of 100 questions. You answered 88 of them right and 12 wrong.

If there's no guessing penalty, your score is simply 88. But if there's a one-third point guessing penalty, the scorers take your 12 wrong answers and divide by 3 to come up with 4. Then they *subtract* that 4 from your correct-answer score of 88 to leave you with a score of 84. Thus, you would have been better off if you had simply not answered those 12 questions that you weren't sure of. Then your total score would still be 88, because there wouldn't be anything to subtract.

What You Should Do About the Guessing Penalty

That's how a guessing penalty works. The first thing this means for you is that marking your answer sheet at random doesn't pay. If you're running out of time on an exam that has a guessing penalty, you should not use your remaining seconds to mark a pretty pattern on your answer sheet. Take those few seconds to try to answer one more question right.

But as soon as you get out of the realm of random guessing, the "guessing penalty" no longer works against you. If you can use the process of elimination to get rid of even one wrong answer choice, the odds stop being against you and start working in your favor.

Sticking with our example of an exam that has four answer choices, eliminating just one wrong answer makes your odds of choosing the correct answer one in three. That's the same as the one-out-of-three guessing penalty—even odds. If you eliminate two answer choices, your odds are one in two—better than the guessing penalty. In either case, you should go ahead and choose one of the remaining answer choices.

(continued on page 20)

Your Guessing Ability

The following are ten really hard questions. You're not supposed to know the answers. Rather, this is an assessment of your ability to guess when you don't have a clue. Read each question carefully, just as if you did expect to answer it. If you have any knowledge at all of the subject of the question, use that knowledge to help you eliminate wrong answer choices. Use this answer grid to fill in your answers to the questions.

ANSWER GRID

1. (a) (b) (c) (d)   5. (a) (b) (c) (d)   9. (a) (b) (c) (d)
2. (a) (b) (c) (d)   6. (a) (b) (c) (d)   10. (a) (b) (c) (d)
3. (a) (b) (c) (d)   7. (a) (b) (c) (d)
4. (a) (b) (c) (d)   8. (a) (b) (c) (d)

1. September 7 is Independence Day in
    a. India
    b. Costa Rica
    c. Brazil
    d. Australia √

2. Which of the following is the formula for determining the momentum of an object?
    a. $p = mv$
    b. $F = ma$
    c. $P = IV$
    d. $E = mc^2$ √

3. Because of the expansion of the universe, the stars and other celestial bodies are all moving away from each other. This phenomenon is known as
    a. Newton's first law
    b. the big bang
    c. gravitational collapse
    d. Hubble flow

4. American author Gertrude Stein was born in
    a. 1713
    b. 1830
    c. 1874
    d. 1901

5. Which of the following is NOT one of the Five Classics attributed to Confucius?
   a. the I Ching
   b. the Book of Holiness
   c. the Spring and Autumn Annals
   d. the Book of History

6. The religious and philosophical doctrine that holds that the universe is constantly in a struggle between good and evil is known as
   a. Pelagianism
   b. Manichaeanism
   c. neo-Hegelianism
   d. Epicureanism

7. The third Chief Justice of the U.S. Supreme Court was
   a. John Blair
   b. William Cushing
   c. James Wilson
   d. John Jay

8. Which of the following is the poisonous portion of a daffodil?
   a. the bulb
   b. the leaves
   c. the stem
   d. the flowers

9. The winner of the Masters golf tournament in 1953 was
   a. Sam Snead
   b. Cary Middlecoff
   c. Arnold Palmer
   d. Ben Hogan

10. The state with the highest per capita personal income in 1980 was
    a. Alaska
    b. Connecticut
    c. New York
    d. Texas

Answers

Check your answers against the correct answers below.

1. c.   **5.** b.   **9.** d.
2. a.   **6.** b.   **10.** a.
3. d.   **7.** b.
4. c.   **8.** a.

How Did You Do?

You may have simply gotten lucky and actually known the answer to one or two questions. In addition, your guessing was more successful if you were able to use the process of elimination on any of the questions. Maybe you didn't know who the third Chief Justice was (question 7), but you knew that John Jay was the first. In that case, you would have eliminated answer **d** and therefore improved your odds of guessing right from one in four to one in three.

According to probability, you should get 2 1/2 answers correct, so getting either two or three right would be average. If you got four or more right, you may be a really terrific guesser. If you got one or none right, you may be a really bad guesser.

Keep in mind, though, that this is only a small sample. You should continue to keep track of your guessing ability as you work through the sample questions in this book. Circle the numbers of questions you guess on as you make your guess; or, if you don't have time while you take the practice tests, go back afterward and try to remember which questions you guessed at. Remember, on a test with four answer choices, your chances of getting a right answer is one in four. So keep a separate "guessing" score for each exam. How many questions did you guess on? How many did you get right? If the number you got right is at least one-fourth of the number of questions you guessed on, you are at least an average guesser, maybe better—and you should always go ahead and guess on the real exam. If the number you got right is significantly lower than one-fourth of the number you guessed on, you should not guess on exams where there is a guessing penalty unless you can eliminate a wrong answer. If there's no guessing penalty, you would, frankly, be safe in guessing anyway, but maybe you'd feel more comfortable if you guessed only selectively, when you can eliminate a wrong answer or at least have a good feeling about one of the answer choices.

WHEN THERE IS NO GUESSING PENALTY

As noted above, most firefighter exams don't have a guessing penalty. That means that, all other things being equal, you should always go ahead and guess, even if you have no idea what the question means. Nothing can happen to you if you're wrong. But all other things aren't necessarily equal. The other factor in deciding whether or not to guess, besides the exam and whether or not it has a guessing penalty, is you. There are two things you need to know about yourself before you go into the exam:

- Are you a risk-taker?
- Are you a good guesser?

Your risk-taking temperament matters most on exams with a guessing penalty. Without a guessing penalty, even if you're a play-it-safe person, guessing is perfectly safe. Overcome your anxieties, and go ahead and mark an answer.

But what if you're not much of a risk-taker, *and* you think of yourself as the world's worst guesser? Complete the worksheet Your Guessing Ability to get an idea of how good your intuition is.

STEP 7: REACH YOUR PEAK PERFORMANCE ZONE

Time to complete: 10 minutes to read; weeks to complete!
Activity: Complete the Physical Preparation Checklist
To get ready for a challenge like a big exam, you have to take control of your physical, as well as your mental, state. Exercise, proper diet, and rest will ensure that your body works with, rather than against, your mind on test day, as well as during your preparation.

EXERCISE

If you don't already have a regular exercise program going, the time during which you're preparing for an exam is actually an excellent time to start one. You'll have to be pretty fit to pass your physical ability test anyway. And if you're already keeping fit—or trying to get that way—don't let the pressure of preparing for an exam fool you into quitting now. Exercise helps reduce stress by pumping wonderful good-feeling hormones called endorphins into your system. It also increases the oxygen supply throughout your body, including your brain, so you'll be at peak performance on test day.

A half hour of vigorous activity—enough to raise a sweat—every day should be your aim. If you're really pressed for time, every other day is OK. Choose an activity you like and get out there and do it. Jogging with a friend always makes the time go faster, or take a radio.

But don't overdo. You don't want to exhaust yourself. Moderation is the key.

DIET

First of all, cut out the junk. Go easy on caffeine and nicotine, and eliminate alcohol and any other drugs from your system at least two weeks before the exam. Promise yourself a binge the night after the exam, if need be.

(continued on page 22)

Physical Preparation Checklist

For the week before the test, write down 1) what physical exercise you engaged in and for how long and 2) what you ate for each meal. Remember, you're trying for at least half an hour of exercise every other day (preferably every day) and a balanced diet that's light on junk food.

Exam minus 7 days
Exercise: _____ for _____ minutes
Breakfast: _____
Lunch: _____
Dinner: _____
Snacks: _____

Exam minus 6 days
Exercise: _____ for _____ minutes
Breakfast: _____
Lunch: _____
Dinner: _____
Snacks: _____

Exam minus 5 days
Exercise: _____ for _____ minutes
Breakfast: _____
Lunch: _____
Dinner: _____
Snacks: _____

Exam minus 4 days
Exercise: _____ for _____ minutes
Breakfast: _____
Lunch: _____
Dinner: _____
Snacks: _____

Exam minus 3 days
Exercise: _____ for _____ minutes
Breakfast: _____
Lunch: _____
Dinner: _____
Snacks: _____

Exam minus 2 days

Exercise: _____ for _____ minutes

Breakfast: _____

Lunch: _____

Dinner: _____

Snacks: _____

Exam minus 1 day

Exercise: _____ for _____ minutes

Breakfast: _____

Lunch: _____

Dinner: _____

Snacks: _____

What your body needs for peak performance is simply a balanced diet. Eat plenty of fruits and vegetables, along with protein and carbohydrates. Foods that are high in lecithin (an amino acid), such as fish and beans, are especially good "brain foods."

The night before the exam, you might "carbo-load" the way athletes do before a contest. Eat a big plate of spaghetti, rice and beans, or whatever your favorite carbohydrate is.

REST

You probably know how much sleep you need every night to be at your best, even if you don't always get it. Make sure you do get that much sleep, though, for at least a week before the exam. Moderation is important here, too. Extra sleep will just make you groggy.

If you're not a morning person and your exam will be given in the morning, you should reset your internal clock so that your body doesn't think you're taking an exam at 3 a.m. You have to start this process well before the exam. The way it works is to get up half an hour earlier each morning, and then go to bed half an hour earlier that night. Don't try it the other way around; you'll just toss and turn if you go to bed early without having gotten up early. The next morning, get up another half an hour earlier, and so on. How long you will have to do this depends on how late you're used to getting up.

STEP 8: GET YOUR ACT TOGETHER

Time to complete: 10 minutes to read; time to complete will vary

Activity: Complete Final Preparations worksheet

You're in control of your mind and body; you're in charge of test anxiety, your preparation, and your test-taking strategies. Now it's time to take charge of external factors, like the testing site and the materials you need to take the exam.

FIND OUT WHERE THE TEST IS AND MAKE A TRIAL RUN

The exam bulletin will tell you when and where your exam is being held. Do you know how to get to the testing site? Do you know how long it will take you to get there? If not, make a trial run, preferably on the same day of the week at the same time of day. Make note, on the worksheet Final Preparations, of the amount of time it will take you to get to the exam site. Plan on arriving 10–15 minutes early so you can get the lay of the land, use the bathroom, and calm down. Then figure out how early you will have to get up that morning, and make sure you get up that early every day for a week before the exam.

GATHER YOUR MATERIALS

The night before the exam, lay out the clothes you will wear and the materials you have to bring with you to the exam. Plan on dressing in layers; you won't have any control over the temperature of the examination room. Have a sweater or jacket you can take off if it's warm. Use the checklist on the worksheet Final Preparations to help you pull together what you'll need.

DON'T SKIP BREAKFAST

Even if you don't usually eat breakfast, do so on exam morning. A cup of coffee doesn't count. Don't do doughnuts or other sweet foods, either. A sugar high will leave you with a sugar low in the middle of the exam. A mix of protein and carbohydrates is best: cereal with milk and just a little sugar, or eggs with toast, will do your body a world of good.

STEP 9: DO IT!

Time to complete: 10 minutes, plus test-taking time

Activity: Ace the Firefighter Exam!

Fast forward to exam day. You're ready. You made a study plan and followed through. You practiced your test-taking strategies while working through this book. You're in control of your physical, mental, and emotional state. You know when and where to show up and what to bring with you. In other words, you're better prepared than most of the other people taking the exam with you. You're psyched.

Just one more thing. When you're done with the firefighter exam, you will have earned a reward. Plan a celebration. Call up your friends and plan a party, or have a nice dinner for two—whatever your heart desires. Give yourself something to look forward to.

And then do it. Go into the exam, full of confidence, armed with test-taking strategies you've practiced till they're second nature. You're in control of yourself, your environment, and your performance on the exam. You're ready to succeed. So do it. Go in there and ace the exam. And look forward to your future career as a firefighter!

Final Preparations

Getting to the Exam Site

Location of exam: _____

Date of exam: _____

Time of exam: _____

Do I know how to get to the exam site? Yes _____ No _____
If no, make a trial run.

Time it will take to get to the exam site: _____

Things to lay out the night before

Clothes I will wear   _____

Sweater/jacket   _____

Watch   _____

Photo ID   _____

Admission card   _____

4 No. 2 pencils   _____

_____   _____

_____   _____

C·H·A·P·T·E·R 4

FIREFIGHTER EXAM 1

CHAPTER SUMMARY

This is the first practice exam in this book based on the most commonly tested areas on the firefighter written exams. Use this test to see how you would do if you had to take the exam today.

The skills tested on the exam that follows are the ones that have been tested in the past on firefighter exams that focus on job-related skills. The exam you take may *look* somewhat different from this exam, but you'll find that this exam provides vital practice in the skills you need to pass a firefighter exam. For a somewhat different type of test, see Firefighter Exam 2 in the next chapter.

The practice exam consists of 100 multiple-choice questions in the following areas: memory and observation, reading comprehension, verbal expression, spatial relations, judgment, and following procedures.

Normally you would have about three hours for this test; however, for now don't worry about timing. Just take the test in as relaxed a manner as you can. The answer sheet you should use for answering the questions is on the following page. Then comes the exam itself, and after that is the answer key, with each correct answer explained. The answer key is followed by a section on how to score your exam.

1.	ⓐ	ⓑ	ⓒ	ⓓ	35.	ⓐ	ⓑ	ⓒ	ⓓ	69.	ⓐ	ⓑ	ⓒ	ⓓ
2.	ⓐ	ⓑ	ⓒ	ⓓ	36.	ⓐ	ⓑ	ⓒ	ⓓ	70.	ⓐ	ⓑ	ⓒ	ⓓ
3.	ⓐ	ⓑ	ⓒ	ⓓ	37.	ⓐ	ⓑ	ⓒ	ⓓ	71.	ⓐ	ⓑ	ⓒ	ⓓ
4.	ⓐ	ⓑ	ⓒ	ⓓ	38.	ⓐ	ⓑ	ⓒ	ⓓ	72.	ⓐ	ⓑ	ⓒ	ⓓ
5.	ⓐ	ⓑ	ⓒ	ⓓ	39.	ⓐ	ⓑ	ⓒ	ⓓ	73.	ⓐ	ⓑ	ⓒ	ⓓ
6.	ⓐ	ⓑ	ⓒ	ⓓ	40.	ⓐ	ⓑ	ⓒ	ⓓ	74.	ⓐ	ⓑ	ⓒ	ⓓ
7.	ⓐ	ⓑ	ⓒ	ⓓ	41.	ⓐ	ⓑ	ⓒ	ⓓ	75.	ⓐ	ⓑ	ⓒ	ⓓ
8.	ⓐ	ⓑ	ⓒ	ⓓ	42.	ⓐ	ⓑ	ⓒ	ⓓ	76.	ⓐ	ⓑ	ⓒ	ⓓ
9.	ⓐ	ⓑ	ⓒ	ⓓ	43.	ⓐ	ⓑ	ⓒ	ⓓ	77.	ⓐ	ⓑ	ⓒ	ⓓ
10.	ⓐ	ⓑ	ⓒ	ⓓ	44.	ⓐ	ⓑ	ⓒ	ⓓ	78.	ⓐ	ⓑ	ⓒ	ⓓ
11.	ⓐ	ⓑ	ⓒ	ⓓ	45.	ⓐ	ⓑ	ⓒ	ⓓ	79.	ⓐ	ⓑ	ⓒ	ⓓ
12.	ⓐ	ⓑ	ⓒ	ⓓ	46.	ⓐ	ⓑ	ⓒ	ⓓ	80.	ⓐ	ⓑ	ⓒ	ⓓ
13.	ⓐ	ⓑ	ⓒ	ⓓ	47.	ⓐ	ⓑ	ⓒ	ⓓ	81.	ⓐ	ⓑ	ⓒ	ⓓ
14.	ⓐ	ⓑ	ⓒ	ⓓ	48.	ⓐ	ⓑ	ⓒ	ⓓ	82.	ⓐ	ⓑ	ⓒ	ⓓ
15.	ⓐ	ⓑ	ⓒ	ⓓ	49.	ⓐ	ⓑ	ⓒ	ⓓ	83.	ⓐ	ⓑ	ⓒ	ⓓ
16.	ⓐ	ⓑ	ⓒ	ⓓ	50.	ⓐ	ⓑ	ⓒ	ⓓ	84.	ⓐ	ⓑ	ⓒ	ⓓ
17.	ⓐ	ⓑ	ⓒ	ⓓ	51.	ⓐ	ⓑ	ⓒ	ⓓ	85.	ⓐ	ⓑ	ⓒ	ⓓ
18.	ⓐ	ⓑ	ⓒ	ⓓ	52.	ⓐ	ⓑ	ⓒ	ⓓ	86.	ⓐ	ⓑ	ⓒ	ⓓ
19.	ⓐ	ⓑ	ⓒ	ⓓ	53.	ⓐ	ⓑ	ⓒ	ⓓ	87.	ⓐ	ⓑ	ⓒ	ⓓ
20.	ⓐ	ⓑ	ⓒ	ⓓ	54.	ⓐ	ⓑ	ⓒ	ⓓ	88.	ⓐ	ⓑ	ⓒ	ⓓ
21.	ⓐ	ⓑ	ⓒ	ⓓ	55.	ⓐ	ⓑ	ⓒ	ⓓ	89.	ⓐ	ⓑ	ⓒ	ⓓ
22.	ⓐ	ⓑ	ⓒ	ⓓ	56.	ⓐ	ⓑ	ⓒ	ⓓ	90.	ⓐ	ⓑ	ⓒ	ⓓ
23.	ⓐ	ⓑ	ⓒ	ⓓ	57.	ⓐ	ⓑ	ⓒ	ⓓ	91.	ⓐ	ⓑ	ⓒ	ⓓ
24.	ⓐ	ⓑ	ⓒ	ⓓ	58.	ⓐ	ⓑ	ⓒ	ⓓ	92.	ⓐ	ⓑ	ⓒ	ⓓ
25.	ⓐ	ⓑ	ⓒ	ⓓ	59.	ⓐ	ⓑ	ⓒ	ⓓ	93.	ⓐ	ⓑ	ⓒ	ⓓ
26.	ⓐ	ⓑ	ⓒ	ⓓ	60.	ⓐ	ⓑ	ⓒ	ⓓ	94.	ⓐ	ⓑ	ⓒ	ⓓ
27.	ⓐ	ⓑ	ⓒ	ⓓ	61.	ⓐ	ⓑ	ⓒ	ⓓ	95.	ⓐ	ⓑ	ⓒ	ⓓ
28.	ⓐ	ⓑ	ⓒ	ⓓ	62.	ⓐ	ⓑ	ⓒ	ⓓ	96.	ⓐ	ⓑ	ⓒ	ⓓ
29.	ⓐ	ⓑ	ⓒ	ⓓ	63.	ⓐ	ⓑ	ⓒ	ⓓ	97.	ⓐ	ⓑ	ⓒ	ⓓ
30.	ⓐ	ⓑ	ⓒ	ⓓ	64.	ⓐ	ⓑ	ⓒ	ⓓ	98.	ⓐ	ⓑ	ⓒ	ⓓ
31.	ⓐ	ⓑ	ⓒ	ⓓ	65.	ⓐ	ⓑ	ⓒ	ⓓ	99.	ⓐ	ⓑ	ⓒ	ⓓ
32.	ⓐ	ⓑ	ⓒ	ⓓ	66.	ⓐ	ⓑ	ⓒ	ⓓ	100.	ⓐ	ⓑ	ⓒ	ⓓ
33.	ⓐ	ⓑ	ⓒ	ⓓ	67.	ⓐ	ⓑ	ⓒ	ⓓ					
34.	ⓐ	ⓑ	ⓒ	ⓓ	68.	ⓐ	ⓑ	ⓒ	ⓓ					

You will have 5 minutes to study the diagram on the following page, after which you must turn the page and answer questions 1–7 from memory. You will not be permitted to look back at the diagram in order to answer the questions.

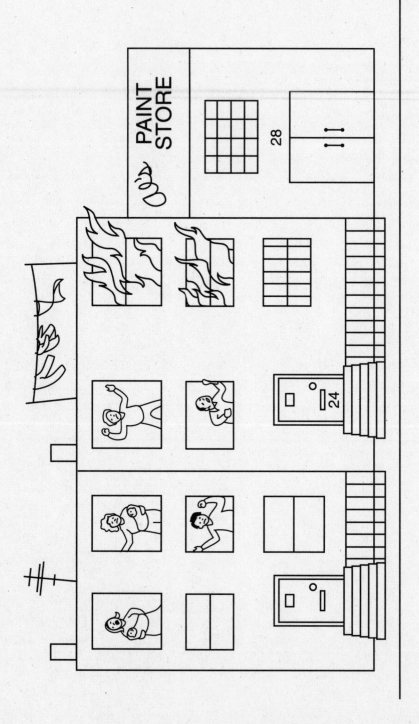

After you have spent 5 minutes studying the diagram on the previous page, turn the page and answer questions 1–7 based on the diagram. DO NOT turn back to the diagram to answer these questions. When you have finished questions 1–7, you may go on to the next memory diagram.

1. Upon arriving at the scene, you can see flames leaping inside the windows on which floor(s)?
   a. second floor only
   b. third floor only
   c. first and third floors
   ✓ d. second and third floors

2. How many victims can you see in the building that is on fire?
   a. none
   b. one
   ✓ c. two
   d. three

3. What is the address of the business next door to the fire scene?
   a. 22
   b. 20
   c. 24
   ✓ d. 28

4. You must evacuate the victims in the fire building from the roof. What are the obstructions that are in your way?
   a. a clothesline and two smoke stacks
   b. a TV antenna and two smoke stacks
   c. a clothesline and a TV antenna
   ✓ d. a clothesline and a smoke stack

5. How many people are standing in the windows of the dwelling adjacent to the fire?
   a. two adults
   b. three adults
   c. three adults and two babies
   ✓ d. two adults and two babies

6. When you arrive at the scene, you evacuate the business next door to the fire for all of the following reasons EXCEPT
   a. paints can be extremely flammable
   b. the fire has spread to the roof of the store
   c. smoke may endanger the employees and patrons of the store
   d. the store shares the fire wall with the building on fire

7. There is one window of the fire building that firefighters do not have access to. On which floor is it located?
   ✓ a. first
   b. third
   c. basement
   d. second

You will have 5 minutes to study the diagram on the next page, after which you must turn the page and answer questions 8–15 from memory. You will not be permitted to look back at the diagram in order to answer the questions.

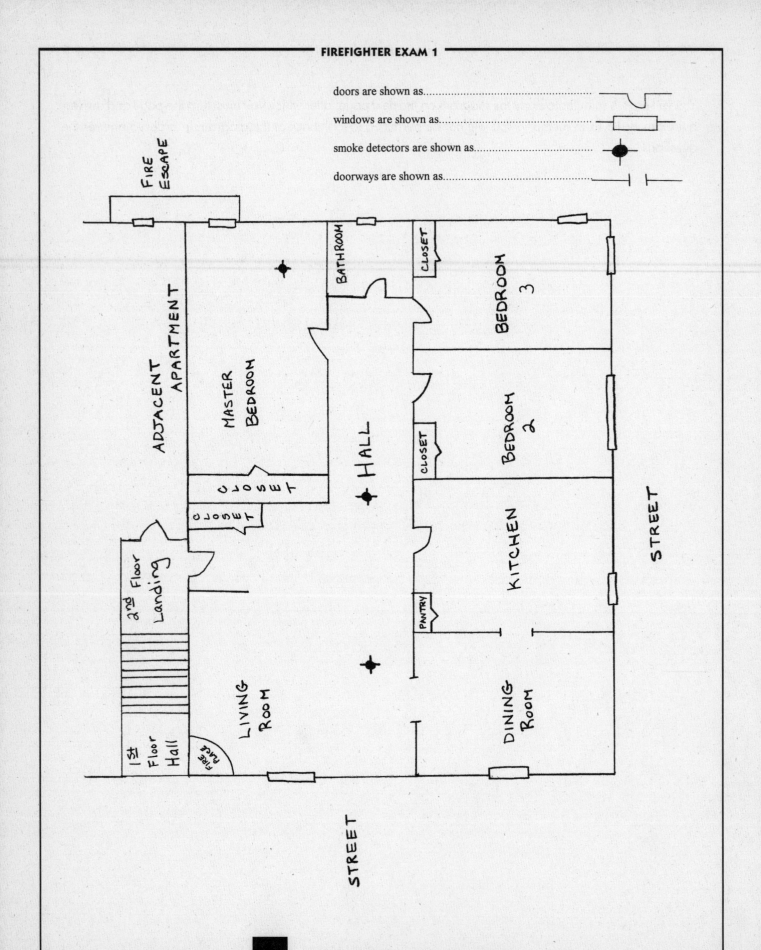

doors are shown as..

windows are shown as...

smoke detectors are shown as...

doorways are shown as...

After you have spent 5 minutes studying the diagram, turn the page and answer questions 8–15 based on the diagram. DO NOT turn back to the diagram to answer these questions. When you have finished questions 8–15, you may go on with the rest of the test.

8. The number of rooms in the apartment is
   a. eight
   b. seven
   c. six
   d. five

9. The firefighters enter the first floor hall and proceed up the stairs and into the apartment. What is the first room they encounter?
   a. the living room
   b. the master bedroom
   c. the bathroom
   d. the kitchen

10. How many smoke detectors are in the bedrooms?
   a. none
   b. one
   c. two
   d. three

11. While searching a room firefighters notice there are two windows. Which room are they in?
   a. bedroom 3
   b. the dining room
   c. bedroom 2
   d. the master bedroom

12. During the night a spark from the fireplace starts the carpet smoldering, which causes the drapes to catch fire. The fire begins to spread. The areas most affected by the fire are the
   a. kitchen and bedroom 2
   b. living room and bathroom
   c. master bedroom and bedroom 2
   d. living room and dining room

13. The residents of the apartment like to smoke in bed. One of them falls asleep in the master bedroom and drops a lit cigarette on the floor. The nearest smoke detector to be activated would be located in the
   a. hall
   b. living room
   c. master bedroom
   d. bedroom 3

14. The number of windows in the apartment is
   a. seven
   b. eight
   c. nine
   d. ten

15. The firefighters who need to get into the apartment can do so by the
   a. fire escape only
   b. windows, hall stairway, and fire escape
   c. hall stairway and fire escape only
   d. windows and hall stairway only

Answer questions 16–19 based on the following information.

The preferred order for removal of civilians from a fire building is as follows:

1. Interior stairs
2. Adjoining building
3. Fire escape
4. Ladder
5. Roof rescue rope
6. Life net

16. Which of the following is the preferred means of removing fire victims from a burning building?
a. leading them down a fire escape
b. using the aerial ladder or tower ladder
c. using the stairway inside the building
d. using a life net

17. What means of saving civilians trapped by fire would be used only as a last resort?
a. using a roof rescue rope and removing the victims through a window
b. taking them out via an adjoining building
c. telling them to jump into the life net
d. raising a portable ladder to a window

18. Several firefighters suddenly become trapped by the fire they are fighting. They cannot get out by the interior stairs or through the adjoining building. What method of escape should they try next?
a. the fire escape
b. a ladder
c. the roof rescue rope
d. the life net

19. Before resorting to using the ladder, a firefighter should try all the following escape methods, EXCEPT
a. going through the adjoining building
b. sliding down the roof rescue rope
c. using the interior stairs
d. using the fire escape

Answer question 20 based on your best judgment and common sense.

20. Firefighters are required to check the air supply on their self-contained breathing apparatus each day. If there is any reduction in pressure, the firefighter should change the air tank and replace it with a full tank. The main reason firefighters should have full air tanks is that
a. a full air tank permits the firefighters to operate for a maximum length of time in a fire area
b. firefighters won't have to check their air tank for the rest of the week if the tanks are not used
c. a full air tank allows the firefighters to have a feeling of confidence and protection against heat, flame, and toxic gases
d. checking and replacing tanks provides work for the firefighters assigned to the Mask Maintenance Unit

Answer questions 21–23 based on the following information.

Firefighters may require the use of supplemental oxygen while fighting a fire. The equipment consists of a compressed air tank with an off/on valve and a pressure gauge that indicates how much air is remaining in the tank. There is also a flexible hose connecting the air tank to the face mask. Firefighters should follow the standard procedure for use of this equipment as outlined below.

1. Upon arrival at a fire scene, determine if entry into the building is absolutely necessary.

2. If entry is necessary, remove supplemental breathing equipment from the truck.

3. Check the pressure gauge to insure that it contains sufficient compressed air.

4. Turn on the air valve.

5. Put on the air tank using the attached shoulder straps.

6. Put on the face mask, and take a few deep breaths to insure that air is flowing to the mask.

7. Once inside the building, continually monitor the pressure gauge to prevent running out of air. If the gauge drops below the minimum recommended pressure, exit the building.

21. Firefighters have arrived at the scene of a residential house fire. What is the first thing the firefighters should do prior to entering the building?
    a. remove supplemental breathing equipment from the truck
    b. check the pressure gauges on the breathing equipment
    c. strap the air tanks on their shoulders
    d. determine whether they really have to go in to the building

22. What should a firefighter do if she notices that the pressure gauge on the supplemental breathing equipment has dropped below the minimum recommended pressure?
    a. sit down and rest to conserve air
    b. leave the fire building
    c. continue searching the building if occupants are known to be inside
    d. connect her mask to her partner's tank

23. After putting on the air tank shoulder straps, a firefighter should
    a. put on the face mask
    b. enter the building
    c. turn on the water pumps
    d. turn on the air valve

Answer questions 24–28 based solely on the information in the following passage.

Firefighters know that the dangers of motor vehicle fires are too often overlooked. In the United States, one out of five fires involves motor vehicles, resulting each year in 600 deaths, 2,600 civilian injuries, and 1,200 injuries to firefighters. The reason for so many injuries and fatalities is that a vehicle can generate heat of up to 1,500°F. (The boiling point of water is 212°F., and the cooking temperature for most foods is 500°F.)

Because of the intense heat generated in a vehicle fire, parts of the car or truck may burst, causing debris to shoot great distances and turning bumpers, tire rims, drive shafts, axles, and even engine parts into lethal shrapnel. Gas tanks may rupture and spray highly flammable fuel. In addition, hazardous materials such as battery acid, even without burning, can cause serious injury.

Vehicle fires can also produce toxic gases. Carbon monoxide, which is produced during a fire, is an odorless and colorless gas but in high concentrations is deadly. Firefighters must wear self-contained breathing devices and full protective fire-resistant gear when attempting to extinguish a vehicle fire.

24. One reason that firefighters wear self-contained breathing devices is to protect themselves against
    a. flying car parts
    b. intense heat
    c. flammable fuels
    d. carbon monoxide

25. The passage suggests that most injuries in motor-vehicle fires are caused by
    a. battery acid
    b. odorless gases
    c. extremely high temperatures
    d. firefighters' mistakes

26. The main focus of this passage is
    a. how firefighters protect themselves against motor vehicle fires
    b. the dangers of motor-vehicle fires
    c. the amount of heat generated in motor vehicle fires
    d. the dangers of odorless gases in motor vehicle fires

27. The cooking temperature for food (500°F) is most likely included in the passage to show the reader
    a. how hot motor vehicle fires really are
    b. at what point water boils
    c. why motor vehicle fires produce toxic gases
    d. why one out of five fires involves a motor vehicle

28. One reason that firefighters must be aware of the possibility of carbon monoxide in motor vehicle fires is because carbon monoxide
    a. is highly concentrated
    b. cannot be seen or smelled
    c. cannot be protected against
    d. can shoot great distances into the air

Answer questions 29 and 30 based on your best judgment and common sense.

29. When a firefighter uses a ladder to rescue a citizen, the firefighter should assist the person down the ladder. The most important reason for giving this assistance is that
   a. even the best fire ladders tend to be unstable
   b. firefighters should do everything they can to improve public relations
   c. if there is an accident, the fire department might be held liable
   d. firefighters should keep individuals being rescued as safe as possible

30. When firefighters remove a refrigerator from an apartment, the door or door lock is removed. The chief reason for this action is that
   a. children may play in the refrigerator and lock themselves inside
   b. vagrants may use the refrigerator to store their belongings
   c. a disreputable refrigerator company may attempt to resell the refrigerator
   d. the refrigerator will develop unhealthy fumes if the door is tightly closed

31. Choose the sentence that is most clearly written.
   a. For three weeks the Merryville Fire Chief received taunting calls from an arsonist, who would not say where he intended to set the next fire.
   b. The Merryville Fire Chief received taunting calls from an arsonist, but he would not say where he intended to set the next fire, for three weeks.

   c. He would not say where he intended to set the next fire, but for three weeks the Merryville Fire Chief received taunting calls from an arsonist.
   d. The Merryville Police Chief received taunting calls from an arsonist for three weeks, not saying where he intended to set the next fire.

32. Choose the sentence that is most clearly written.
   a. Kate Meyers received a recent well-deserved promotion and several firefighters also.
   b. Having received a well-deserved promotion, recently Kate Meyers was included with several other firefighters.
   c. Kate Meyers, and including several firefighters recently, they all received a well-deserved promotion.
   d. Several firefighters, including Kate Meyers, have recently received well-deserved promotions.

Answer questions 33–35 based solely on the information in the following passage.

So that the Fire Agency Specialties Team (F.A.S.T.) can maintain a high level of efficiency and preparedness for emergency response situations, its members must meet certain requirements. In order for you to be considered for membership on F.A.S.T., your department must be a member of the F.A.S.T. organization, and you must have written permission from your fire chief or your department's highest ranking administrator.

Once active, you must meet further requirements to maintain active status. These include completion of technician level training and certification in hazardous material (hazmat) operations. In addition, after becoming a member, you must also attend a minimum of 50 percent of all drills conducted by F.A.S.T. and go to at least one F.A.S.T. conference. You may qualify for alternative credit for drills by proving previous experience in actual hazmat emergency response.

If you fail to meet minimum requirements, you will be considered inactive, and the director of your team will be notified. You will be placed back on active status only after you complete the training necessary to meet the minimum requirements.

A training calendar and schedule will be distributed to all applicants. Training will take place the third week of each month. Classes will be taught on Monday afternoons, Wednesday evenings, and Saturday afternoons.

33. Potential F.A.S.T. members can attend less than half of F.A.S.T. drills if they
   a. complete technician level training requirements
   b. indicate prior real emergency experience
   c. receive permission from their fire chief
   d. enroll in three weekly training sessions

34. Which of the following is the main subject of the passage?
   a. preparing for hazmat certification
   b. the main goal of F.A.S.T.
   c. completing F.A.S.T. membership requirements
   d. learning about your department's F.A.S.T. membership

35. Applicants must be available for training
   a. three days each week
   b. every third month
   c. three months each year
   d. during the third week of each month

Answer questions 36 and 37 based on your best judgment and common sense.

36. When the firehouse receives an alarm, all the firefighters should immediately put their protective clothing on. The most important reason for this rule is that
   a. it allows the firefighters to begin fighting the fire immediately upon arriving at the scene
   b. the firefighters may not be recognized by civilians at the scene of the fire
   c. it is too difficult for firefighters to dress on the truck
   d. if the firefighters on the truck cannot be identified by their attire, other vehicles may not yield

37. The most important reason that tools and equipment are checked and cleaned at the fire station every day is that
   a. fire department members can look for damage and do needed repairs
   b. departmental regulations require this procedure
   c. the procedure keeps the firefighters occupied during the slow periods
   d. all fire department equipment must be well-maintained for inspection purposes

38. Leaving work an hour after a windstorm, Firefighter Garcia is driving north on Washington Street when he comes upon a large tree limb that has fallen and is blocking his lane. About fifty yards north is the intersection of Washington and Fourth Avenue where there is a public telephone booth. Garcia carefully drives around a fallen limb and stops to phone in a report. Which of the following statements most clearly and accurately reports this situation?

a. I'm at the phone booth on Fourth Avenue in my truck, and a tree limb fell, which is blocking my lane.

b. A large tree limb has fallen across the road north of Washington Street near Fourth Avenue.

c. There is a fallen tree limb blocking one lane of Washington Street, about fifty yards south of Fourth Avenue.

d. In the northbound lane of Fourth Avenue and Washington Street, I had to drive around a limb that fell off a tree obstructing traffic.

39. Firefighter Davis is returning to the station after a call. He is driving east on First Avenue when a large dog runs in front of his truck. Davis slams on his brakes but is unable to keep from hitting the dog. Hearing the screeching of the brakes, the dog's owner, James Ramsey, runs out of his house on the corner of First Avenue and Highland Court and discovers that his dog has a leg injury. Davis helps put the dog into Ramsey's car so that Ramsey can take the animal to the vet. Later, Davis files a report. Which of the following reports describes the incident most clearly and accurately?

a. The dog's owner, James Ramsey, whose leg appeared to be hurt, took him to the vet after I helped him into the car on First Avenue at Highland Court.

b. Near the intersection of First Avenue and Highland Court, a dog ran out in front of my truck and I could not avoid hitting it. I stopped to help the dog's owner, James Ramsey, who took the injured animal to the vet.

c. I was driving along First Avenue when I hit a dog. We picked the dog up with a leg injury and put him in the car, which then drove to the vet. James Ramsey was the man's name.

d. James Ramsey, who owned a dog, came running out of his house at First and Highland and saw me hit him with my truck. Though I didn't mean to do it, I helped him into a car so that Ramsey could get to the vet for medical treatment.

Answer questions 40 and 41 based on the following information.

When obtaining water from a hydrant, the firefighters should perform the following steps in the order shown below.

1. Lay out hoses between fire truck and fire hydrant.
2. Attach hoses to fire hydrant and then to fire truck holding tank.
3. Attach secondary hose to fire truck holding tank discharge fitting and lay out hose to fire location.
4. Use a wrench to turn on the water at the fire hydrant valve.
5. When the firefighters on the end of the hose are ready, open the truck valves and activate the pumps.

40. Firefighters on the scene of a residential fire have attached the hose from the hydrant to the truck holding tank. They have also attached the secondary hose to the holding tank discharge connection and laid out the hose to the fire location. What is their next step?

a. activate the pump

b. turn on the hydrant valve

c. turn on the fire truck siren

d. warn other firefighters that the internal combustion engine is operating

41. What mechanical device is used to turn on the fire hydrant valve?

a. a pump

b. a hose

c. a wrench

d. a holding tank

Answer questions 42–46 based solely on the information in the following passage.

Following a recent series of arson fires in public-housing buildings, the mayor of a large U.S. city has decided to expand the city's Community Patrol, made up of 18- to 21-year-olds, to about 400 people. The Community Patrol is an important part of the city's efforts to at least reduce the number of these crimes.

In addition to the expanded patrol, the city also plans to reduce the seriousness of these fires, which are most often started in stairwells, by stripping the paint from the stairwell walls. Fed by the thick layers of oil-based paint, these arson fires race up the stairwells at an alarming speed.

Although the city attempted to control the speed of these fires by covering walls with a flame retardant, it is now clear that the retardant failed to work in almost all cases. In the most recent fire, the flames raced up ten stories after the old paint under the newly applied fire retardant ignited. Because the retardant failed to stop the flames, the city decided to stop applying it and will now strip the stairwells down to the bare walls.

42. One of the main points of the passage is that flame retardants

a. reduce the number of arson fires in large cities

b. are being stripped from walls by the Community Patrol

c. have not prevented stairwell fires from spreading

d. have increased the speed of flames in stairwell fires

43. The mayor expanded the size of the Community Patrol in an effort to

a. arrest and convict the city's arsonists

b. increase jobs for 18- to 21-year-olds

c. apply flame retardants in public-housing buildings

d. prevent some of the stairwell fires from occurring

44. The city's MOST RECENT decision in an attempt to reduce the seriousness of stairwell fires is to

a. remove all paint and retardants from stairwell walls

b. increase the age range of community-patrol members

c. develop a new flame-retardant material

d. apply a non-oil-based paint to stairwell walls

45. The passage indicates stairwell fires spread extremely rapidly because
   a. the stairwells have no ventilation from the outdoors
   b. arsonists set the fires in several locations at once
   c. the stairwell walls are old and often bare
   d. the flames are fed by the oil-based paint on the walls

46. The city has decided to stop using flame retardants because the retardants
   a. have failed to control the speed of stairwell fires
   b. send toxic fumes and gases into the buildings
   c. are thick and have a flammable oil base
   d. increase the speed at which flames travel up stairs

Answer question 47 based on your best judgment and common sense.

47. After every fire, firefighters are required to clean and check their protective clothing when they return to the firehouse. The most important reason for this requirement is that the firefighters
   a. take pride in their firehouses and want their equipment to be neat and clean
   b. need to get any chemicals, toxins, or fire ash off the clothing and check that the clothing doesn't require replacement
   c. must demonstrate that they know how to clean their protective clothing
   d. must verify that all their protective clothing has come back to the firehouse with them

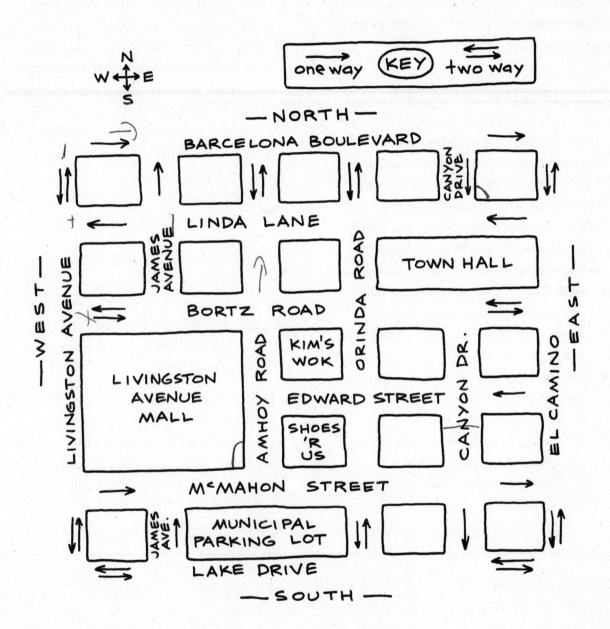

Answer questions 48–50 solely on the basis of the map on the previous page. The arrows indicate traffic flow; one arrow indicates a one-way street going in the direction of the arrow; two arrows represent a two-way street. You are not allowed to go the wrong way on a one-way street.

48. Your company has been called to a trash can fire in the Livingston Avenue Mall at the southeast corner of the building. Dispatch notifies you of an alarm going off in a residence located at the northwest corner of Canyon Drive and Linda Lane. What is the quickest route for the fire engine to take from the mall to the residence?

   a. Turn north on Amhoy Road, then east on Linda Lane, then north on Canyon Drive.

   b. Turn east on McMahon Street, then north on El Camino, then west on Linda Lane, then north on Orinda Road, then east on Barcelona Blvd. to Canyon Drive, and south on Canyon Drive.

   c. Turn north on Amhoy Road, then east on Barcelona Blvd., then south on Canyon Drive.

   d. Turn north on Amhoy Road, then east on Bortz Road, then north on Orinda Road, then east on Barcelona Blvd., and south on Canyon Drive.

49. Returning from a false alarm, your company's fire engine is southbound on Canyon Drive and has just crossed Edward Street, when a call comes in that someone has set fire to a bus parked at a bus stop located at Livingston Avenue and Bortz Road. What is the quickest route for the engine to take to the bus stop?

   a. Continue south on Canyon Drive, then turn west on McMahon Street, then north on Orinda Road, then west on Edward Street, then north on Amhoy Road, then west on Bortz Road to Livingston.

   b. Continue south on Canyon Drive, then turn west on Lake Drive, then north on Livingston Avenue to Bortz Road.

   c. Make a U-turn on Canyon Drive, then go west on Bortz Road to Livingston Avenue.

   d. Continue south on Canyon Drive, then turn east on Lake Drive, then north on El Camino, and then west on Bortz Road to Livingston Avenue.

50. Firefighter Ricardo has just come off duty and is driving west on Bortz Road. She makes a right onto James Avenue, then a left onto Linda Lane, then a right onto Livingston, and then a right onto Barcelona Boulevard. What direction is she facing?

   a. east

   b. south

   c. west

   d. north

Answer questions 51 and 52 based on your best judgment and common sense.

51. A woman walks into the firehouse and tells you she has locked her keys in the car. She is frantic because her three-year-old daughter is in the back seat. You should
   a. leave the firehouse and break the car window
   b. advise the woman to call a locksmith, and then go stand by the car to reassure the child
   c. ask the woman the location of her car, and inform your superior officer immediately
   d. suggest the woman call a locksmith, and advise her not to be so careless in the future

52. The fire department has replaced its wooden ladders with aluminum ladders. Which of the following is NOT a sensible reason for this change?
   a. Wooden ladders are harder to repair and keep clean.
   b. Wooden ladders are less expensive than aluminum ladders.
   c. Wooden ladders are heavier than aluminum ladders.
   d. Wooden ladders catch on fire more readily than aluminum ladders.

Answer questions 53–55 based solely on the information in the following passage.

If a building is to be left in a safe condition, firefighters must search for hidden fires that may rekindle. Typically this process, known as overhaul, begins in the area of actual fire involvement. Before searching for hidden fires, however, firefighters must first determine the condition of the building.

The fire's intensity and the amount of water used to fight the fire are both factors that affect a building. Fire can burn away floor joists and weaken roof trusses. Heat from the fire can weaken concrete and the mortar in wall joints and elongate steel roof supports. Excess water can add dangerous weight to floors and walls.

Once it has been determined that it is safe to enter a building, the process of overhauling begins. A firefighter can often detect hidden fires by looking for discoloration, peeling paint, cracked plaster, and smoke emissions; by feeling walls and floors with the back of the hand; by listening for popping, cracking, and hissing sounds; and by using electronic sensors to detect heat variances.

53. The main purpose of overhauling a building is to
   a. make sure the fire will not start up again
   b. strengthen wall joints and roof supports
   c. make sure excess water has not damaged floors
   d. test for heat damage by using electronic sensors

54. Before overhauling a building, what is the
FIRST thing a firefighter should do?
a. Look for discoloration in the paint.
b. Detect differences in heat along walls and
floors.
c. Listen for sounds that may indicate a fire.
d. Determine the extent of fire and water damage.

55. According to the passage, cracked plaster is a
sign that
a. a wall may be about to fall in
b. a fire may be smoldering inside a wall
c. a wall is dangerously weighted with water
d. firefighters should exit the building
immediately

Answer question 56 based on your best judgment
and common sense.

56. While reading the latest edition of *Firefighters
Magazine*, you see an article that explains a
faster, more efficient way to connect a hose to a
standpipe. You think this is a terrific idea that
will save precious time at the scene of a fire.
Which of the following is the most appropriate
first action for you to take?
a. At the next fire, implement the procedure
you read about.
b. Write a letter to the fire commissioner
reporting your findings.
c. Show the article to your superior officer and
ask if your company can change its procedure.
d. Call the union and ask them if you can
advise the fire department to change its
procedure.

57. The fire department's new fire safety drive will
take place at the fire station during the month
of June. At that time, each family in the community will be able to purchase up to three fire
alarms at a cost of only $3 each. Each family is
also entitled to one fire extinguisher at a cost of
$8. Which of the following statements describes
the city's new program most clearly and accurately?
a. In June, every person in the community will
purchase 3 fire alarms and fire extinguishers
that cost $3 and $8 each.
b. During the month of June, each family may
buy one fire extinguisher for $8 and up to
three fire alarms, which cost $3 each.
c. During the fire safety drive in June, families
can purchase fire extinguishers and fire
alarms, up to three of these, costing $3 and
$8.
d. The purchase of up to three fire alarms at a
cost of $3 each and one fire extinguisher at
$8 each may be bought in June at the fire
station's safety drive.

58. During a major snowstorm, Firefighter O'Neal is driving a fire truck along the 1200 block of Arden Drive, one of the city's main snow routes. When the snow is more than two inches deep, residents are restricted from parking on streets that are designated snow routes. The snow on this day is already four inches deep. Suddenly, O'Neal sees a parked car on the left side of the street and barely manages to drive the truck around it. When she returns to the station, she phones in a request to have the car towed. Which of the following most clearly and accurately describes the situation?

   a. Because I almost did not see the car on Arden Drive during this snowstorm, it should be removed immediately.

   b. I am calling for a tow truck in the 1200 block of a main snow route, because I almost hit a car with the snow falling, which made it impossible to see cars on my left side.

   c. As I was driving on the 1200 block of Arden Drive, I almost ran into an illegally parked car. Please send a tow truck and have the car removed.

   d. There is a car in the 1200 block of Arden Drive. The snow is four inches deep, which may cause an accident and should be towed immediately.

59. Firefighter Caruso is washing a fire truck in front of the station when nine-year-old Joey Tremont asks if he would help get Joey's kitten, Sugar, down from a tree across the street. After checking with his chief, Caruso walks across the street and sees that he can easily reach the limb where the kitten is trapped. As he is pulling the kitten to safety, the kitten scratches him on the face. The next day, Caruso's face is swollen; the scratch has become infected. He must file a medical report. Which of the following reports describes the incident most clearly and accurately?

   a. A kitten scratched me as I was washing the truck in front of the station when a boy named Joey asked me to retrieve Sugar. The scratch has become infected.

   b. Joey Tremont asked me to save his kitten, but when he did he scratched me on the face and an infection ensued.

   c. While I was washing the truck in front of the station, a boy named Joey asked me to rescue his kitten from a tree across the street. As I was lifting the kitten, it scratched me, and the scratch became infected.

   d. Having rescued a kitten named Sugar from a tree across the street after washing the truck, Joey, the boy's name, had asked me to. The kitten then scratched me on the face, which became infected the next day.

Answer questions 60–62 solely on the basis of this map. The arrows indicate traffic flow; one arrow indicates a one-way street going in the direction of the arrow; two arrows represent a two-way street. You are not allowed to go the wrong way on a one-way street.

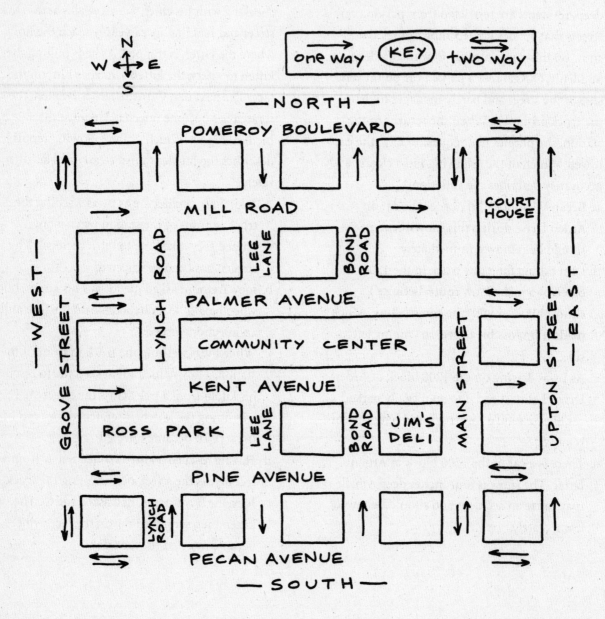

60. Your company's fire engine is eastbound on Kent Avenue at Lee Lane when a call comes in from dispatch about a gas heater explosion at a residence located at the northeast corner of Lynch Road and Mill Road. What is the quickest route for the engine to take?

a. Continue east on Kent Avenue, then turn north on Main Street to Mill Road, then west on Mill Road to the northeast corner of Lynch Road and Mill Road.

b. Continue east on Kent Avenue, then turn north on Main Street, then east on Pomeroy Blvd., then south on Lynch Road.

c. Continue east on Kent Avenue, then turn south on Main Street, then west on Pine Avenue, then north on Grove Street, then east on Mill Road to Lynch Road.

d. Continue east on Kent Avenue, then turn north on Main Street, then west on Palmer Avenue, then north on Lynch Road to Mill Road.

61. Firefighter McElhaney is off duty and driving by the court house, northbound on Upton Street. He receives a call on his car phone about a bomb having gone off at Ross Park on the Grove Street side of the park. He decides he may be able to be of some help. What is the most direct route for Firefighter McElhaney to take?

a. Continue north on Upton Street, turn west on Pomeroy Blvd., then south on Main Street, then west on Kent Avenue to Grove Street.

b. Continue north on Upton Street, then turn west on Pomeroy Blvd., then south on Grove Street to Ross Park.

c. Continue north on Upton Street, then turn west on Pomeroy Avenue, then south on Main Street, then west on Palmer Avenue, then south on Grove Street to Ross Park.

d. Make a U-turn on Upton Street, then go west on Palmer Avenue, then south on Grove Street to Ross Park.

62. Firefighter Kearney has just had lunch at Jim's Deli and is now heading west on Pine Avenue. She turns left on Lee Lane, then left again onto Pecan Avenue. She turns left on Main Street and finally turns right on Palmer Avenue. What direction is she facing?

a. west

b. south

c. north

d. east

Answer question 63 based on your best judgment and common sense.

63. You arrive at an apartment building for a routine inspection. During the inspection you notice several fire safety violations in the building across the street. The best course of action for you to take would be to

a. notify the police to arrest the owner of the building across the street

b. issue violation orders for the building across the street

c. disregard the building across the street, since it is not due for inspection

d. call your company into the building across the street to fix the violations

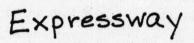

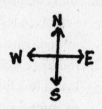

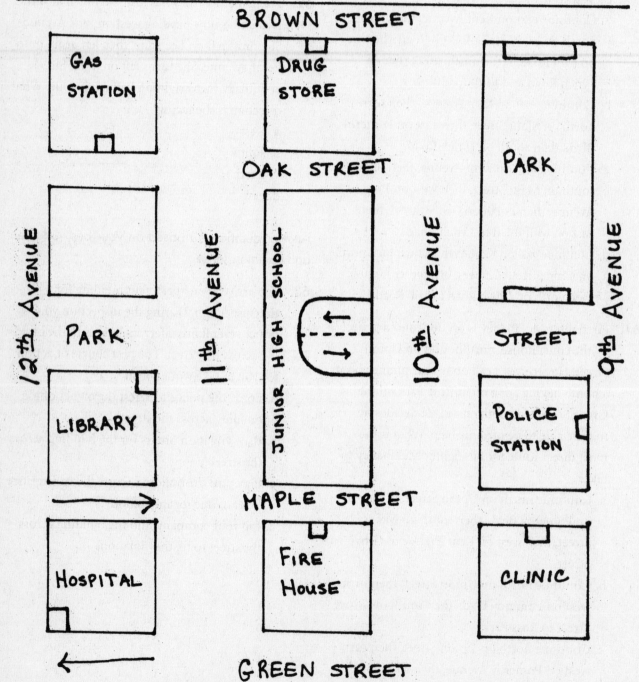

Answer questions 64–67 solely on the basis of the map on the previous page. The arrows indicate traffic flow; one arrow indicates a one-way street going in the direction of the arrow; no arrows represent a two-way street. You are not allowed to go the wrong way on a one-way street.

64. There is a vehicular accident at the corner of Brown Street and 9th Avenue, and a fire has started. What is the most direct legal way for the fire engine to travel from the fire station to the accident scene?
    a. east on Maple Street and north on 9th Avenue to the accident
    b. west on Maple Street, north on 12th Avenue, and east on Brown Street to the accident
    c. east on Maple Street and north on 11th Avenue to the accident
    d. west on Maple Street, north on 11th Avenue, and east on Brown Street to the accident

65. What streets run north and south of the park?
    a. Brown Street and Oak Street
    b. Maple Street and Park Street
    c. Brown Street and Park Street
    d. Green Street and Oak Street

66. A civilian leaving the clinic needs to drive to the drug store. If you were giving her directions from the clinic, what would be the most direct route?
    a. east on Maple Street, north on 9th Avenue, and west on Brown Street to the store entrance
    b. west on Maple Street, north on 10th Avenue, and west on Brown Street to the store entrance
    c. west on Green Street, north on 12th Avenue, and east on Brown Street to the store entrance
    d. east on Oak Street, north on 11th Avenue, and east on Brown Street to the store entrance

67. Someone at the junior high school has been injured and needs to go to the hospital. What directions would you give to the ambulance driver?
    a. Go north on 10th Avenue, west on Brown Street, and south on 12th Avenue to the hospital entrance.
    b. Go south on 10th Avenue and west on Green Street to the hospital entrance.
    c. Go north on 10th Avenue and south on Brown Street to the hospital entrance.
    d. Go south on 10th Avenue, south on Maple Street, and east on Green Street to the hospital entrance.

Answer questions 68 and 69 based on your best judgment and common sense.

68. You are finishing up operations after an apartment building fire. Outside on the ground, you find a box containing jewelry and believe it to be of considerable value. There is no owner's name on the box. What should you do?
- a. Leave the box where you found it, as the owner will probably return to reclaim it.
- b. Turn the box over to your superior officer.
- c. Keep the box, because you have no way of knowing who it belongs to.
- d. Since the owner is unknown, bring the box to the firehouse and share the contents with your company.

69. You have been invited by the local elementary school to give a fire safety talk. While you are there, one of the children asks you, "What do I do if my clothes catch on fire?" Which of the following should you tell the child?
- a. "Stop where you are, drop to the ground, and roll around to put the fire out."
- b. "Call the operator or dial the emergency number 911."
- c. "Try to locate a fire extinguisher and use it to put out the fire."
- d. "Call the fire department and ask them for help."

Answer questions 70–73 based solely on the information in the following passage.

As a firefighter, you may be assigned the important task of conducting school fire inspections. At the school, you should first meet with school officials to discuss fire safety policy. Be certain all those involved—including administrators, teachers, and support staff—understand their roles during emergencies. Ask about the school's fire drill schedule and inquire about your department's participation in future drills. Next, conduct a check of all alarms on the premises. If an alarm has been tampered with, notify school officials immediately. If an alarm is not functioning properly and cannot be repaired immediately, notify school officials and fill out a repair request form. Next, inspect all exits to be sure none are obstructed. Review evacuation plans to make certain primary and secondary exits are viable. Walk the routes yourself. Next, inspect all extinguishers. Remember, pressurized water extinguishers must NOT be located near electrical equipment. If this is the case, they should be replaced immediately with foam units, which are safer. Next, inspect wall and ceiling decorations. Depending on regulations, it is often a violation of fire codes to have more than 20 percent of any wall or ceiling covered with artwork or other hangings. Last, report your findings to your supervisor.

70. According the passage, why should fire personnel review evacuation plans?
- a. to confirm that all exits listed are workable options
- b. to inspect the alarms located near exits
- c. to replace pressurized water extinguishers
- d. to notify school officials if alarms are malfunctioning

71. Why should pressurized water extinguishers located near electrical equipment be replaced?
a. They cannot be easily repaired.
b. They obstruct emergency exits.
c. Their use requires extensive training.
d. They are a potential threat to safety.

72. Which of the following is NOT included in this passage?
a. instructions on what to do if an alarm is damaged
b. a review of staff responsibility during an emergency
c. a description of the procedure to follow if an exit is blocked
d. mention of the significance of material attached to ceilings

73. Which of the following safety measures is covered in the passage?
a. how to correctly perform a fire drill
b. how to tell if an alarm has been tampered with
c. how to identify a particularly hazardous wall or ceiling hanging
d. how to tell if a certain pressurized water extinguisher should be replaced

Answer questions 74 and 75 based on the following information.

Firefighters must routinely fight structure fires that require more water than is carried on the fire truck. Water must be obtained from a fire hydrant. This water is fed through fire hoses to the truck holding tank and then pumped through additional hoses to the fire as needed. Several mechanical devices are used in this process.

1. Wrenches are used to attach the hose to the hydrant and to turn on the water.
2. Centrifugal pumps are used to pump the water from the truck to the fire.
3. Electric motors are used to drive the centrifugal pumps.
4. The truck's internal combustion engine is used to run the electric motors.
5. Pressure gauges are used to insure that the system is operating properly.
6. Valves are used to control the flow of water from the hydrant and from the fire truck.

74. Firefighters respond to an industrial fire. Water must be obtained from a hydrant one block away. What are four of the mechanical devices that will be used to get the water from the hydrant to the fire?
a. electric motors, pumps, temperature gauges, and valves
b. pumps, pulleys, internal combustion engine, and electric motors
c. pressure gauges, electric motors, wrenches, and internal combustion engine
d. internal combustion engine, a winch, valves, and pressure gauges

75. Which of the following is used to drive the centrifugal pumps?
   a. electric motors
   b. an internal combustion engine
   c. pressure gauges
   d. valves

Answer questions 76–81 based on your best judgment and common sense.

76. After a fire is extinguished, the water in the hose lines must be removed before the hose lines are reloaded on the fire truck. The best place to remove this water is
   a. near a large body of water if there is one close by
   b. inside the building where the fire was
   c. back at the fire station
   d. just outside the building where the fire was

77. Because subway fires take place underground, they are difficult to work on and require that firefighters take extra precautions to keep the fire contained. One such precaution is to cover the sidewalk grates. This is one of the first actions firefighters should take because
   a. citizens walking by may complain
   b. citizens walking by may become very emotional
   c. the fire must be prevented from reaching the grates on the sidewalk
   d. the precaution enables the firefighters to keep their equipment in one place

78. Lieutenant James has ordered you to clean his breathing apparatus. While cleaning the apparatus, you drop it and think you may have damaged it. The best course of action would be to
   a. keep quiet unless you are certain it is badly damaged
   b. watch Lieutenant James when you go to the next fire, to make sure the equipment is working properly
   c. keep quiet because Lieutenant James may bring you up on charges for damaging his equipment
   d. tell Lieutenant James about the suspected damage

79. The first thing a firefighter should do upon arriving at the scene of an automobile accident is to
   a. check for any gasoline leaks
   b. call the police so they can fill out an accident report
   c. do nothing until the ambulance arrives
   d. remove victims who are trapped inside the automobile

80. A fire company is called to a house fire. When the engine arrives at the street supplied by the caller, there is no house at the number given, nor is there a fire elsewhere on the street. Which of the following is NOT a reasonable assumption about false alarms?
   a. False alarms waste the time and money of the fire department.
   b. The fire department cannot answer another call while out on a false alarm.
   c. Sometimes what seems to be a false alarm is simply a mistake made by the caller.
   d. False alarms, although illegal, serve a positive role in keeping firefighters alert.

81. Your company is doing a building inspection of your favorite restaurant. You know the owner and all of the servers. You discover the restaurant's permits have all expired; therefore, you should
    a. take the owner aside out of courtesy and issue a verbal warning, without writing a formal summons
    b. inform your superior officer, and let that officer handle the situation
    c. leave the restaurant immediately because your involvement with the owner might reflect badly on the fire department
    d. call the police and have the owner arrested

Answer questions 82–84 based on the following information.

After a fire is put out, the firefighter must routinely write a report on what occurred at the scene. This is normally done back at the firehouse on a computer in the following manner:

1. Log on to the computer.
2. Go to the directory that contains the report forms.
3. If there were injuries on the scene, complete report form 103.
4. If there was a death on the scene, complete report form 111.
5. If there was loss of or damage to equipment, complete form 107.
6. If there was no injury, death, equipment loss, or equipment damage, complete form 101.
7. If form 107 and form 103 are required, complete form 122 also.
8. Complete form 106, which is a general report and must be filled out for ALL fire reports.
9. Print and file all forms that have been completed, and fax a copy to division headquarters.

82. A firefighter has just returned to the firehouse after a fire and is preparing the necessary report forms. One of the residents of the house that burned was injured and sent to the hospital. Also, one of the fire hoses was damaged. There were no deaths at the fire. Which forms must the firefighter complete?
    a. forms 101 and 106
    b. forms 111 and 107
    c. forms 106, 111, and 122
    d. forms 103, 106, 107, and 122

83. A firefighter is filling out fire reports on a fire in which there was one death, no equipment damage or loss, and one injury in addition to the death. Which forms must the firefighter complete?
    a. forms 103, 106, and 122
    b. forms 103 and 111
    c. forms 101, 106, and 122
    d. forms 103, 106, and 111

84. A firefighter is preparing a report on a grass fire that was put out with no injuries, no deaths, and no equipment damage or loss. Which form, in addition to form 101, must the firefighter complete?
    a. form 106
    b. form 111
    c. form 107
    d. form 103

Answer question 85 based on your best judgment and common sense.

85. You are a firefighter at the scene of a fire caused by damaged wiring. The civilian who owns the building approaches you and complains about the windows broken by firefighters extinguishing the fire. You should
   a. deny the firefighters did it unless you are absolutely sure they did
   b. chastise the civilian for being reckless and causing the fire, and then direct him to your superior officer
   c. advise the civilian to write a letter to the fire commissioner
   d. explain that breaking the window was necessary in order to release heat and smoke from the fire

Answer questions 86–90 based solely on the information in the following passage.

While preserving evidence is not the firefighter's main priority, certain steps can be taken, while fighting a fire, to maintain site integrity and maximize efforts of investigators.

Try to determine the point of origin from wind direction or the way the fire is spread. Take notes, mentally and on paper, of suspicious people or vehicles. Use ribbon or other practical material to flag potential evidence, such as tracks near the suspected point of origin and items such as matches, bottles, rags, cigarette butts, lighters, paper, or exposed wires. Keep other personnel away from these areas unless doing so would hamper firefighting efforts.

After flagging the evidence, notify the commanding officer as soon as possible. If evidence must be removed, handle it carefully to maintain fingerprint integrity.

Once the fire is declared under control, create a map of the scene, indicating the point of origin and areas where evidence is or was located. Compose an inventory of any evidence that was removed. Record any other useful information, such as conversations with witnesses, names, and descriptions. Before leaving, share your findings with the lead investigator.

Remember, safety is the main priority while you are fighting the fire. But by keeping an alert eye for clues, you can also contribute to an efficient investigation into its cause.

86. According to the passage, which of the following is the main responsibility of a firefighter?
   a. to maintain the integrity of the site
   b. to flag evidence and keep an inventory of it
   c. to operate in a safe manner
   d. to provide support for investigators

87. The passage suggests that the first step the firefighter should take after evidence is flagged is to
   a. bring it to the attention of the officer in command
   b. create a map of the scene
   c. see how it relates to the point of origin
   d. indicate its location to investigators

88. Which of the following would a firefighter NOT necessarily do after the fire is brought under control?
   a. create an inventory
   b. carefully remove the evidence from the scene
   c. log witness descriptions
   d. record flagged evidence areas

89. Which of the following best expresses the main idea of this passage?

a. how to aid investigation into the cause of a fire

b. how to maintain safety while investigating a fire

c. the importance of flagging evidence during the fighting of a fire

d. what to do with flagged evidence of the cause of a fire

90. According to the passage, fire personnel should be instructed to avoid areas where evidence is found

a. only after the fire has been brought under control

b. only if the fire can also be fought effectively

c. only if the evidence points directly to the cause of the fire

d. only until the commanding officer is informed

Answer question 91 based on your best judgment and common sense.

91. One of the duties of the fire department is to raise public awareness of fire prevention methods. To this end, firefighters often speak with the public at schools, churches, and other meeting places. When speaking to the public, which of the following would NOT be an appropriate subject for a firefighter to address?

a. how to advise one's neighbors on fire prevention

b. how to choose the most inexpensive fire-protection equipment

c. how to purchase tickets for the firefighters' charity ball

d. how to make an escape plan in case of a fire in one's home

Answer questions 92–94 based on the following information.

The rescue rope is an important tool in the fire department. It must be maintained in top condition and ready for the members' use at all times. The rope is inspected weekly, then rewound so it will be ready for immediate use. A rescue rope may be placed out of service for the following reasons:

1. The rope has been used to carry the weight of two people during a rescue.
2. The strands have become frayed.
3. The rope has abrasions.
4. The rope has been exposed to extreme heat.
5. There are persistent rust stains on the rope.
6. The rope has been frozen during operations.
7. The rope has been exposed to acid or acid-containing substances.
8. There is any doubt as to the rope's suitability to remain in service.

92. Which of the following would NOT be a reason to place the rescue rope out of service?

a. Battery acid has leaked onto the rope.

b. The rope is more than two years old.

c. One end of the rope is frayed.

d. The rope has been exposed to extreme heat.

93. Firefighters use the rope to rescue a woman and child. After the rescue, the rope should be
   a. rewound for the next use
   b. inspected at the fire station
   c. placed out of service
   d. left to burn at the fire scene

94. During inspection of the rescue rope, you notice a rust stain. With a brush and soapy water you clean the stain off. After this, the rope should be
   a. placed out of service
   b. replaced with a new rope
   c. rewound for immediate use
   d. re-inspected by another firefighter

95. On his way to work at 6:40 A.M., Firefighter Marshall's car gets a flat tire. He manages to pull the car over to the shoulder of the road and decides to change the tire himself. Though his shift begins at 7:00 A.M., he now estimates that he will not arrive on the job until about 7:20 A.M. He phones his supervisor from a public telephone to report that he will be late. Which of the following reports most clearly and accurately describes the situation?
   a. I was driving to work. I won't be there until about 20 minutes later than was expected.
   b. On my way to work, there was a flat tire, which I am about to fix. It is now about 6:40.
   c. I would have been on time, but now I am unable to make it by 7:00 because the car is on the shoulder of the road.
   d. I am stuck on the side of the road with a flat tire. I will change it and should be able to report to work around 7:20.

96. Firefighters Ellis and Wong have responded to what appears to be a false alarm in the alley behind the building at 1412 Longview Avenue. They are about to return to the station when Wong notices a suspicious-looking receptacle in one of the dumpsters. When Ellis agrees that this receptacle may possibly contain an explosive, the two workers follow department policy by keeping people away from the area and phoning the police department. Which of the following reports describes the situation most clearly and accurately?
   a. There may be an explosive in a dumpster in the alley behind 1412 Longview Avenue.
   b. Something looks suspicious on Longview Avenue which could possibly explode.
   c. There is a receptacle in a dumpster in the alley on Longview Avenue, and it is in the trash.
   d. At 1412 Longview, there is something suspicious-looking sitting behind it in the dumpster in the alley.

97. Firefighter Camillo is driving to a high school to speak to students. He stops for a red light at Lucas Drive, and when the light turns green, he drives slowly forward into the intersection of Lucas Drive and Manchester Way. There, his truck is broadsided from the left by a gray, late-model station wagon. Although he is shaken, Camillo has not been injured. The driver of the car is also uninjured, but he accuses Camillo of having driven through the red light. Someone in a nearby building saw the accident and phoned the police, who arrive within minutes. Which of the following reports would Camillo give to the police to describe the accident most clearly and accurately?

a. I was on Lucas, completely stopped for the red light. Then, when the light turned green, I pulled forward and was immediately broadsided by the wagon.

b. He's accusing me of going through a red light, but before I drove through I stopped. I didn't see the station wagon as it hit the left side of the truck coming down Manchester Way.

c. The station wagon drove into the side of my truck when I tried to drive forward on Lucas Drive. It was after the red light. Then he accused me of causing the accident.

d. I was driving straight ahead on Lucas Drive, and when I was at the light at the intersection of Manchester Way, I pulled forward and he hit me. It was a gray station wagon.

Answer questions 98–100 based on the following information.

Firefighters must monitor water pressure gauges while fighting a fire. If the water pressure becomes too low, the water may stop flowing through the hose. This can be very dangerous for the firefighters on the front line. The following facts must be observed and procedure used while monitoring the pressure gauges.

1. There are three primary pressure gauges which must be monitored. Gauge #1 monitors incoming pressure from the hydrant. Gauge #2 monitors discharge pressure to the hose. Gauge #3 monitors the oil pressure of the internal combustion engine of the fire truck.

2. The minimum acceptable pressure for Gauge #1 is 30 psi.

3. The minimum acceptable pressure for Gauge #2 is 20 psi.

4. The minimum acceptable pressure for Gauge #3 is 10 psi.

5. If the pressure on Gauge #1 drops below 30 psi, the fire hydrant valve must be opened one revolution using a special wrench. The maximum allowable Gauge #1 pressure is 50 psi. If Gauge #1 approaches 50 psi, the hydrant valve must be closed one revolution.

6. If the pressure on Gauge #2 drops below 20 psi, the discharge control valve on the truck must be opened one revolution.

98. A firefighter is monitoring the pressure gauges on the fire truck. She notices that Gauge #2 reads 19 psi. What should she do next?

a. open the discharge control valve by two revolutions

b. open the discharge control valve by one revolution

c. open the hydrant valve by one revolution

d. close the hydrant valve by one revolution

99. A firefighter is monitoring the pressure gauges on the fire truck. He notices that Gauge #1 reads 51 psi. What should he do next?

a. close the discharge control valve by one revolution

b. open the discharge control valve by one revolution

c. open the hydrant valve by one revolution

d. close the hydrant valve by one revolution

100. A firefighter is monitoring the pressure gauges on the fire truck. He notices that Gauge #1 reads 29 psi. What should he do next?

a. open the hydrant valve by one revolution

b. close the discharge control valve by one revolution

c. open the discharge control valve by one revolution

d. close the hydrant valve by one revolution

ANSWERS

1. **d.** In the drawing, flame is showing from the second and third floors.

2. **c.** Two victims can be seen in the second and third floors, of the fire building.

3. **d.** The business next door to the fire scene is Al's Paint Store; the address is #28.

4. **d.** The drawing shows a clothesline and a smoke stack on the roof of the fire building.

5. **c.** Three adults and two babies can be seen in the windows of the building on the left.

6. **b.** The drawing does not show that fire has spread to the paint store.

7. **a.** The window on the first floor is blocked by security bars.

8. **b.** A living room, a dining room, a kitchen, three bedrooms, and a bathroom are shown in the diagram.

9. **a.** The living room is the first room off the entryway.

10. **b.** A smoke detector is located in the master bedroom.

11. **a.** Two windows can be found in bedroom 3.

12. **d.** The fireplace is in the living room, and the dining room is closest to the living room.

13. **c.** The smoke detector in the master bedroom is the first to be activated.

14. **b.** The diagram indicates that there are eight windows in the apartment.

15. **b.** All may provide means of entry.

16. **c.** Interior stairs is the preferred method of removal.

17. **c.** The last item in the order of removal is the life net.

18. **a.** The fire escape immediately follows adjoining building in the order.

19. **b.** Roof rescue rope follows ladder as a means of egress.

20. **a.** Maximum time in the fire area will allow a firefighter to operate more efficiently and extinguish the fire faster, a priority. Choices **b** and **d** are much less important. A full air tank will not necessarily protect against heat, flame, and toxic gases (choice **c**).

21. **d.** This is the first step of the procedure.

22. **b.** Step 7 clearly states that the firefighter must exit the building. To do otherwise endangers the firefighter's own life, as well as that of other firefighters who might have to rescue her when her air tank fails.

23. **a.** See step 6 of the procedure.

24. **d.** The discussion of carbon monoxide in the last paragraph serves to demonstrate why firefighters should wear breathing apparatus.

25. **c.** The dangers outlined in the first and second paragraphs of the passage are all caused by extreme heat.

26. **b.** The other choices are mentioned in the passage but are not the main idea.

27. **a.** The cooking temperature is given to show the difference of 1,000 degrees of heat between a motor vehicle fire and cooking.

28. **b.** The last paragraph states that *carbon monoxide . . . is odorless and colorless.*

29. **d.** A priority of firefighting is always the safety of members and civilians.

30. **a.** Safety of the public is a firefighter's main concern.

31. **a.** The other choices are unclear because they are awkwardly constructed, obscuring who intends to set the fire.

32. d. This is the only clear statement. In choice **a**, it is not clear that several firefighters received the promotion. Choice **b** makes no logical sense. Choice **c** is grammatically unsound.

33. b. See the last sentence of the second paragraph.

34. c. Virtually the whole passage deals with this. The other choices are too narrow.

35. d. See the last paragraph.

36. a. Firefighters must arrive at the scene ready to work. If they are not, precious minutes can be lost, and lives and property are at stake.

37. a. All tools used in firefighting must be in good condition. This has priority, as many lives depend on the equipment's working properly.

38. c. This is the only clear and accurate statement. Choice **a** is incorrect because it leaves out information; choices **b** and **d** give incorrect information with regard to the location.

39. b. This is the only accurate statement. Choice **a** is incorrect because it implies that James Ramsey broke his leg. Choice **c** leaves out information. In choice **d**, it is not clear who was helped into the car.

40. b. See step 4 of the procedure.

41. c. See step 4 of the procedure.

42. c. The passage is mainly about how the flame retardant failed to work.

43. d. This is clearly stated in the first paragraph. The other options are not mentioned in the passage.

44. a. The answer can be found in the last sentence of the passage.

45. d. See the last sentence of the second paragraph.

46. a. See the first sentence of the third paragraph.

47. b. After each fire, equipment must be cleaned and inspected to be sure it is in acceptable condition and immediately available for its next use, when minutes will count. The other options are not nearly as important.

48. c. This is the simplest way around the one-way streets and Town Hall. Because Linda Lane is one-way the wrong way, some backtracking is inevitable. However, the residence is only one block off of Barcelona Blvd., and so turning eastbound on Barcelona requires the least amount of backtracking. Choice **a** directs the engine to turn the wrong way down a one-way street. Choice **b** requires too much backtracking because Barcelona Blvd. is a one-way street going east. Choice **d** requires too many turns and is the least direct route.

49. b. This route is most direct because it requires the fewest turns. Choice **a** requires the engine to go the wrong way on McMahon Street. Choice **c** is not correct because Canyon Drive is a one-way street south. Choice **d** is a much longer route.

50. a. If firefighter Ricardo turns right onto James Avenue she will be facing north. A left turn onto Linda Lane turns her west again, and a right turn onto Livingston Avenue turns her north. The final right turn onto Barcelona Blvd. turns her east.

51. c. In any emergency situation, teamwork is necessary, because firefighters work as a unit. Responding on your own (choices **a** and **b**) would be improper. Choice **d** is inappropriate because a firefighter should treat others with respect and take all requests for help seriously.

52. b. The lower cost is an advantage of wooden ladders over aluminum. The other statements are negative statements regarding wooden ladders.

53. a. The answer is found in the first sentence of the passage. The other choices give information from the passage, but they do not indicate the main purpose of an overhaul.

54. d. The answer is implied in the third sentence of the first paragraph in combination with the conditions described in the second paragraph.

55. b. The answer can be found in the last sentence. Choices **a**, **c**, and **d** are not in the passage.

56. c. A firefighter must always go to the superior officer before making any changes in standard operating procedures; therefore, this would be your first course of action.

57. b. This is the only clear choice. Choice **a** gives incorrect information; choice **c** is unclear; choice **d** leaves out information.

58. c. This is the only clear and accurate description. Choice **a** is incorrect because it leaves out important information; choices **b** and **d** are unclear.

59. c. This is the only clear and accurate report. Choice **a** implies that Caruso was rescuing the kitten at the same time as he was washing the truck. Choice **b** sounds as though the boy made the scratch. Choice **d** is unclear.

60. d. This is the most direct route because it does not require any backtracking. Choice **a** is not correct because it would require the engine to go the wrong way on Mill Road. Choice **b** requires the engine to go the wrong way on Lynch Road. Choice **c** is not as direct because it requires the engine to move in the opposite direction from the call.

61. b. This is the fastest route, requiring the fewest turns. Choice **a** is not correct because Kent is a one-way street going east. Choice **c** requires too many turns and is not the most direct route. Choice **d** is not correct because Upton Street is one-way going north.

62. d. A left turn onto Lee Lane turns firefighter Kearney south. Another left turn onto Pecan Avenue turns her east. Left onto Main Street turns her north and the final right turn onto Palmer turns her back east.

63. b. You should not ignore violations that you can see from across the street. They are likely to pose a threat to civilians as well as to firefighters responding to an alarm at the location.

64. a. The other routes are impossible or illegal.

65. c. Brown Street and Park Street are the two streets that run north and south of the Park.

66. a. The other routes are impossible or illegal.

67. b. The other routes are impossible (choices **c** and **d**) or circuitous (choice **a**).

68. b. Firefighters must follow the chain of command and so must report such lost or unclaimed property to their superior officer. The superior officer then reports to his or her superior officer, and so on up the chain of command. It is a firefighter's duty to safeguard property; therefore, leaving the valuables (choice **a**) would not be an option. Keeping the box (choices **c** and **d**) would be illegal and unethical.

69. a. A person whose clothes are on fire should stop, drop, and roll. As a firefighter, you should explain to the children they need to take immediate action in this situation. The other choices would be appropriate in a situation that is not immediately life threatening.

70. a. Roughly in the middle, the passage states, *Review evacuation plans to make sure primary and secondary exits are viable.*

71. d. Near the end, the passage recommends replacing water-filled extinguishers with foam units, *which are safer.*

72. c. Choice **a** is mentioned in the sections on alarms. Choice **b** is mentioned in the third sentence. Choice **d** is mentioned near the conclusion. Blocked exits are mentioned near the middle of the passage, but there is no discussion of relevant procedures with regard to them.

73. d. Near the end, the passage advises replacing pressurized extinguishers if they are located near electrical equipment. The other choices are not covered.

74. c. The procedure does not mention the use of temperature gauges (choice **a**), pulleys (choice **b**) or a winch (choice **d**).

75. a. See step 3 of the procedure.

76. d. Hoses are drained outside the fire building. Dumping into a large body of water nearby (choice **a**) could cause pollution and would probably be illegal. Draining inside (choice **b**) would cause unnecessary damage, and transporting the hoses full of water (choice **c**) is not feasible.

77. c. One of the highest priorities in firefighting is to confine the fire and keep it from spreading and causing additional damage or injury.

78. d. Damaged equipment should never be used in an emergency situation, regardless of interpersonal relationships.

79. a. Checking for gasoline leaks is the top priority here because it protects against the possibility of an explosion, which might injure or kill everyone, including the people trapped in the car.

80. d. Firefighters don't need false alarms to keep them alert—real alarms will do that. Choices **a** and **b** are reasonable criticisms of false alarms. Choice **c** is reasonable because people do make mistakes, especially if they are in a panic.

81. b. Your superior officer must be made aware of any situation that is a potential hazard to firefighters or the public. Again, safety has priority.

82. d. There was an injury, so form 103 must be completed, as stated in step 3 of the procedure. There was equipment damage, so form 107 must be completed, as stated in step 5 of the procedure. Step 8 says that form 106 must be completed for all fire reports. Step 7 says that form 122 must be completed, because forms 107 and 103 were both required.

83. d. There was an injury, so form 103 must be completed, as stated in step 3 of the procedure. Since there was a death on the scene, form 111 must be completed, according to step 4 of the procedure. As always, form 106 must be completed, as stated in step 8 of the procedure.

84. a. Since there were no injuries, deaths, or equipment loss or damage, step 8 indicates that form 106 must be completed.

85. d. A polite and direct explanation of the necessity of breaking windows for ventilation will help the civilian understand your actions. Firefighters should always be honest and courteous when dealing with the public.

86. c. See the next to last sentence.

87. a. See the third paragraph.

88. b. The fourth paragraph gives the steps to take after the fire is brought under control, and removal of evidence is not one of them.

89. a. The first sentence states that, while fighting a fire, firefighters can take steps to *maximize efforts of investigators.* Virtually all of the passage deals with those steps. Do not confuse the "main idea" of the passage with the firefighter's "main responsibility" (choice **b**). Choices **c** and **d** are only details relating to the main idea.

90. b. The second paragraph states that personnel shall be kept away from flagged evidence, *unless doing so would hamper firefighting efforts.*

91. c. Soliciting the public is not a good method of encouraging fire prevention and is detrimental to the reputation of the department.

92. b. The reasons for removing the rope from service do not specify age of the rope.

93. c. As per item 1 of the list, the rope was subject to the weight of two people.

94. c. The stain was removed and therefore was not *persistent*, so the rope should be returned to service.

95. d. This is the only clear and accurate report. Choice **a** doesn't report why Marshall will be late for work. Choice **b** doesn't say when he will report to work. Choice **c** doesn't say what happened.

96. a. This is the only clear and accurate statement. Choice **b** implies that Longview Avenue could explode. Choices **c** and **d** do not mention that there might be an explosive in the dumpster.

97. a. This is the only clear and accurate statement. Choices **b**, **c**, and **d** are incorrect because they leave out information and distort what really happened.

98. b. See step 6 of the procedure.

99. d. See step 5 of the procedure, which says that the hydrant valve must be closed one revolution when the pressure approaches 50 psi.

100. a. See step 5 of the procedure. The pressure is too low, so the firefighter should open the hydrant valve one revolution.

FIREFIGHTER EXAM 1		
Question Type	**Question Numbers**	**Chapter**
Memory and Observation (15 questions)	1–15	7, "Memory and Observation"
Reading Comprehension (25 questions)	24–28, 33–35, 42–46, 53–55, 70–73, 86–90	6, "Reading Comprehension"
Map Reading (10 questions)	48–50, 60–62, 64–67	11, "Spatial Relations"
Judgment (20 questions)	20, 29–30, 36–37, 47, 51–52, 56, 63, 68–69, 76–81, 85, 91	9, "Judgment and Reasoning"
Following Procedures (20 questions)	16–19, 21–23, 40–41, 74–75, 82–84, 92–94, 98–100	9, "Judgment and Reasoning"
Verbal Expression (10 questions)	31–32, 38–39, 57–59, 95–97	12, "Verbal Reasoning"

SCORING

Generally, you need a score of 70–80 percent on the actual firefighter exam in order to pass. But just passing isn't likely to be enough to ensure that you will be called for the next steps in the process. Often, a score of 95 percent or higher is necessary to go on to the physical ability test. Once you take the physical test, your score on that test may be combined with your score on the written exam to determine your rank on the eligibility list. Or your written exam score alone may determine your rank on the list. So your goal should be to achieve the highest score you possibly can.

If you want to raise your score, you should review your exam results carefully. Use the table on the preceding page to find the number of questions you answered correctly in each of the five question types. Then calculate the percentage for each type. For example, if you answered 15 judgment questions correctly, your percentage is 75%. Next, rank your performance according to question type. In which types were your results highest? Which were lowest? Once you have ranked your performance, you can set priorities in your study plan. For instance, if your lowest score was in following procedures, you should plan on spending the most time reviewing the appropriate section in Chapter 9. Use the following suggestions to help direct your test preparation between now and the day of the exam:

- If you had trouble with memory and observation questions, then you should plan to spend a lot of time on Chapter 7, "Memory and Observation."

- If the verbal expression questions were the most difficult, carefully review Chapter 12, "Verbal Expression."
- If you had difficulty understanding the reading passages, then you should plan to spend more time on Chapter 6, "Reading Comprehension."
- If you had difficulty with the questions on reading maps, then you should spend a longer period of time on Chapter 11, "Spatial Relations."
- If you had trouble with the questions testing judgment and following procedures, then you should spend a lot of time on Chapter 9, "Judgment and Reasoning."

Each of these chapters includes lots of tips and hints for doing well on the given kind of question. As you probably noticed, the various kinds of questions are all mixed up together on the exam. So take out your completed answer sheet and compare it to the table on the previous page in order to find out which kinds of questions you did well in and which kinds gave you more trouble. Then you can plan to spend more of your preparation time on the chapters of this book that correspond to the questions you found hardest and less time on the chapters in areas in which you did well.

Even if you got a perfect score on a particular kind of question, you'll probably want to at least glance through the relevant chapter. After you work through all the chapters, take the third practice exam in Chapter 13 to see how much you've improved.

C · H · A · P · T · E · R

FIREFIGHTER EXAM 2

CHAPTER SUMMARY

This is the second of four practice exams in this book covering the areas most often tested on firefighter exams. If your exam tests the basic skills you need to be trained as a firefighter, the test that follows will give you the practice you need.

The practice test that follows is another type of test often used to see if firefighter candidates have what it takes to do the job. Actually, a test like this mostly tries to assess if you have what it takes to *learn* the job; it tests some of the basic skills you need to be able to do well in your firefighter training program. This practice test includes five areas: reading comprehension, verbal expression, logical reasoning, mathematics, and mechanical aptitude.

Normally you would have about two hours to take an exam like this, but for now don't worry about timing; just take the test in as relaxed a manner as you can. The answer sheet you should use is on the next page. After the exam is an answer key, with an explanation of each correct answer, followed by a section on scoring your exam.

1.	ⓐ	ⓑ	ⓒ	ⓓ
2.	ⓐ	ⓑ	ⓒ	ⓓ
3.	ⓐ	ⓑ	ⓒ	ⓓ
4.	ⓐ	ⓑ	ⓒ	ⓓ
5.	ⓐ	ⓑ	ⓒ	ⓓ
6.	ⓐ	ⓑ	ⓒ	ⓓ
7.	ⓐ	ⓑ	ⓒ	ⓓ
8.	ⓐ	ⓑ	ⓒ	ⓓ
9.	ⓐ	ⓑ	ⓒ	ⓓ
10.	ⓐ	ⓑ	ⓒ	ⓓ
11.	ⓐ	ⓑ	ⓒ	ⓓ
12.	ⓐ	ⓑ	ⓒ	ⓓ
13.	ⓐ	ⓑ	ⓒ	ⓓ
14.	ⓐ	ⓑ	ⓒ	ⓓ
15.	ⓐ	ⓑ	ⓒ	ⓓ
16.	ⓐ	ⓑ	ⓒ	ⓓ
17.	ⓐ	ⓑ	ⓒ	ⓓ
18.	ⓐ	ⓑ	ⓒ	ⓓ
19.	ⓐ	ⓑ	ⓒ	ⓓ
20.	ⓐ	ⓑ	ⓒ	ⓓ
21.	ⓐ	ⓑ	ⓒ	ⓓ
22.	ⓐ	ⓑ	ⓒ	ⓓ
23.	ⓐ	ⓑ	ⓒ	ⓓ
24.	ⓐ	ⓑ	ⓒ	ⓓ
25.	ⓐ	ⓑ	ⓒ	ⓓ
26.	ⓐ	ⓑ	ⓒ	ⓓ
27.	ⓐ	ⓑ	ⓒ	ⓓ
28.	ⓐ	ⓑ	ⓒ	ⓓ
29.	ⓐ	ⓑ	ⓒ	ⓓ
30.	ⓐ	ⓑ	ⓒ	ⓓ
31.	ⓐ	ⓑ	ⓒ	ⓓ
32.	ⓐ	ⓑ	ⓒ	ⓓ
33.	ⓐ	ⓑ	ⓒ	ⓓ
34.	ⓐ	ⓑ	ⓒ	ⓓ

35.	ⓐ	ⓑ	ⓒ	ⓓ
36.	ⓐ	ⓑ	ⓒ	ⓓ
37.	ⓐ	ⓑ	ⓒ	ⓓ
38.	ⓐ	ⓑ	ⓒ	ⓓ
39.	ⓐ	ⓑ	ⓒ	ⓓ
40.	ⓐ	ⓑ	ⓒ	ⓓ
41.	ⓐ	ⓑ	ⓒ	ⓓ
42.	ⓐ	ⓑ	ⓒ	ⓓ
43.	ⓐ	ⓑ	ⓒ	ⓓ
44.	ⓐ	ⓑ	ⓒ	ⓓ
45.	ⓐ	ⓑ	ⓒ	ⓓ
46.	ⓐ	ⓑ	ⓒ	ⓓ
47.	ⓐ	ⓑ	ⓒ	ⓓ
48.	ⓐ	ⓑ	ⓒ	ⓓ
49.	ⓐ	ⓑ	ⓒ	ⓓ
50.	ⓐ	ⓑ	ⓒ	ⓓ
51.	ⓐ	ⓑ	ⓒ	ⓓ
52.	ⓐ	ⓑ	ⓒ	ⓓ
53.	ⓐ	ⓑ	ⓒ	ⓓ
54.	ⓐ	ⓑ	ⓒ	ⓓ
55.	ⓐ	ⓑ	ⓒ	ⓓ
56.	ⓐ	ⓑ	ⓒ	ⓓ
57.	ⓐ	ⓑ	ⓒ	ⓓ
58.	ⓐ	ⓑ	ⓒ	ⓓ
59.	ⓐ	ⓑ	ⓒ	ⓓ
60.	ⓐ	ⓑ	ⓒ	ⓓ
61.	ⓐ	ⓑ	ⓒ	ⓓ
62.	ⓐ	ⓑ	ⓒ	ⓓ
63.	ⓐ	ⓑ	ⓒ	ⓓ
64.	ⓐ	ⓑ	ⓒ	ⓓ
65.	ⓐ	ⓑ	ⓒ	ⓓ
66.	ⓐ	ⓑ	ⓒ	ⓓ
67.	ⓐ	ⓑ	ⓒ	ⓓ
68.	ⓐ	ⓑ	ⓒ	ⓓ

69.	ⓐ	ⓑ	ⓒ	ⓓ
70.	ⓐ	ⓑ	ⓒ	ⓓ
71.	ⓐ	ⓑ	ⓒ	ⓓ
72.	ⓐ	ⓑ	ⓒ	ⓓ
73.	ⓐ	ⓑ	ⓒ	ⓓ
74.	ⓐ	ⓑ	ⓒ	ⓓ
75.	ⓐ	ⓑ	ⓒ	ⓓ
76.	ⓐ	ⓑ	ⓒ	ⓓ
77.	ⓐ	ⓑ	ⓒ	ⓓ
78.	ⓐ	ⓑ	ⓒ	ⓓ
79.	ⓐ	ⓑ	ⓒ	ⓓ
80.	ⓐ	ⓑ	ⓒ	ⓓ
81.	ⓐ	ⓑ	ⓒ	ⓓ
82.	ⓐ	ⓑ	ⓒ	ⓓ
83.	ⓐ	ⓑ	ⓒ	ⓓ
84.	ⓐ	ⓑ	ⓒ	ⓓ
85.	ⓐ	ⓑ	ⓒ	ⓓ
86.	ⓐ	ⓑ	ⓒ	ⓓ
87.	ⓐ	ⓑ	ⓒ	ⓓ
88.	ⓐ	ⓑ	ⓒ	ⓓ
89.	ⓐ	ⓑ	ⓒ	ⓓ
90.	ⓐ	ⓑ	ⓒ	ⓓ
91.	ⓐ	ⓑ	ⓒ	ⓓ
92.	ⓐ	ⓑ	ⓒ	ⓓ
93.	ⓐ	ⓑ	ⓒ	ⓓ
94.	ⓐ	ⓑ	ⓒ	ⓓ
95.	ⓐ	ⓑ	ⓒ	ⓓ

SECTION 1: READING COMPREHENSION

Answer questions 1–5 based solely on the information in the following passage.

Beginning next month, the city of Wellmont will institute a program intended to remove the graffiti from city-owned delivery trucks. Any truck that finishes its assigned route before the end of the driver's shift will return to its lot where supervisors will provide materials for that driver to use in cleaning the truck. Because the length of time it takes to complete different tasks and routes varies, trucks within the same department will no longer be assigned to specific routes but will be rotated among the routes. Therefore, workers should no longer leave personal items in the trucks, as they will not necessarily be driving the same truck each day as in the past.

1. The main purpose of this passage is to
   a. explain why graffiti should be removed from delivery trucks
   b. announce a plan to remove graffiti from delivery trucks
   c. show that graffiti is a problem for the city of Wellmont
   d. tell drivers that their jobs are changing

2. According to the passage, the removal of graffiti from trucks will be done by
   a. a small group of drivers specifically assigned to the task
   b. custodians who work for the city
   c. any supervisor or driver who finishes a route first
   d. each driver as that driver finishes his or her route

3. According to the passage, routes within particular departments
   a. vary in the amount of time they take to complete
   b. vary in the amount of graffiti they're likely to have on them
   c. are all of approximately equal length
   d. vary according to the truck's driver

4. According to the passage, prior to instituting the graffiti clean-up program, city workers
   a. were not responsible for cleaning the trucks
   b. had to re-paint the trucks at intervals
   c. usually drove the same truck each workday
   d. were not allowed to leave personal belongings in the trucks

5. Which of the following does the passage suggest is the greatest problem for the city of Wellmont?
   a. drivers leaving their belongings in city trucks
   b. drivers not finishing their routes on time
   c. people who are defacing city-owned property
   d. drivers who do not want to change routes

Answer questions 6 and 7 by referring to the following table, which gives the causes of major home fires.

MAJOR CAUSES OF HOME FIRES IN THE PREVIOUS 4-YEAR PERIOD

Cause	Fires (% of Total)	Civilian Deaths (% of Total)
Heating equipment	161,500 (27.5%)	770 (16.8%)
Cooking equipment	104,800 (17.8%)	350 (7.7%)
Incendiary, suspicious	65,400 (11.1%)	620 (13.6%)
Electrical equipment	45,700 (7.8%)	440 (9.6%)
Other equipment	43,000 (7.3%)	240 (5.3%)
Smoking materials	39,300 (6.7%)	1,320 (28.9%)
Appliances, air conditioning	36,200 (6.2%)	120 (2.7%)
Exposure and other heat	28,600 (4.8%)	191 (4.2%)
Open flame	27,200 (4.6%)	130 (2.9%)
Child play	26,900 (4.6%)	370 (8.1%)
Natural causes	9,200 (1.6%)	10 (0.2%)

6. What is the percentage of the total fires caused by electrical equipment and other equipment combined?
   a. 7.8%
   b. 14.9%
   c. 15.1%
   d. 29.9%

7. Of the following causes, which one has the highest ratio of total fires to percentage of deaths?
   a. heating equipment
   b. smoking materials
   c. child play
   d. natural causes

Answer questions 8–12 based solely on the information in the following passage.

Before you turn up your boom box or buy front-row seats to a rock concert, you might want to consider how excessive noise affects your hearing. According to Nancy Hadler, Director of the League for the Hard of Hearing's Noise Center, dance clubs, over-amped stereos, noisy vehicles, and even movie soundtracks can contribute to hearing loss.

Hearing loss is sly, slow, and irreversible. There are 30,000 tiny fibers inside each cochlea, which is the spiral-shaped cavity of the inner ear. These hair cells bend in response to sound and create a charge that stimulates the nerve endings at the bottom of each cell. With repeated noise bombardment, these nerve cells can burn out. Hadler compares the nerve fibers to a shag carpet. A good vacuuming will restore the fluffy nap, but if you walk across the same spot too many times, all the vacuuming in the world won't bring the dead fibers back.

Protect yourself from excessive, loud noise. If you are <u>routinely</u> exposed, wear earplugs. And turn down the sound on all your machines.

8. This passage is mainly about how
   a. to protect yourself from loud noise
   b. the inner ear works
   c. loud noise affects hearing
   d. a person's nerve cells are destroyed

9. According to the passage, the cochlea is
   a. a tiny nerve fiber
   b. part of the inner ear
   c. part of the outer ear
   d. synonym for the term *hearing loss*

10. The passage includes a metaphor (comparison) that compares a shag carpet to
   a. loud music
   b. ear plugs
   c. hearing loss
   d. tiny fibers in the ear

11. Which of the following most likely states the opinion of the author?
   a. Wear ear plugs when you operate any loud machinery.
   b. Give up going to the movie theater.
   c. Have your hearing tested every six months.
   d. Don't listen to music on a boom box.

12. A synonym for the word *routinely*, as it is underlined and used in the last paragraph, is
   a. sometimes
   b. regularly
   c. carelessly
   d. periodically

Answer questions 13 and 14 by referring to the following table, which shows forest fires in a certain region during the month of June.

FOREST FIRES, TRI-COUNTY REGION, JUNE 1995			
Date	**Area**	**#Acres Burned**	**Probable Cause**
June 2	Burgaw Grove	115	Lightning
June 3	Fenner Forest	200	Campfire
June 7	Voorhees Air Base Training Site	400	Equipment Use
June 12	Murphy County Nature Reserve	495	Children
June 13	Knoblock Mountain	200	Misc.
June 14	Cougar Run Ski Center	160	Unknown
June 17	Fenner Forest	120	Campfire
June 19	Stone River State Park	526	Arson
June 21	Burgaw Grove	499	Smoking
June 25	Bramley Acres Resort	1,200	Arson
June 28	Hanesboro Crossing	320	Lightning
June 30	Stone River State Park	167	Campfire

13. According to the table, suspected arson fires
   a. occurred at Stone River State Park and Hanesboro Crossing
   b. consumed over 1,700 acres
   c. occurred less frequently than fires caused by smoking
   d. consumed fewer acres than fires caused by lightning

14. One week after the Voorhees Air Base fire, where did a fire occur?
   a. Knoblock Mountain
   b. Fenner Forest
   c. Cougar Run Ski Center
   d. Burgaw Grove

Answer questions 15–19 based solely on the information in the following passage.

A healthy diet with proper nutrition is essential for maintaining good overall health. Since vitamins were discovered early in the twentieth century, people have routinely been taking vitamin supplements for this purpose. The Recommended Dietary Allowance (RDA) is a frequently used nutritional standard for maintaining optimal health. The RDA specifies the recommended amount of a number of nutrients for people in many different age and gender groups. The National Research Council's Committee on Diet and Health has proposed a definition of the RDA to be the amount of a nutrient that meets the needs of 98 percent of the population.

The RDA approach has a number of <u>shortcomings.</u> First, it is based on the assumption that it is possible to accurately define nutritional requirements for a given group. However, individual nutritional requirements can vary widely within each group. The efficiency with which a person converts food intake into nutrients can also vary widely. Certain foods when eaten in combination actually prevent the absorption of nutrients. For example, spinach combined with milk reduces the amount of calcium available to the body from the milk. Also, the RDA approach specifies a different dietary requirement for each age and gender, and it is clearly unrealistic to expect a homemaker to prepare a different menu for each family member. Still, although we cannot rely solely upon RDA to ensure our overall long-term health, it can be a useful guide so long as its limitations are recognized.

15. In the first paragraph, the author focuses on
   a. proper nutrition for various age groups
   b. the definition of the RDA
   c. the discovery of vitamins in the twentieth century
   d. the number of nutrients people need

16. With which of the following would the author most likely agree?
   a. The RDA approach should be replaced by a more realistic nutritional guide.
   b. The RDA approach should be supplemented with more specific nutritional guides.
   c. In spite of its flaws, the RDA approach is definitely the best guide to good nutrition.
   d. The RDA approach is most suitable for a large family.

17. According to the passage, a woman will get less calcium from the milk she drinks if she
   a. does not take in the recommended daily allowance of calcium
   b. is older than 98 percent of the population
   c. eats spinach during the same meal
   d. eats unhealthy foods during the same meal

18. A synonym for the word *shortcomings*, as it is underlined and used in the second paragraph, is
   a. aspects
   b. phases
   c. viewpoints
   d. drawbacks

19. The passage suggests that people have been taking vitamins
   a. for about 200 years
   b. for the past 20 years
   c. since the beginning of the 1900s
   d. since the 1950s

Answer questions 20–22 by referring to the following table, which shows arson statistics for 1998 and 1999.

ARSON STATISTICS FOR 1998 AND 1999			
Type of Structure	**1998**	**1999**	**Percent Change**
Single Occupancy	674	750	+ 11.3
Other Residence	219	236	+ 7.8
Storage	116	112	– 3.4
Industrial	21	19	– 9.5
Other Commercial	124	117	– 5.6
Public	154	175	+ 13.6
All Other Structures	266	496	+ 86.5
Motor Vehicle	491	582	+ 18.5

20. In comparison to 1998, in 1999 "other residence" arson fires
   a. decreased by 9.5 percent
   b. increased by 11.3 percent
   c. decreased by 3.4 percent
   d. increased by 7.8 percent

21. If the trends between 1998 and 1999 continued in 2000, there would be
   a. about 34 percent more storage structure fires
   b. almost 10 percent more industrial fires
   c. almost 10 percent fewer industrial fires
   d. about 8 percent more motor vehicle fires

22. Other than the "all other structures" category, which kinds of fires showed the most dramatic increase?
   a. motor vehicle fires
   b. single occupancy structure fires
   c. public structure fires
   d. other residence structure fires

Answer questions 23–27 based solely on the information in the following passage.

By using tiny probes as neural prostheses, scientists may be able to restore nerve function in quadriplegics and make the blind see or the deaf hear. Thanks to advanced techniques, a single, small, implanted probe can stimulate individual neurons in the brain electrically or chemically and then record responses. Preliminary results suggest that the microprobe telemetry systems can be permanently implanted and replace damaged or missing nerves.

The tissue-compatible microprobes represent an advance over the typical aluminum wire electrodes previously used in studies of the cortex and other brain structures. Researchers accumulate much data using traditional electrodes, but there is a question of how much damage they cause to the nervous system. Microprobes, which are about as thin as a human hair, cause minimal damage and disruption of neurons when inserted into the brain.

In addition to recording nervous system impulses, the microprobes have minuscule channels that open the way for delivery of drugs, cellular growth factors, neurotransmitters, and other neuroactive compounds to a single neuron or to groups of neurons. Also, patients who lack certain biochemicals could receive doses via prostheses. The probes can have up to four channels, each with its own recording/stimulating electrode.

23. One feature that microprobes and wire electrodes have in common is
   a. a minimal disturbance of neurons
   b. the density of the material
   c. the capacity for multiple leads
   d. their ability to generate information

24. Which of the following best expresses the main idea of the passage?
   a. Microprobes require further technological advances before they can be used in humans.
   b. Wire electrodes are antiquated as a means for delivering neuroactive compounds to the brain.
   c. Microprobes have great potential to help counteract neural damage.
   d. Technology now exists that may enable repair of the nervous system.

25. All of the following are mentioned in the passage as potential uses for prostheses EXCEPT
   a. transportation of medication
   b. induction of physical movement
   c. transportation of growth factor
   d. removal of biochemicals from the cortex

26. The initial function of microprobe channels is to
   a. create pathways
   b. disrupt neurons
   c. replace ribbon cables
   d. study the brain

27. The passage suggests that one reason microprobes cause less damage than aluminum-wire electrodes do is that microprobles
   a. are much thinner
   b. can reach groups of neurons
   c. are made of human hair
   d. inserted in the cortex of the brain

Answer questions 28–30 by referring to the following graph, which shows wildfire trends in a particular region

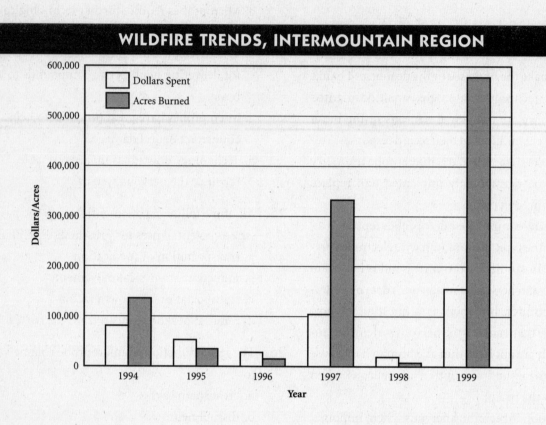

WILDFIRE TRENDS, INTERMOUNTAIN REGION

28. In which of the following years were the fewest acres burned?
  a. 1994
  b. 1995
  c. 1996
  d. 1997

29. About how much money was spent fighting wildfires in the Intermountain Region during 1997?
  a. $ 90,000
  b. $100,000
  c. $110,000
  d. $320,000

30. In which of the following years was the cost per acre of fighting wildfires the lowest?
  a. 1995
  b. 1996
  c. 1998
  d. 1999

SECTION 2: VERBAL EXPRESSION

For numbers 31–35, choose the word that most nearly means the same as the italicized word.

31. The city's computer system, having been installed fifteen years ago, was *obsolete*.
   a. typical
   b. usable
   c. outmoded
   d. unnecessary

32. For all the problems faced by his district, Congressman Owly regarded budget cuts as a the answer to every problem, a complete *panacea*.
   a. cure
   b. result
   c. cause
   d. necessity

33. The residents of the area, knowing that seat belts save lives, are *compliant* with the seat-belt law.
   a. skeptical
   b. obedient
   c. forgetful
   d. appreciative

34. Not wanting to commit itself wholeheartedly, the City Council gave *tentative* approval to the idea of banning smoking from all public buildings.
   a. provisional
   b. ambiguous
   c. wholehearted
   d. necessary

35. He based his conclusion on what he *inferred* from the evidence, not on what he actually observed.
   a. intuited
   b. imagined
   c. surmised
   d. implied

For numbers 36–38, choose the word that best fills the blank.

36. In order to keep our customers' business, their complaints must be handled in a _____ manner.
   a. diplomatic
   b. delaying
   c. elaborate
   d. combative

37. The captain often _____ responsibility to his subordinates, so as to have time to do the important tasks himself.
   a. analyzed
   b. respected
   c. criticized
   d. delegated

38. The spokesperson must _____ the philosophy of an entire department so that outsiders can understand it completely.
   a. entrust
   b. defend
   c. verify
   d. articulate

For numbers 39–43, replace the underlined portion with the phrase that best completes the sentence. If the sentence is correct as is, choose option **a**.

39. The news reporter who <u>had been covering the story suddenly became ill, and I was called</u> to take her place.
- a. had been covering the story suddenly became ill, and I was called
- b. was covering the story suddenly becomes ill, and they called me
- c. is covering the story suddenly becomes ill, and I was called
- d. would have been covering the story suddenly became ill, and I am called

40. The troposphere is the lowest layer of Earth's <u>atmosphere, it extends</u> from ground level to an altitude of seven to ten miles.
- a. atmosphere, it extends
- b. atmosphere of which it extends
- c. atmosphere. Extending
- d. atmosphere; it extends

41. <u>Along with your membership to our health club and</u> two months of free personal training.
- a. Along with your membership to our health club, and
- b. Along with your membership to our health club go
- c. With your membership to our health club,
- d. In addition to your membership to our health club being

42. <u>To determine the speed of automobiles, radar is often used by the state police.</u>
- a. To determine the speed of automobiles, radar is often used by the state police.
- b. In determining the speed of automobiles, the use of radar by state police is often employed.
- c. To determine the speed of automobiles, the state police often use radar.
- d. Radar by state police in determining the speed of automobiles is often used.

43. Which of these expresses the idea most clearly and accurately?
- a. Ethics and the law having no true relationship.
- b. There is no true relationship between ethics and the law.
- c. Between ethics and the law, no true relationship.
- d. Ethics and the law is no true relationship.

44. Which of these expresses the idea most clearly and accurately?
- a. Some people say jury duty is a nuisance that just takes up their precious time and that we don't get paid enough.
- b. Some people say jury duty is a nuisance that just takes up your precious time and that one doesn't get paid enough.
- c. Some people say jury duty is a nuisance that just takes up precious time and that doesn't pay enough.
- d. Some people say jury duty is a nuisance that just takes up our precious time and that they don't get paid enough.

45. Which of these expresses the idea most clearly and accurately?

   a. By the time they are in the third or fourth grade, the eyes of most children in the United States are tested.

   b. Most children by the time they are in the United States have their eyes tested in the third or fourth grade.

   c. Most children in the United States have their eyes tested by the time they are in the third or fourth grade.

   d. In the United States by the time of third or fourth grade, there is testing of the eyes of most children.

SECTION 3: LOGICAL REASONING

46. Look at this series: 10, 34, 12, 31, __, 28, 16,... What number should fill the blank?

   a. 14

   b. 18

   c. 30

   d. 34

47. Look at this series: 17, __, 28, 28, 39, 39,... What number should fill the blank?

   a. 50

   b. 39

   c. 25

   d. 17

48. Look at this series: 0.15, 0.3, __, 1.2, 2.4,... What number should fill the blank?

   a. 4.8

   b. 0.006

   c. 0.6

   d. 0.9

49. Look at this series: J14, L16, __, P20, R22,... What letter and numbers should fill the blank?

   a. S24

   b. N18

   c. M18

   d. T24

50. Look at this series: QPO, NML, KJI, ___, EDC,... What letters should fill the blank?

   a. HGF

   b. CAB

   c. JKL

   d. GHI

For numbers 51–53, find the pattern in the sequence.

51.

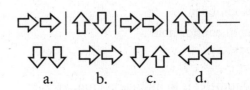

52.

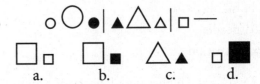

53.

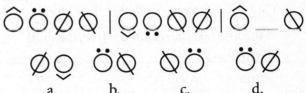

For numbers 54–57, complete the analogy.

54. Communication is to telephone as transportation is to
a. aviation
b. travel
c. information
d. bus

55. Bicycle is to pedal as canoe is to
a. water
b. kayak
c. oar
d. fleet

56. Tactful is to diplomatic as bashful is to
a. timid
b. confident
c. uncomfortable
d. bold

57. Odometer is to mileage as compass is to
a. speed
b. hiking
c. needle
d. direction

58. City A has a higher population than City B.
City C has a lower population than City B.
City A has a lower population than City C.

If the first two statements are true, the third statement is
a. true
b. false
c. uncertain

59. The Shop and Save Grocery is south of Greenwood Pharmacy.
Rebecca's house is northeast of Greenwood Pharmacy.
Rebecca's house is west of the Shop and Save Grocery.

If the first two statements are true, the third statement is
a. true
b. false
c. uncertain

60. Oat cereal has more fiber than corn cereal but less fiber than bran cereal.
Corn cereal has more fiber than rice cereal but less fiber than wheat cereal.
Of the five kinds of cereal, rice cereal has the least amount of fiber.

If the first two statements are true, the third statement is
a. true
b. false
c. uncertain

SECTION 4: MATHEMATICS

61. If a fire truck travels at the speed of 62 mph for 15 minutes, how far will it travel? (Distance = Rate × Time)
a. 9.3 miles
b. 15.5 miles
c. 16 miles
d. 24.8 miles

62. Pumper Truck A pumps at a rate of 500 gallons of water per minute. Pumper Truck B pumps at a rate of 425 gallons per minute. If both trucks begin pumping at the same time, how many more gallons of water will Truck A pump in 12 minutes than will Truck B?
  a. 75
  b. 600
  c. 900
  d. 1,500

63. The cost of a list of supplies for a fire station is as follows: $19.98, $52.20, $12.64, and $7.79. What is the total cost?
  a. $91.30
  b. $92.61
  c. $93.60
  d. $93.61

64. Nationwide, in one year there were about 21,500 residential fires associated with furniture. Of these, 11,350 were caused by smoking materials. About what percent of the residential fires were smoking related?
  a. 47%
  b. 49%
  c. 51%
  d. 53%

65. A firefighter checks the gauge on a cylinder that normally contains 45 cubic feet of air and finds that the cylinder has only 10 cubic feet of air. The gauge indicates that the cylinder is
  a. $\frac{1}{4}$ full
  b. $\frac{7}{9}$ full
  c. $\frac{1}{3}$ full
  d. $\frac{4}{5}$ full

66. A firefighter determines that the length of hose needed to reach a particular building is 175 feet. If the available hoses are 45 feet long, how many sections of hose, when connected together, will it take to reach the building?
  a. 2
  b. 3
  c. 4
  d. 5

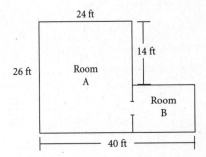

67. The smallest waterproof tarpaulin that will entirely cover Room B is
  a. 10 ft ×14 ft
  b. 12 ft × 14 ft
  c. 10 ft × 16 ft
  d. 12 ft × 16 ft

68. A fire station receives an alarm on August 3 at 10:42 P.M. and another alarm at 1:19 A.M. on August 4. How much time has elapsed between alarms?
  a. 1 hour 37 minutes
  b. 2 hours 23 minutes
  c. 2 hours 37 minutes
  d. 3 hours 23 minutes

69. Each sprinkler head in an office sprinkler system sprays water at an average of 16 gallons per minute. If 5 sprinkler heads are flowing at the same time, how many gallons of water will be released in 10 minutes?
   a. 80
   b. 160
   c. 1,650
   d. 800

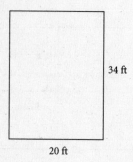

34 ft

20 ft

70. How many feet of rope will a firefighter need to tie off a protective area that is 34 feet long and 20 feet wide?
   a. 54
   b. 88
   c. 108
   c. 680

71. About how many liters of water will a 5-gallon container hold? (1 liter = 1.06 quarts)
   a. 5
   b. 11
   c. 20
   d. 21

72. A locked ammunition box is about $2\frac{1}{2}$ centimeters thick. About how thick is this box in inches? (1 cm = 0.39 inches)
   a. $\frac{1}{4}$ inch
   b. 1 inch
   c. 2 inches
   d. 5 inches

73. What is the approximate total weight of four firefighters who weigh 152 pounds, 168 pounds, 182 pounds, and 201 pounds?
   a. 690 pounds
   b. 700 pounds
   c. 710 pounds
   d. 750 pounds

74. If a tank on the back of a fire truck is 10 feet long, 6 feet wide, and 4 feet high, how many cubic feet of water will it hold? ($V = lwh$)
   a. 20
   b. 64
   c. 210
   d. 240

75. If the diameter of a metal spool is 3.5 feet, how many times will a 53-foot hose wrap completely around it? ($C = \pi d, \pi = \frac{22}{7}$)
   a. 2
   b. 3
   c. 4
   d. 5

SECTION 5: MECHANICAL APTITUDE

Use the information provided in the question, as well as any diagrams provided, to answer the questions below.

76. A fire engine has become stuck in a ditch. Which of the following tools would most likely be used to help extract the fire engine from the ditch?
   a. a clamp
   b. an electric winch
   c. a speedometer
   d. a centrifugal pump

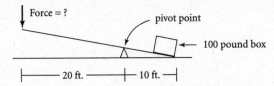

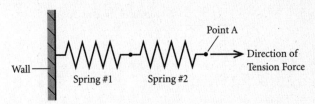

77. In the diagram shown above, Joe must lift a 100-pound box using a lever. How many pounds of force must he apply to the left side of the lever to lift the box? (The product of the weight of the box times the distance of the box from the pivot point must be equal to the product of the required force times the distance from the force to the pivot point:

$w \times d_1 = f \times d_2$)

   a. 100 pounds
   b. 200 pounds
   c. 50 pounds
   d. 33 pounds

78. The purpose of a spark plug in an internal combustion engine is to provide
   a. lubrication of the engine
   b. rotation of the piston
   c. cooling of the manifold
   d. ignition of the fuel

79. A carpenter's square is primarily used to
   a. insure that a cut is straight
   b. measure the length of a stud
   c. saw a board to the correct length
   d. check that a building is level

80. Two springs are arranged in series as shown above. Spring #1 is very stiff and will become 1 inch longer when a tension force of 10 pounds is applied to it. Spring #2 is very soft and will become 2 inches longer when a tension force of 5 pounds is applied to it. What will be the change in length of the two springs when a force of 20 pounds is applied—that is, how far will point A move to the right?
   a. 10 inches
   b. 6 inches
   c. 8 inches
   d. 3 inches

81. What primary principle of physics is used by the "Jaws of Life?"
   a. a rotor
   b. a lever
   c. a spring
   d. a pulley

82. Which of the following items is used to measure angles?
   a. a lever
   b. a tachometer
   c. a gear
   d. a protractor

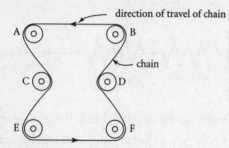

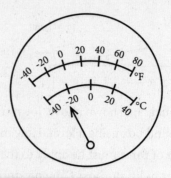

83. In the diagram shown above, which gears are turning clockwise?

a. A, C, and E

b. B, D, and F

c. C and D

d. E and F

84. Which of the following is NOT a type of wrench?

a. crescent

b. box end

c. ratchet

d. drill

85. What type of gauge is read in units of psi (pounds per square inch)?

a. pressure gauge

b. depth gauge

c. speed gauge

d. RPM gauge

86. The gauge shown above is

a. a pressure gauge

b. an altitude gauge

c. a temperature gauge

d. a flow meter gauge

87. If a truck is traveling at constant speed of 50 miles per hour for a total time period of 1 hour and 30 minutes, how many miles does it travel? (Distance = Rate × Time)

a. 75 miles

b. 50 miles

c. 5 miles

d. 130 miles

88. What common mechanical device is typically used on a push button—such as that found on a push-button telephone, a computer keyboard, or an electric garage door opener—in order to return the button to its original position?

a. a wheel

b. a pulley

c. a spring

d. a gear

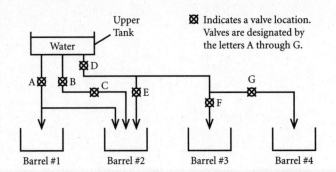

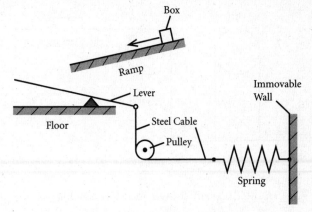

89. In the diagram shown above, all valves are initially closed. Gravity will cause the water to drain down into the barrels when the valves are opened. Which barrels will be filled if valves A, B, E, F, and G are opened and valves C and D are left closed?
   a. barrels #1 and #2
   b. barrels #3 and #4
   c. barrels #1, #2, #3, and #4
   d. barrels #1, #2, and #3

90. Which of the mechanical devices listed below is used to control the flow of liquids and gases in a piping system?
   a. a gear
   b. a valve
   c. a piston
   d. a spring

91. The purpose of a radiator on a car is to
   a. cool the engine
   b. maximize gas mileage
   c. increase the engine horsepower
   d. reduce engine noise

92. In the diagram shown above, if the box slides down the ramp and drops onto the left side of the lever, what will happen to the spring?
   a. It will touch the box.
   b. It will remain as it is.
   c. It will be compressed or shortened.
   d. It will be stretched or lengthened.

93. Which mechanical device is NOT typically found on an automobile?
   a. a valve
   b. a pump
   c. a drill
   d. a fan

94. A solar panel, a windmill, an atomic reactor, a dam on a river, and a steam turbine are ALL examples of methods that could be used to create
   a. ice
   b. electricity
   c. steel
   d. rain

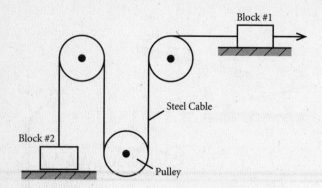

95. In the diagram shown above, if block #1 is moved 10 feet to the right, how far upward is block #2 lifted?

   a. 3 feet

   b. 5 feet

   c. 10 feet

   d. 20 feet

ANSWERS

SECTION 1: READING COMPREHENSION

1. b. The first sentence clearly states that this is an announcement of a new program. There is no support for choices **a** or **c**. Although the drivers' jobs may change somewhat (choice **d**), this is not the main focus of the passage.

2. d. The second sentence of the passage indicates that each driver who finishes a route will clean a truck.

3. a. The third sentence of the passage indicates that routes vary in the length of time they take to complete. The other choices are not included in the passage.

4. c. According to the last sentence of the passage, in the past city workers usually drove the same truck each day.

5. c. Because the city wants to clean up the graffiti, it is reasonable to conclude that this is a problem for the city of Wellmont. Choice **a** may be a problem, but the graffiti is a greater problem. There is no support for **b** or **d**.

6. c. Adding 7.8 (electrical equipment) and 7.3 (other equipment) is the way to arrive at the correct response.

7. b. Smoking materials account for only 6.7% of the fires but for 28.9% of the deaths.

8. c. The main focus of this passage is how loud noises can cause hearing loss. Although choices **a** and **b** are mentioned, these are not the main focus of the passage. The passage also mentions the destruction of nerve cells (choice **d**), but the passage discusses only those cells in the inner ear, not nerve cells in general.

9. b. The second paragraph clearly states that the cochlea is *the spiral-shaped cavity of the inner ear.*

10. d. The second paragraph compares the fibers in a shag carpet to the fibers in the inner ear.

11. a. This is the only choice that can reasonably be inferred from the information in the passage; the basis for this inference is the last paragraph. There is no support that the author believes either **b** or **c**. As for **d**, the author suggests turning down the boom box, not giving up listening.

12. b. This is the only choice that is in keeping with the context of the passage. Choices **a** and **d** both mean on occasion, not steadily. Choice **c** can be ruled out because there is no context to support this answer.

13. b. 1,200 acres at Bramley Acres Resort and 526 acres at Stone River Park adds up to 1,726 acres.

14. c. The Voorhees fire occurred June 7. The Cooper Run fire occurred June 14.

15. b. This paragraph concentrates on defining the RDA. Choices **a**, **c**, and **d** are mentioned, but none is the main focus of the paragraph.

16. b. Choice **b** is indicated by the final sentence, which indicates that the RDA approach is useful, but has limitations, implying that a supplemental guide would be a good thing. Choice **a** is contradicted by the final sentence of the passage. Choice **c** is incorrect because the passage says the RDA approach is a *useful guide*, but does NOT say it is the best guide to good nutrition. Choice **d** is contradicted by the next-to-last sentence of the passage.

17. c. This is a detail item, and the answer is clearly stated in the middle of the second paragraph.

There is no support in the passage for the other choices.

18. d. If you read the paragraph, you will see that the sentences that follow this opening sentence list some of the deficiencies of the RDA; this is why *drawbacks* is the only possible choice. Although the other choices fit into the sentence, they do not fit into the context of the paragraph.

19. c. The first paragraph states that people have been taking vitamins since early in the twentieth century.

20. d. See the *Other Residence, Percent Change* row on the table.

21. c. See the *Industrial, Percent Change* row on the table.

22. a. See the last row of the table.

23. d. The second sentence of the first paragraph states that probes record responses. The second paragraph says that electrodes *accumulate much data*.

24. c. The tone throughout the passage suggests the potential for microprobes. They can be permanently implanted, they have advantages over electrodes, they are promising candidates for neural prostheses, they will have great accuracy, and they are flexible. The other choices are too narrow to be main ideas.

25. d. According to the third paragraph, people who *lack* biochemicals could receive doses via prostheses. However, there is no suggestion that removing biochemicals would be viable.

26. a. The first sentence of the third paragraph says that microprobes have channels that *open the way for delivery of drugs*. Studying the brain (choice **d**) is not the initial function of channels, though it is one of the uses of the probes themselves.

27. a. This inference is made in the second paragraph, which states that microprobes *are about as thin as a human hair*. This statement suggests that this is the reason microprobes cause less damage than the aluminum wires do. Although choice **c** is attractive, it can be ruled out because the passage does not say the probes are made of human hair.

28. c. According to the graph, about 15,000 acres burned in 1996. Although fewer acres burned in 1998, this is not one of the choices.

29. c. The bar on the graph is over the 100,000 mark.

30. d. To answer this question, both *Acres Burned* and *Dollars Spent* must be considered. The ratio between the two is greater in 1999 than in the other years.

SECTION 2: VERBAL EXPRESSION

31. c. To be *obsolete* is to be out-of-date or *outmoded*. The key to the meaning is the context—that is, the phrase *having been installed fifteen years ago....*

32. a. A *panacea* is an all-encompassing remedy or cure. The key here is the phrase *answer to every problem*.

33. b. When one is *compliant*, one is acquiescent or *obedient*.

34. a. When something is *tentative*, it is of an *experimental* or *provisional* nature.

35. c. To *infer* something is to *surmise* it or deduce it from the evidence.

36. a. To be *diplomatic* is to be or sensitive in dealing with others. In the context of the sentence, this is the only choice that makes sense.

37. d. To *delegate* a task is to assign it or to appoint another to do it. This is the only choice that fits the context of the sentence.

38. d. To *articulate* something is to give words to it or express it. The other choices do not fit the context of the sentence.

39. a. When constructing sentences, unnecessary shifts in verb tenses should be avoided. Choice **a** is best because all three verbs in the sentence indicate that the action occurred in the past (*had been covering, became,* and *was called*). In choice **b**, there is a shift to the present (*becomes*). Choice **c** begins in the present (*is covering, becomes*), then shifts to the past (*called*). Choice **d** makes two tense shifts.

40. d. The correct punctuation between two independent clauses is a semicolon. Choice **a** is wrong because it creates a comma splice. Choice **b** creates faulty subordination. Choice **c** creates a sentence fragment.

41. b. This is the correct choice because it is the only one that is a complete sentence.

42. d. Choice **d** is best because it is written in the active voice, and the sentence is constructed so that all modifiers are appropriately placed.

43. b. Answers **a** and **c** are sentence fragments. Answer **d** represents confused sentence structure as well as lack of agreement between subject and verb.

44. c. The other choices contain unnecessary shifts in person, from *people* to *their* and *we* in answer **a**, to *your* and *one* in answer **b**, and to *our* and *they* in answer **d**.

45. c. This is the only choice that is clear and logical. Choice **a** reads as though the eyes are in the third or fourth grade. Choices **b** and **d** are unclear.

SECTION 3: LOGICAL REASONING

46. a. This is a simple alternating addition and subtraction series. The first series begins with 10 and adds 2; the second begins with 34 and subtracts 3.

47. d. In this simple addition with repetition series, each number in the series repeats itself, and then increases by 11 to arrive at the next number.

48. c. This is a simple multiplication series. Each number is 2 times greater than the previous number.

49. b. In this series, the letters progress by 2, and the numbers increase by 2.

50. a. This series consists of letters in a reverse alphabetical order.

51. b. Look at each segment. In the first segment, the arrows are both pointing to the right. In the second segment, the first arrow is up and the second is down. The third segment repeats the first segment. In the fourth segment, the arrows are up and then down. Because this is an alternating series, the two arrows pointing right will be repeated, so option **b** is the only possible choice.

52. b. Notice that in each segment, the figures are all the same shape, but the one in the middle is larger than the two on either side. Also, notice that one of the figures is shaded and that this shading alternates first right and then left. To continue this pattern in the third segment, you will look for a square. Choice **b** is correct because this choice will put the large square between the two smaller squares, with the shading on the right.

53. d. This is an alternating series. The first and third segments are repeated. The second segment is simply upside down.

54. d. The telephone is a means of communication. The bus is a means of transportation. Aviation (choice **a**) is not the answer because it is a type of transportation, not a means. The answer is not choice **b** or choice **c** because neither of these represents a means of transportation.

55. c. A bicycle is put in motion by means of a pedal. A canoe is put into motion by means of an oar. The answer is not choice **a** because the substance water does not necessarily put the canoe into motion. Kayak (choice **b**) is incorrect because it is a type of boat similar to a canoe. Choice **d** is incorrect because a fleet is a group of boats.

56. a. *Tactful* and *diplomatic* are synonyms (they mean about the same thing). *Bashful* and *timid* are also synonyms. The answer is not choice **b** or **c** because neither of these means the same as *bashful*. Choice **d** is incorrect because *bold* means the opposite of *bashful*.

57. d. An odometer is an instrument used to measure mileage. A compass is an instrument used to determine direction. Choices **a**, **b**, and **c** are incorrect because none are instruments.

58. b. From the first two statements we know that of the three cities, City A has the highest population, so the third statement must be false.

59. b. Because the first two statements are true, Rebecca's house is also northeast of the Shop and Save Grocery, which means that the third statement is false.

60. a. From the first statement, we know that bran cereal has more fiber than both oat cereal and corn cereal. From the second statement we know that rice cereal has less fiber than both corn and wheat cereals. Therefore, rice cereal has the least amount of fiber.

SECTION 4: MATHEMATICS

61. b. Solving this problem requires converting 15 minutes to 0.25 hour, which is the time, then using the formula: 62 mph × 0.25 hour = 15.5 miles.

62. c. The simplest way to solve this problem is to first subtract 425 from 500. The remainder of 75 is the number of gallons per minute more that Truck A is pumping. The second step is to multiply 75 by 12 minutes for a total of 900 gallons.

63. b. You simply add all the numbers together to solve this problem.

64. d. Division is used to arrive at a decimal, which can then be rounded to the nearest hundredth and converted to a percentage: 11,350 ÷ 21,500 = 0.5279. 0.5279 rounded to the nearest hundredth is 0.53, or 53%.

65. b. Because the answer is a fraction, the best way to solve the problem is to convert the known to a fraction: $\frac{10}{45}$ of the cylinder is full. By dividing both the numerator and the denominator by 5, you can reduce the fraction to $\frac{2}{9}$.

66. c. The answer is arrived at by first dividing 175 by 45. Since the answer is 3.89, not a whole number, the firefighter needs 4 sections of hose. Three sections of hose would be too short.

67. d. To solve the problem, the dimensions of Room B must be determined. The width of Room B is determined by subtracting 14 feet from 26 feet. The length is determined by subtracting 24 feet (the width of Room A) from 40 feet (the length of both Room A and Room B).

68. c. Subtraction and addition will solve this problem. From 10:42 to 12:42 two hours have elapsed. From 12:42 to 1:00, another 18 minutes has elapsed (60 − 42 = 18). Then from 1:00 to 1:19 there is another 19 minutes.

69. d. Multiply 16 times 5 to find out how many gallons all five sprinklers will release in one minute. Then multiply the result (80 gallons per minute) by the number of minutes (10) to get 800 gallons.

70. c. There are two sides 34 feet long and two sides 20 feet long. Using the formula P = 2L + 2W will solve this problem. Therefore, you should multiply 34 times 2 and 20 times 2, and then add the results: 68 + 40 = 108.

71. d. The answer to this question lies in knowing that there are four quarts to a gallon. There are therefore 20 quarts in a 5-gallon container. Multiply 20 by 1.06 quarts per liter to get 21.2 liters and then round off to 21.

72. b. The problem is solved by first converting a fraction to a decimal, then multiplying $2.5 \times 0.39 = 0.975$, which is rounded to 1.

73. b. Add all four weights for a total of 703. 703 rounded to the nearest ten is 700.

74. d. This is a multiplication problem using the volume formula given: $10 \times 6 \times 4 = 240$.

75. c. Solving this problem requires determining the circumference of the spool by multiplying $\frac{22}{7}$ by $3\frac{1}{2}$ $(\frac{7}{2})$. Divide the total (11) into 53. The answer is 4.8 so the hose will completely wrap only 4 times.

SECTION 5: MECHANICAL APTITUDE

76. b. An electric winch would be used to remove a fire truck from a ditch. The other devices would not be useful in this situation.

77. c. The distance from the pivot point to the point of application of the force (20 feet) is twice the distance from the pivot point to the box (10 feet). Therefore, in order to lift the box, the required force will be one half of the weight of the box (100 pounds), or 50 pounds.

78. d. The spark plug produces a spark inside the cylinder of the engine. This spark causes the fuel to burn.

79. a. A carpenter's square is typically an L-shaped piece of metal used to draw a straight line on a board on which a cut is to be made.

80. a. Because the springs are in series, their amount of stretch is additive. Spring #1 will stretch 1 inch under 10 pounds, so its total stretch under 20 pounds will be 2 inches. Spring #2 is being subjected to a load of 20 pounds, which is four times the load that will stretch it 2 inches. Therefore, its total stretch will be 8 inches. Adding the amount of stretch for the two springs together gives you 10 inches.

81. b. The "Jaws of Life" consists of two levers that combine to form one tool. The jaws pivot around a center point and use the mechanical advantage of a lever to pry apart strong pieces of metal.

82. d. A protractor is typically a half circle made of metal or plastic, which has tick marks around the edge spaced at one-degree intervals—a complete circle has 360 degrees. The protractor can be used to measure angles of various geometric shapes, plots of land, and other items.

83. c. The other gears are turning counter-clockwise. It helps to follow the direction of the chain, which is directly connected to all of the gears.

84. d. A drill is not a type of wrench. A drill is used to create holes in such materials as wood, plastic, metal, or concrete.

85. a. A pressure gauge is measured in psi. The other gauges are read in the following units: A depth gauge uses a unit of length such as feet or meters; a speed gauge uses a unit of velocity such as miles per hour (mph) or kilometers per hour (kph); the RPM gauge measures revolutions per minute.

86. c. That this gauge measures temperature can be determined by the units of degrees Fahrenheit and degrees Celsius shown on the gauge. These are units of temperature.

87. a. The truck travels for 1 hour and 30 minutes, which is 1.5 hours. According to the formula, then, the distance traveled is 1.5 hours times 50 mph, or 75 miles.

88. c. A compression coil spring is typically placed behind the button. When the button is pressed, the spring is compressed and then springs back to return the button to its original position.

89. a. Since valve D is closed, water will not flow to barrels #3 and #4. Water will flow through valve B but be stopped at valve C. Water will flow through valve A into barrels #1 and #2.

90. b. A valve is used to control the flow of liquids and gases in a piping system. An example is the faucet on a sink.

91. a. The radiator contains fluid (water and antifreeze) that is circulated around the engine block by the water pump. The fluid becomes hot as it passes around the engine and is then cooled as air passes through the radiator.

92. d. The box will force the left side of the lever down and the right side of the lever up, which will pull the cable up. The cable will pass across the pulley and apply a pulling force on the spring, so that the spring will stretch.

93. c. A drill is a common carpenter's hand tool. The other items are common parts of a car.

94. b. The systems listed produce electric power; none generate ice, steel, or rain.

95. c. The two blocks are directly connected by a fixed length of steel cable. Therefore, regardless of the number of pulleys between the two blocks, the distance moved by one block will be the same as that moved by the other block.

SCORING

In most cities, a score of 70 or higher places you onto the eligibility list, and anything less than a 70 usually eliminates you from the selection process. But your goal shouldn't be just to get a 70 and make it onto the list. Though in some cities the written exam is only pass/fail, other cities use the test scores to rank candidates in the beginning stages of the selection process. Whether your city ranks candidates after this exam or not, your score is usually recorded in the file that will be reviewed before final firefighter selection. Thus, the higher you score on the exam, the better.

To best help you prepare, you should review your exam results carefully. First of all, you can apply your total score to the self-evaluation section of the Learning-Express Test Preparation System in Chapter 3 of this book to help you decide on a study plan.

Next, calculate the percentage of questions you answered correctly in each section. In which section were your results highest? Lowest? Rank the sections in order of performance so you can set priorities in your study plan. For example, if your lowest score was in reading comprehension, you should plan on paying the most attention to that chapter. The following suggestions will help direct your preparation between now and the day of the exam:

- If you had difficulty understanding the passages in the reading comprehension section, then you should plan to spend a lot of time on Chapter 6, "Reading Comprehension."
- If you had trouble with the vocabulary or grammar questions, plan to review Chapter 12, "Verbal Expression," carefully.
- If you had trouble with logical reasoning questions, spend a lot of time on Chapter 9.
- If you had trouble with the mechanical aptitude questions, carefully review Chapter 10.
- If you had difficulty with the math problems, focus on Chapter 8.

Each of these chapters includes lots of tips and hints for doing well on the given kind of question. You should decide how much time to spend on each chapter based on the results of this exam. Of course, if your exam doesn't include all of the kinds of questions included in this practice exam, you don't need to spend much time on the chapters covering those kinds of questions—though all of these skills will be useful to you when you become a firefighter.

When you've finished these chapters, take the third and fourth practice exams in Chapters 13 and 14 to see how much you've improved.

C·H·A·P·T·E·R 6
READING COMPREHENSION

CHAPTER SUMMARY

Because reading is such a vital skill, most firefighter exams include a reading comprehension section that tests your ability to understand what you read. The tips and exercises in this chapter will help you improve your comprehension of written passages as well as of tables, charts, and graphs, so that you can increase your score in this area.

M emos, policies, procedures, reports—these are all things you'll be expected to understand if you become a firefighter. Understanding written materials is part of almost any job. That's why most firefighter tests attempt to measure how well applicants understand what they read.

Reading comprehension tests are usually in a multiple-choice format and ask questions based on brief passages, much like the standardized tests that are offered in schools. For that matter, almost all standardized test questions test your reading skill. After all, you can't answer the question if you can't read it! Similarly, you can't study your training materials or learn new procedures once you're on the job if you can't read well. So reading comprehension is vital not only on the test but also for the rest of your career.

TYPES OF READING COMPREHENSION QUESTIONS

You have probably encountered reading comprehension questions before, where you are given a passage to read and then have to answer multiple-choice questions about it. This kind of question has two advantages for you as a test taker:

1. You don't have to know anything about the topic of the passage because
2. You're being tested only on the information the passage provides.

But the disadvantage is that you have to know where and how to find that information quickly in an unfamiliar text. This makes it easy to fall for one of the wrong answer choices, especially since they're designed to mislead you.

The best way to do well on this passage/question format is to be very familiar with the kinds of questions that are typically asked on the test. Questions most frequently ask you to:

1. identify a specific **fact or detail** in the passage
2. note the **main idea** of the passage
3. make an **inference** based on the passage
4. define a **vocabulary** word from the passage

In order for you to do well on a reading comprehension test, you need to know exactly what each of these questions is asking. **Facts and details** are the specific pieces of information that support the passage's **main idea**. The main idea is the thought, opinion, or attitude that governs the whole passage. Generally speaking, facts and details are indisputable—things that don't need to be proven, like statistics (18 million people) or descriptions (a green overcoat). Let's say, for example, you read a sentence that says *"After the department's reorganization, workers were 50% more productive."* A sentence like this, which gives you the **fact** that 50% of workers were more productive, might support a **main idea** that says, *"Every department should be reorganized."* Notice that this main idea is not something indisputable; it is an opinion. The writer thinks all departments should be reorganized, and because this is his opinion (and not everyone shares it), he needs to support his opinion with facts and details.

An **inference**, on the other hand, is a conclusion that can be drawn based on fact or evidence. For example, you can infer—based on the fact that workers became 50% more productive after the reorganization, which is a dramatic change—that the department had not been efficiently organized. The fact sentence, *"After the department's reorganization, workers were 50% more productive,"* also implies that the reorganization of the department was the reason workers became more productive. There may, of course, have been other reasons, but we can infer only one from this sentence.

As you might expect, **vocabulary** questions ask you to determine the meaning of particular words. Often, if you've read carefully, you can determine the meaning of such words from their context, that is, how the word is used in the sentence or paragraph.

PRACTICE PASSAGE 1: USING THE FOUR QUESTION TYPES

The following is a sample test passage, followed by four questions. Read the passage carefully, and then answer the questions, based on your reading of the text, by circling your choice. Then refer to the list above and note under your answer which type of question has been asked. Correct answers appear immediately after the questions.

Community policing has been frequently touted as the best way to reform urban law enforcement. The idea of putting more officers on foot patrol in high crime areas, where relations with police have frequently been strained, was initiated in Houston in 1983 under the leadership of then-Commissioner Lee Brown. He believed that officers should be accessible to the community at the street level. If officers were assigned to the same area over a period of time, those officers would eventually build a network of trust with neighborhood residents. That trust would mean that merchants and residents in the community would let officers know about criminal activities in the area and would support police intervention. Since then, many large cities have experimented with Community-Oriented Policing (COP) with mixed results. Some have found that police and citizens are grateful for the opportunity to work together. Others have found that unrealistic expectations by citizens and resistance from officers have combined to hinder the effectiveness of COP. It seems possible, therefore, that a good idea may need improvement before it can truly be considered a reform.

1. Community policing has been used in law enforcement since
    a. the late 1970s
    b. the early 1980s
    c. the Carter administration
    d. Lee Brown was New York City Police Commissioner

    Question type_____

2. The phrase "a network of trust" in this passage suggests that
    a. police officers can rely only on each other for support
    b. community members rely on the police to protect them
    c. police and community members rely on each other
    d. community members trust only each other

    Question type_____

3. The best title for this passage would be
    a. Community Policing: The Solution to the Drug Problem
    b. Houston Sets the Pace in Community Policing
    c. Communities and Cops: Partners for Peace
    d. Community Policing: An Uncertain Future

    Question type_____

4. The word "touted" in the first sentence of the passage most nearly means
    a. praised
    b. denied
    c. exposed
    d. criticized

    Question type_____

ANSWERS AND EXPLANATIONS FOR PRACTICE PASSAGE 1

Don't just look at the right answers and move on. The explanations are the most important part, so read them carefully. Use these explanations to help you understand how to tackle each kind of question the next time you come across it.

1. **b.** Question type: 1, fact or detail. The passage says that community policing began "in the last decade." A decade is a period of ten years. In addition, the passage identifies 1983 as the first large-scale use of community policing in Houston. Don't be misled by trying to figure out when Carter was president. Also, if you happen to know that Lee Brown was New York City's police commissioner, don't let that information lead you away from the information contained in the passage alone. Brown was commissioner in Houston when he initiated community policing.

2. **c.** Question type: 3, inference. The "network of trust" referred to in this passage is between the community and the police, as you can see from the sentence where the phrase appears. The key phrase in the question is *in this passage*. You may think that police can rely only on each other, or one of the other answer choices may appear equally plausible to you. But your choice of answers must be limited to the one suggested *in this passage*. Another tip for questions like this: Beware of absolutes! Be suspicious of any answer containing words like *only, always*, or *never*.

3. **d.** Question type: 2, main idea. The title always expresses the main idea. In this passage, the main idea comes at the end. The sum of all the details in the passage suggests that community policing is not without its critics and that therefore its future is uncertain. Another key phrase is *mixed results*, which means that some communities haven't had full success with community policing.

4. **a.** Question type: 4, vocabulary. The word *touted* is linked in this passage with the phrase *the best way to reform*. Most people would think that a good way to reform something is praiseworthy. In addition, the next few sentences in the passage describe the benefits of community policing. Criticism or a negative response to the subject doesn't come until later in the passage.

DETAIL AND MAIN IDEA QUESTIONS

Main idea questions and fact or detail questions are both asking you for information that's right there in the passage. All you have to do is find it.

DETAIL OR FACT QUESTIONS

In detail or fact questions, you have to identify a specific item of information from the test. This is usually the simplest kind of question. You just have to be able to separate important information from less important information. However, the choices may often be very similar, so you must be careful not to get confused.

Be sure you read the passage and questions carefully. In fact, it is usually a good idea to read the questions first, *before* you even read the passage, so you'll know what details to look out for.

MAIN IDEA QUESTIONS

The main idea of a passage, like that of a paragraph or a book, is what it is *mostly* about. The main idea is like an umbrella that covers all of the ideas and details in the passage, so it is usually something general, not specific. For example, in Practice Passage 1, question 3 asked you what title would be best for the passage, and the correct answer was "Community Policing: An Uncertain Future." This is the best answer because it's the only one that includes both the positive and negative sides of community policing, both of which are discussed in the passage.

Sometimes the main idea is stated clearly, often in the first or last sentence of the passage—the main idea is expressed in the *last* sentence of Practice Passage 1, for example. The sentence that expresses the main idea is often referred to as the **topic sentence**.

At other times, the main idea is not stated in a topic sentence but is *implied* in the overall passage, and you'll need to determine the main idea by inference. Because there may be much information in the passage, the trick is to understand what all that information adds up to— the gist of what the author wants you to know. Often some of the wrong answers on main idea questions are specific facts or details from the passage. A good way to test yourself is to ask, "Can this answer serve as a *net* to hold the whole passage together?" If not, chances are you've chosen a fact or detail, not a main idea.

PRACTICE PASSAGE 2: DETAIL AND MAIN IDEA QUESTIONS

Practice answering main idea and detail questions by working on the questions that follow this passage. Circle the answers to the questions, and then check your answers against the key that appears immediately after the questions.

There are three different kinds of burns: first degree, second degree, and third degree. It is important for firefighters to be able to recognize each of these types of burns so that they can be sure burn victims are given proper medical treatment. The least serious burn is the first-degree burn, which causes the skin to turn red but does not cause blistering. A mild sunburn is a good example of a first-degree

burn, and, like a mild sunburn, first-degree burns generally do not require medical treatment other than a gentle cooling of the burned skin with ice or cold tap water.

Second-degree burns, on the other hand, do cause blistering of the skin and should be treated immediately. These burns should be immersed in warm water and then wrapped in a sterile dressing or bandage. (Do not apply butter or grease to these burns; despite the old wives' tale, butter does *not* help burns heal and actually increases chances of infection.) If second-degree burns cover a large part of the body, then the victim should be taken to the hospital immediately for medical care.

Third-degree burns are those that char the skin and turn it black, or burn so deeply that the skin shows white. These burns usually result from direct contact with flames and have a great chance of becoming infected. All third-degree burns should receive immediate hospital care. They should not be immersed in water, and charred clothing should not be removed from the victim. If possible, a sterile dressing or bandage should be applied to burns before the victim is transported to the hospital.

1. Which of the following would be the best title for this passage?
   a. Dealing with Third-Degree Burns
   b. How to Recognize and Treat Different Burns
   c. Burn Categories
   d. Preventing Infection in Burns

2. Second-degree burns should be treated with
   a. butter
   b. nothing
   c. cold water
   d. warm water

3. First-degree burns turn the skin
   a. red
   b. blue
   c. black
   d. white

4. Which of the following best expresses the main idea of the passage?
   a. There are three different types of burns.
   b. Firefighters should always have cold compresses on hand.
   c. Different burns require different types of treatment.
   d. Butter is not good for healing burns.

ANSWERS AND EXPLANATIONS FOR PRACTICE PASSAGE 2

1. b. A question that asks you to choose a title for a passage is a main idea question. This main idea is expressed in the second sentence, the topic sentence: "It is important for firefighters to be able to recognize each of these types of burns so that they can be sure burn victims are given proper treatment." Answer **b** expresses this idea and is the only title that encompasses all of the ideas expressed in the passage. Answer **a** is too limited; it deals only with one of the kinds of burns discussed in the passage. Likewise, answers **c** and **d** are also too limited. Answer **c** covers types of burns but not their treatment, and **d** deals only with preventing infection, which is only a secondary part of the discussion of treatment.

2. d. The answer to this fact question is clearly expressed in the sentence, "These burns should be immersed in warm water and then wrapped in a sterile dressing or bandage." The hard part is keeping track of whether "These burns" refers to the kind of burns in the question, which is second-

degree burns. It's easy to choose a wrong answer here because all of the answer choices are mentioned in the passage. You need to read carefully to be sure you match the right burn to the right treatment.

3. a. This is another fact or detail question. The passage says that a first-degree burn "causes the skin to turn red." Again, it's important to read carefully because all of the answer choices (except **b**, which can be eliminated immediately) are listed elsewhere in the passage.

4. c. Clearly this is a main idea question, and **c** is the only answer that encompasses the whole passage. Answers **b** and **d** are limited to *particular* burns or treatments, and answer **a** discusses only burns and not their treatment. In addition, the second sentence tells us that "It is important for firefighters to be able to *recognize each of these types of burns so that they can be sure burn victims are given proper medical treatment.*"

INFERENCE AND VOCABULARY QUESTIONS

Questions that ask you about the meaning of vocabulary words in the passage and those that ask what the passage *suggests* or *implies* (inference questions) are different from detail or main idea questions. In vocabulary and inference questions, you usually have to pull ideas from the passage, sometimes from more than one place in the passage.

INFERENCE QUESTIONS

Inference questions can be the most difficult to answer because they require you to draw meaning from the text when that meaning is implied rather than directly stated. Inferences are conclusions that we draw based on the clues the writer has given us. When you draw inferences, you have to be something of a detective, looking for such clues as word choice, tone, and specific details that suggest a certain conclusion, attitude, or point of view. You have to read between the lines in order to make a judgment about what an author was implying in the passage.

A good way to test whether you've drawn an acceptable inference is to ask, "What evidence do I have for this inference?" If you can't find any, you probably have the wrong answer. You need to be sure that your inference is logical and that it is based on something that is suggested or implied in the passage itself—not by what you or others might think. Like a good detective, you need to base your conclusions on evidence—facts, details, and other information—not on random hunches or guesses.

VOCABULARY QUESTIONS

Questions designed to test vocabulary are really trying to measure how well you can figure out the meaning of an unfamiliar word from its context. *Context* refers to the words and ideas surrounding a vocabulary word. If the context is clear enough, you should be able to substitute a nonsense word for the one being sought, and you would still make the right choice because you could determine meaning strictly from the sense of the sentence. For example, you should be able to determine the meaning of the italicized nonsense word below based on its context:

The speaker noted that it gave him great *terivinix* to announce the winner of the Outstanding Leadership Award.

In this sentence, *terivinix* most likely means

a. pain
b. sympathy
c. pleasure
d. anxiety

Clearly, the context of an award makes c, *pleasure,* the best choice. Awards don't usually bring pain, sympathy, or anxiety.

When confronted with an unfamiliar word, try substituting a nonsense word and see if the context gives you the clue. If you're familiar with prefixes, suffixes, and word roots, you can also use this knowledge to help you determine the meaning of an unfamiliar word.

You should be careful not to guess at the answer to vocabulary questions based on how you may have seen the word used before or what you *think* it means. Many words have more than one possible meaning, depending on the context in which they're used, and a word you've seen used one way may mean something else in a test passage. Also, if you don't look at the context carefully, you may make the mistake of confusing the vocabulary word with a similar word. For example, the vocabulary word may be *taut* (meaning *tight*), but if you read too quickly or don't check the context, you might think the word is *tout* (meaning *publicize* or *praise*) or *taunt* (meaning *tease*). Always make sure you read carefully and that what you think the word means fits into the context of the passage you're being tested on.

PRACTICE PASSAGE 3: INFERENCE AND VOCABULARY QUESTIONS

The questions that follow this passage are strictly vocabulary and inference questions. Circle the answers to the questions, and then check your answers against the key that appears immediately after the questions.

Dealing with irritable patients is a great challenge for health-care workers on every level. It is critical that you do not lose your patience when confronted by such a patient. When handling irate patients, be sure to remember that they are not angry at you; they are simply projecting their anger at something else *onto* you. Remember that if you respond to these patients as irritably as they act with you, you will only increase their hostility, making it much more difficult to give them proper treatment. The best thing to do is to remain calm and ignore any imprecations patients may hurl your way. Such patients may be irrational and may not realize what they're saying. Often these patients will purposely try to anger you just to get some reaction out of you. If you react to this behavior with anger, they win by getting your attention, but you both lose because the patient is less likely to get proper care.

1. The word "irate" as it is used in the passage most nearly means
   a. irregular, odd
   b. happy, cheerful
   c. ill-tempered, angry
   d. sloppy, lazy

2. The passage suggests that health-care workers
   a. easily lose control of their emotions
   b. are better off not talking to their patients
   c. must be careful in dealing with irate patients because the patients may sue the hospital
   d. may provide inadequate treatment if they become angry at patients

3. An "imprecation" is most likely
   a. an object
   b. a curse
   c. a joke
   d. a medication

4. Which of the following best expresses the writer's views about irate patients?
   a. Some irate patients just want attention.
   b. Irate patients are always miserable.
   c. Irate patients should be made to wait for treatment.
   d. Managing irate patients is the key to a successful career.

ANSWERS AND EXPLANATIONS FOR PRACTICE PASSAGE 3

1. c. This is a vocabulary question. *Irate* means *ill-tempered, angry*. It should be clear that b, *happy, cheerful*, is not the answer; dealing with happy patients is normally not "a great challenge." Patients that are a, *irregular, odd*, or d, *sloppy, lazy*, may be a challenge in their own way, but they aren't likely to rouse a health-care worker to anger. In addition, the passage explains that irate patients are not "*angry* at you," and *irate* is used as a synonym for *irritable*, which describes the patients under discussion in the very first sentence.

2. d. This is an inference question, as the phrase "the passage *suggests*" might have told you. The idea that angry health-care workers might give inadequate treatment is implied by the passage as a whole,

which seems to be an attempt to prevent angry reactions to irate patients. Furthermore, the last sentence in particular makes this inference possible: "If you react to this behavior with anger . . . you both lose because the patient is less likely to get proper care." Answer **c** is not correct, because while it may be true that some irate patients have sued the hospital in the past, there is no mention of suits anywhere in this passage. Likewise, answer **b** is incorrect; the passage does suggest ignoring patients' insults, but nowhere does it recommend not talking to patients—it simply recommends not talking angrily. And while it may be true that some health-care workers may lose control of their emotions, the passage does not provide any facts or details to support answer **a**, that they "*easily* lose control." Watch out for key works like *easily* that may distort the intent of the passage.

3. b. If you didn't know what an imprecation is, the context should reveal that it's something you can ignore, so neither **a**, an *object*, nor **d**, a *medication*, is a likely answer. Furthermore, **c** is not likely either, since an irate patient is not likely to be making jokes.

4. a. The writer seems to believe that some irate patients just want attention, as is suggested when the writer says, "Often these patients will purposely try to anger you just to get some reaction out of you. If you react to this behavior with anger, they win *by getting your attention*." It should be clear that **b** cannot be the answer, because it includes an absolute: "Irate patients are *always* miserable." Perhaps *some* of the patients are *often* miserable, but an absolute like *always* is almost always wrong. Besides, this passage refers to patients who may be irate in the hospital, but we have no indication of what these patients are like at other times, and *miserable* and *irate* are not exactly the same thing,

either. Answer **c** is also incorrect because the purpose of the passage is to ensure that patients receive "proper treatment" and that irate patients are not discriminated against because of their behavior. Thus, "irate patients should be made to wait for treatment" is not a logical answer. Finally, **d** cannot be correct because though it may be true, there is no discussion of career advancement in the passage.

REVIEW: PUTTING IT ALL TOGETHER

A good way to solidify what you've learned about reading comprehension questions is for *you* to write the questions. Here's a passage, followed by space for you to write your own questions. Write one question of each of the four types: fact or detail, main idea, inference, and vocabulary.

The "broken window" theory was originally developed to explain how minor acts of vandalism or disrespect can quickly escalate to crimes and attitudes that break down the entire social fabric of an area. It is a theory that can easily be applied to any situation in society. The theory contends that if a broken window in an abandoned building is not replaced quickly, soon all the windows will be broken. In other words, a small violation, if condoned, leads others to commit similar or greater violations. Thus, after all the windows have been broken, the building is likely to be looted and perhaps even burned down.

According to this theory, violations increase exponentially. Thus, if disrespect to a superior is tolerated, others will be tempted to be disrespectful as well. A management crisis could erupt literally overnight. For example, if one firefighter begins to disregard proper housewatch procedure by neglecting to keep

If English Isn't Your First Language

When non-native speakers of English have trouble with reading comprehension tests, it's often because they lack the cultural, linguistic, and historical frame of reference that native speakers enjoy. People who have not lived in or been educated in the U.S. often don't have the background information that comes from reading American newspapers, magazines, and textbooks.

A second problem for non-native English speakers is the difficulty in recognizing vocabulary and idioms (expressions like "chewing the fat") that assist comprehension. In order to read with good understanding, it's important to have an immediate grasp of as many words as possible in the text. Test takers need to be able to recognize vocabulary and idioms immediately so that the ideas those words express are clear.

The Long View

Read newspapers, magazines, and other periodicals that deal with current events and matters of local, state, and national importance. Pay special attention to articles related to the career you want to pursue.

Be alert to new or unfamiliar vocabulary or terms that occur frequently in the popular press. Use a highlighter pen to mark new or unfamiliar words as you read. Keep a list of those words and their definitions. Review them for 15 minutes each day. Though at first you may find yourself looking up a lot of words, don't be frustrated—you'll look up fewer and fewer as your vocabulary expands.

During the Test

When you are taking the test, make a picture in your mind of the situation being described in the passage. Ask yourself, "What did the writer mostly want me to think about this subject?"

Locate and underline the topic sentence that carries the main idea of the passage. Remember that the topic sentence—if there is one—may not always be the first sentence. If there doesn't seem to be one, try to determine what idea summarizes the whole passage.

up the housewatch administrative journal, and this firefighter is not reprimanded, others will follow suit by committing similar violations of procedure, thinking, "If he can get away with it, why can't I?" So what starts out as a small thing, a violation that may seem not to warrant disciplinary action, may actually ruin the efficiency of the entire firehouse, putting the people the firehouse serves at risk.

1. Detail question:_____
   a.
   b.
   c.
   d.

2. Main idea question:_____
   a.
   b.
   c.
   d.

3. Inference question:_____
   a.
   b.
   c.
   d.

4. Vocabulary question:_____
   a.
   b.
   c.
   d.

POSSIBLE QUESTIONS

Here is one question of each type based on the passage above. Your questions may be very different, but these will give you an idea of the kinds of questions that could be asked.

1. Detail question: According to the passage, which of the following could happen "overnight"?
   a. The building will be burned down.
   b. The firehouse may become unmanageable.
   c. A management crisis might erupt.
   d. The windows will all be broken.

2. Main idea question: Which of the following best expresses the main idea of the passage?
   a. Even minor acts of disrespect can lead to major problems.

   b. Broken windows must be repaired immediately.
   c. People shouldn't be disrespectful to their superiors.
   d. Housewatch procedures must be taken seriously.

3. Inference question: With which of the following statements would the author most likely agree?
   a. The broken window theory is inadequate.
   b. Managers need to know how to handle a crisis.
   c. Firefighters are lazy.
   d. People will get away with as much as they can.

4. Vocabulary question: In the first paragraph, *condoned* most nearly means
   a. punished
   b. overlooked
   c. condemned
   d. applauded

Answers
1. c.
2. a.
3. d.
4. b.

READING TABLES, GRAPHS, AND CHARTS

Depending on what position you're testing for, civil service exams may also include a section testing your ability to read tables, charts, and graphs. These sections are really quite similar to regular reading comprehension exams, but instead of pulling information from a passage of text, you'll need to answer questions about a graphic representation of data. The types of questions asked about tables, charts, and graphs are actually quite similar to those about reading passages, though there usually aren't any questions on vocabulary. The main difference in reading tables, charts, or graphs is that you're "reading" or interpreting data represented in tabular (table) or graphic (picture) form rather than textual (sentence and paragraph) form.

Tables

Tables present data in rows and columns. Here's a very simple table that shows the number of accidents reported in one county over a 24-hour period. Use it to answer the question that follows.

Time of Day	Number of Accidents
6:00 A.M.–9:00 A.M.	11
9:00 A.M.–12:00 P.M.	3
12:00 P.M.–3:00 P.M.	5
3:00 P.M.–6:00 P.M.	7
6:00 P.M.–9:00 P.M.	9
9:00 P.M.–12:00 A.M.	6
12:00 A.M.–3:00 A.M.	5
3:00 A.M.–6:00 A.M.	3

1. Based on the information provided in this table, at what time of day do the most accidents occur?
   a. noon
   b. morning rush hour
   c. evening rush hour
   d. midnight

The correct answer, of course, is **b**, morning rush hour. You can clearly see that the highest number of accidents (11) occurred between 6:00 A.M. and 9:00 A.M.

Graphs

Now, here's the same information presented as a graph. A graph uses two axes rather than columns and rows to create a visual picture of the data:

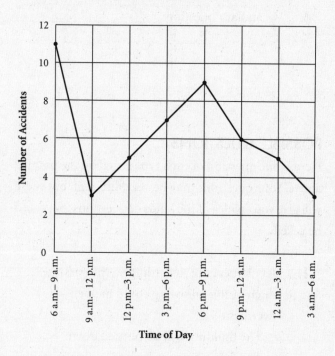

Here you can actually see the time of greatest number of accidents represented by a line that corresponds to the time of day and number. These numbers can also be represented by a box in a bar graph, as shown on the next page.

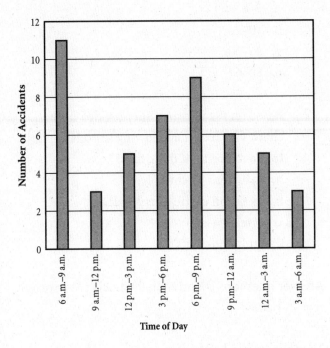

The key to "reading" graphs is to be sure that you know exactly what the numbers on each axis represent. Otherwise, you're likely to grossly misinterpret the information. Here, you see that the horizontal axis represents the time of day and the vertical axis represents the number of accidents that occurred. Thus, the tallest bar shows the time of day with the most accidents.

Like regular reading comprehension questions, questions on tables, charts, and graphs may also ask you to make inferences or even do basic math using the information and numbers the table, chart, or graph supplies. For example, you may be asked questions like the following on the information presented in the table, line graph, or bar graph above. The answers follow immediately after the questions.

2. What is the probable cause for the high accident rate between 6 A.M. and 9 A.M.?
   a. People haven't had their coffee yet.
   b. A lot of drivers are rushing to work.
   c. Sun glare.
   d. Construction.

3. What is the total number of accidents?
   a. 48
   b. 51
   c. 49
   d. 53

2. b. A question like this tests your common sense as well as your ability to read the graph. Though there may indeed be sun glare and though many drivers may not have had their coffee, these items are too variable to account for the high number of accidents. In addition, **d**, construction, is not logical because construction generally slows traffic down. Answer **b** is the best answer, because from 6:00 to 9:00 A.M. there is consistently a lot of rush hour traffic. In addition, many people do *rush*, and this increases the likelihood of accidents.

3. c. This question, of course, tests your basic ability to add. To answer this question correctly, you need to determine the value of each bar and then add those numbers together.

Charts

Finally, you may be presented information in the form of a chart like the pie chart on the next page. Here the accident figures have been converted to percentages. In this figure you don't see the exact number of accidents, but you see how accidents for each time period compare to the others.

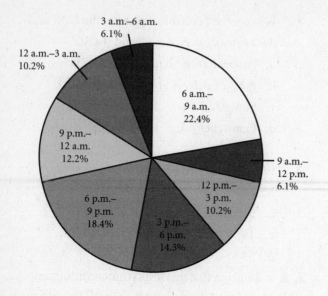

3 a.m.–6 a.m. 6.1%

12 a.m.–3 a.m. 10.2%

6 a.m.– 9 a.m. 22.4%

9 p.m.– 12 a.m. 12.2%

9 a.m.– 12 p.m. 6.1%

6 p.m.– 9 p.m. 18.4%

12 p.m.– 3 p.m. 10.2%

3 p.m.– 6 p.m. 14.3%

PRACTICE

Try the following questions to hone your skill at reading tables, graphs, and charts.

Answer questions 1 and 2 on the basis of the graph shown below.

Causes of household fires, in percentages

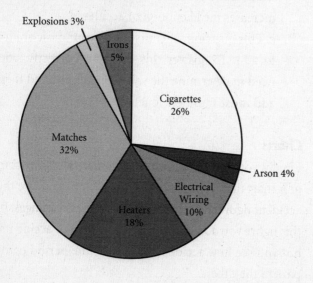

Explosions 3%

Irons 5%

Cigarettes 26%

Matches 32%

Arson 4%

Electrical Wiring 10%

Heaters 18%

1. What is the percentage of smoking-related fires?
   a. 5–8
   b. 10–26
   c. 26–58
   d. 58–62

2. Based on the information provided in the chart, which of the following reasons applies to the majority of these fires?
   a. malicious intent to harm
   b. violation of fire safety codes
   c. carelessness
   d. faulty products

Answer questions 3 and 4 on the basis of the graph shown below.

Number of paid sick days per year of employment

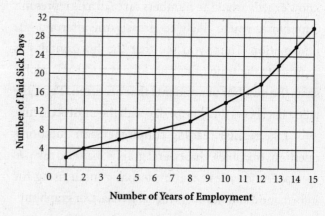

Number of Paid Sick Days

Number of Years of Employment

3. At what point does the rate of increase of sick days change?
   a. 4 years of employment
   b. 10 years of employment
   c. 8 years of employment
   d. 12 years of employment

4. During what years of employment are the number of sick days equal to double the number of years of employment?
   a. 1, 4, and 12
   b. 13, 14, and 15
   c. 1, 2, and 15
   d. 2, 4, and 10

ANSWERS AND EXPLANATIONS TO PRACTICE EXERCISE

1. **c.** Of the causes presented in the chart, both cigarettes (26 percent) and matches (32 percent) are related to smoking. But not all match fires are necessarily smoking related. Thus, the best answer allows for a range between 26 percent and 58 percent.

2. **c.** Fires from cigarettes, heaters, irons, and matches—81 percent in total—are generally the result of carelessness. Only 4 percent of fires are arsons, so **a** cannot be correct. Electrical, heater, and explosion fires *may* be the result of fire safety code violations, but even so, they total only 31 percent. Finally, there's no indication in this chart that there were faulty products involved.

3. **b.** In the first nine years, employees gain an additional two sick days every two years. At ten years of employment, however, the gain increases from two days every two years to four days, that is, from ten days in the eighth year to fourteen days in the tenth year.

4. **c.** In the first year, the number of sick days is two; in the second, four; and not until the fifteenth year does the number of sick days (thirty) again double the number of years of employment.

ADDITIONAL RESOURCES

Here are some other ways you can build the vocabulary and knowledge that will help you do well on reading comprehension questions.

- Practice asking the four sample question types about passages you read for information or pleasure.
- If you belong to a computer network such as America Online or Compuserve, search out articles related to the career you'd like to pursue. Exchange views with others on the Internet. All of these exchanges will help expand your knowledge of job-related material that may appear in a passage on the test.
- Use your library. Many public libraries have sections, sometimes called "Lifelong Learning Centers," that contain materials for adult learners. In these sections you can find books with exercises in reading and study skills. It's also a good idea to enlarge your base of information by reading related books and articles. Many libraries have computer systems that allow you to access information quickly and easily. Library personnel will show you how to use the computers and microfilm and microfiche machines.
- Begin now to build a broad knowledge of your potential profession. Get in the habit of reading articles in newspapers and magazines on job-related issues. Keep a clipping file of those articles. This will help keep you informed of trends in the profession and familiarize you with pertinent vocabulary.

- Consider reading or subscribing to professional journals. Chapter 1 lists several journals written for a general readership of people working in your desired profession. They are available for a reasonable annual fee. They may also be available in your public library.

- If you need more help building your reading skills and taking reading comprehension tests, consider *Reading Comprehension in 20 Minutes a Day* by Elizabeth Chesla and *501 Reading Comprehension Questions,* both published by LearningExpress. Order information is in the back of this book.

C·H·A·P·T·E·R

MEMORY AND OBSERVATION

7

CHAPTER SUMMARY

This chapter contains hints and tips to help you answer questions that test your memory and observation skills. Don't panic when faced with a detailed drawing and questions you have to answer without looking back at the drawing. This chapter will help you deal with them.

t's amazing what your mind will file away in that cabinet we call *memory.* You remember every snippet of dialog uttered by Clint Eastwood in his first Dirty Harry movie from years ago, but you can't remember which bus route you used yesterday to get to the dentist. Some people remember names well, but can't put them with the right faces. Others forget names quickly, but know exactly when, where, and why they met the person whose name they've forgotten. There are a few lucky individuals with what is commonly referred to as photographic memory or total recall. And then there are those of us who wake up every morning to a radio alarm so we can find out what day of the week it is. Fortunately for most of us, a good memory is actually a skill that can be developed—with the right incentive.

A high score on the firefighter exam is plenty of incentive.

Firefighter exams commonly test your short-term memory by presenting you with questions based on drawings or diagrams. You may be shown a sketch of a building on fire with people at the windows needing rescue, or you may be given a diagram showing the floor plan of a building. Usually you'll be given a set amount of time (five minutes is common) to look at the drawing or diagram, and then you'll be asked to answer test questions about what you saw without looking back at the drawing. Your goal is to memorize as much of the drawing or diagram as you can in the allotted time.

This chapter includes tips and techniques for dealing with drawing and diagrams, so you'll be prepared to deal with them effectively.

KINDS OF MEMORY AND OBSERVATION QUESTIONS

Basically, there are two kinds of memory and observation sections: questions based on a drawing of a fire scene, and questions based on a floor plan or similar kind of diagram.

QUESTIONS BASED ON DRAWINGS

Having you look at a sketch of a building on fire is a common way for firefighter exams to test your short-term memory. This is a simple test of your ability to recall details. You won't be asked to suggest ways to fight fires, use judgment skills, or draw conclusions about what you see.

You'll be asked to look at the drawing until a specific time limit is up. Then you'll turn to a set of questions in the test booklet. You have to answer the questions without looking at the drawing. Let's assume you are presented with a drawing showing a building on fire. Several people stand in windows, including an adult figure holding an infant. You might be asked:

1. A figure in one of the windows is holding something. What is it?
   a. a suitcase
   b. a dog
   c. a book
   d. a baby

The questions are simple and the answers are simple. If you don't remember what the adult figure was holding, or didn't notice that figure in the five minutes you had to study the drawing, then you will have to give this question your best guess.

QUESTIONS BASED ON DIAGRAMS

Similarly, you may be presented with a diagram of a floor plan of a building, perhaps filled with smoke. Again, this is a test of your ability to remember details. As mentioned in Chapter 11, "Spatial Relations," the ability of a firefighter to read a floor plan is crucial, as you may someday find yourself making your way through hallways and rooms filled with smoke. When presented with a floor plan, you will want to note the location of potential hazards and dead ends; you may be asked the placement of exits or smoke alarms or where to position a ladder for rescue.

For example, the diagram might show a center hallway with doors leading off of it into certain rooms, and the question might be something like this:

2. You are proceeding east to west down the center hallway and have just passed the den. What is the next room you will pass?
   a. bedroom 1
   b. bathroom
   c. bedroom 2
   d. sewing room

At the end of this chapter you'll find a floor plan and several questions about it that you can use to practice.

HOW TO APPROACH MEMORY AND OBSERVATION QUESTIONS

What to Do

Use a methodical approach to studying what you see. When you read sentences on a page, you read from left to right. This skill is as unconscious as breathing for most English-language readers. Approach memorizing a diagram the same way you read, taking in the information from left to right. Instead of staring at the diagram with the whole picture in focus, make yourself start at the left and work your way across the page until you get to the right.

What Not to Do

- **Do not** go into brain-lock when you first see the diagram. Take a deep breath and decide to be methodical.
- **Do not** try to start memorizing with a shotgun approach, letting your eyes roam all over the page without really taking in the details.
- **Do not** read the questions too quickly, and be sure to read them carefully, so that you answer the question that was actually asked. Haste can produce easily avoidable errors.

MEMORIZATION TIPS

Memorization is much easier if you approach the task with the expectation that you *will* remember what you see. Call it positive thinking, self-hypnosis, or concentration—it doesn't really matter as long as you get results. When you run through the practice questions in this book, prepare your mind before you start. Tell yourself over and over that you will remember what you see as you study the images. Your performance level will rise to meet your expectations.

Yes, it's easy for your brain to seize up when you see a drawing or diagram filled with details, a test section full of questions, and a test proctor standing above you with a stopwatch in one hand intoning, "You have five minutes to study this picture. You may begin." But if you've programmed yourself to stay calm, stay alert,

and execute your plan, you'll remember the details when you need them.

Plan? Yes, you need a plan. If you have a method for memorizing, say, a diagram of a second floor hallway, then you will be more likely to relax and allow yourself to retain what you've seen long enough to answer the test questions. Keep in mind that you aren't trying to memorize the scene to learn it for life, you are doing it to retain the information long enough to answer the test questions. What will it matter if you remember the scene three months from now? Your goal is to retain the information long enough to get through this test.

OBSERVATION TIPS

It's almost impossible to talk about memorization without bringing up observation. Some people are naturally observant. Some frequently drift off into never-never land and have no awareness of the world around them. Whatever category you think you are in, it's never too late to sharpen, or acquire, strong observation skills. How? Practice, of course.

Newspaper photos make great practice tools. News photos are action-oriented and usually have more than one person in the scenes. Sit down in a quiet place, clear your mind, remind yourself for several minutes that you will retain all the details you need when you study the picture, and then turn to a picture and study it for about five minutes. At the end of the time, turn the picture over, get a piece of paper and a pencil, then write down all the details you can think of in the picture. Or you might go to the library and check out a book on architecture that shows the floor plans of buildings. Go over the floor plans and memorize as many details as you can; then put away the book and write down all you remember. Make yourself do this as often as possible before the test.

You can tone up your observation skills on the way to work or school, too. Instead of sitting in your car waiting for the light to change with a blank stare on your face, look around you and say out loud what you see. "On my left is a three-story building with a bank of four windows on the first floor. There are two doorways, one on either side of the bank of windows." (If you are riding a train or subway, note details inside and recite them silently to yourself.) Not only are you practicing a basic skill you will need to become an excellent firefighter, you are training your mind to succeed at whatever memory questions the test maker throws your way.

MEMORY AND OBSERVATION PRACTICE

On the next page is a floor plan like those found on some firefighter exams. Following the floor plan are several questions asking about details of the floor plan. Use this diagram to practice your memory skills. Take five minutes (no more!) to study the diagram and then answer the questions that follow, without looking back at the diagram.

Then check your answers by looking back at the diagram. If you get all the questions right, you know you're well prepared for memory questions. If you miss a few, you know you need to spend more time practicing, using the tips outlined above. Remember, you *can* improve your memory with practice.

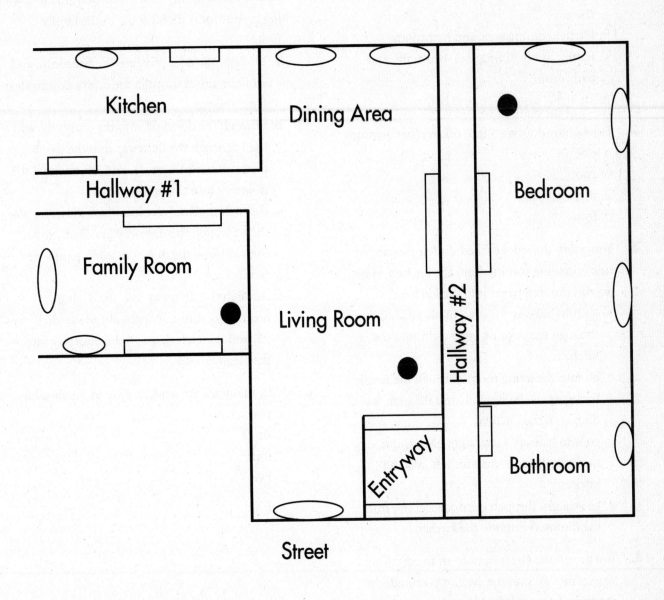

Kitchen

Dining Area

Hallway #1

Family Room

Living Room

Hallway #2

Bedroom

Entryway

Bathroom

Street

doors are shown as ....

windows are shown as ....

smoke detectors are shown as ....

1. Which rooms or areas of the dwelling do NOT have smoke detectors?
   a. kitchen, family room, dining area, and bathroom
   b. kitchen, dining area, and bathroom
   c. family room, dining area, bedroom, and bathroom
   d. kitchen, living room, and bathroom

2. How many doorways lead off the family room?
   a. one
   b. two
   c. three
   d. four

3. You are in the smoke-filled dining area and hear moaning coming from the kitchen. How do you proceed to get into the kitchen?
   a. go into hallway #1, straight ahead, and through the door on your right into the kitchen
   b. go into the living room, through the family room, across hallway #1, and through the door into the kitchen
   c. go into hallway #2, straight ahead, and through the door on your left into the kitchen
   d. go straight through the door leading from the dining room into the kitchen

4. You are on the street in front of the dwelling. You cannot go into the dwelling through the entryway because it is ablaze. To enter directly from the street, what other alternatives do you have?
   a. two windows and one doorway
   b. three windows
   c. two windows and two doorways
   d. one window and one doorway

5. You are in hallway #2. One of your coworkers shouts that there is a person overcome by smoke in the family room. Which of the following is your most direct route to the family room?
   a. through the doorway into the bedroom, and straight ahead through the doorway into the family room
   b. through the doorway into the entryway, and then through the doorway into the living room, down hallway #1, and left through the doorway into the family room
   c. through the doorway into the bathroom, and then through the doorway into hallway #1, then left into the doorway leading into the family room
   d. through the doorway into the dining area/living room, straight ahead into hallway #1, and then left through the doorway into the family room

6. How many smoke detectors are in the dwelling?
   a. two
   b. three
   c. four
   d. five

Tips for Memory and Observation Questions

- Use a methodical approach to memorization.
- Read the picture from left to right.
- Read the questions carefully; make sure you're answering the question that's being asked.
- Practice your memory and observation skills in your daily routine.

C·H·A·P·T·E·R

MATH

8

CHAPTER SUMMARY

This chapter gives you some important tips for dealing with math questions on a firefighter exam and reviews some of the most commonly tested concepts. If you've forgotten most of your high school math or have math anxiety, this chapter is for you.

Not all firefighter exams test your math knowledge, but many do. Knowledge of basic arithmetic, as well as the more complex kinds of reasoning necessary for algebra and geometry problems, are important qualifications for almost any profession. You have to be able to add up dollar figures, evaluate budgets, compute percentages, and other such tasks, both in your job and in your personal life. Even if your exam doesn't include math, you'll find that the material in this chapter will be useful on the job.

The math portion of the test covers the subjects you probably studied in grade school and high school. While every test is different, most emphasize arithmetic skills and word problems.

MATH STRATEGIES

- **Don't work in your head!** Use your test book or scratch paper to take notes, draw pictures, and calculate. Although you might think that you can solve math questions more quickly in your head, that's a good way to make mistakes. Write out each step.
- **Read a math question in *chunks*** rather than straight through from beginning to end. As you read each *chunk*, stop to think about what it means and make notes or draw a picture to represent that *chunk*.
- **When you get to the actual question, circle it.** This will keep you more focused as you solve the problem.
- **Glance at the answer choices for clues.** If they're fractions, you probably should do your work in fractions; if they're decimals, you should probably work in decimals; etc.
- **Make a plan of attack** to help you solve the problem.
- **If a question stumps you, try one of the *backdoor* approaches** explained in the next section. These are particularly useful for solving word problems.
- **When you get your answer, reread the circled question to make sure you've answered it.** This helps avoid the careless mistake of answering the wrong question.
- **Check your work after you get an answer.** Test-takers get a false sense of security when they get an answer that matches one of the multiple-choice answers. Here are some good ways to check your work *if you have time*:
  - Ask yourself if your answer is reasonable, if it makes sense.
  - Plug your answer back into the problem to make sure the problem holds together.
  - Do the question a second time, but use a different method.
- **Approximate when appropriate.** For example:
  - $5.98 + $8.97 is a little less than $15. (Add: $6 + $9)
  - $.9876 \times 5.0342$ is close to 5. (Multiply: 1×5)
- **Skip hard questions and come back to them later.** Mark them in your test book so you can find them quickly.

BACKDOOR APPROACHES FOR ANSWERING QUESTIONS THAT PUZZLE YOU

Remember those word problems you dreaded in high school? Many of them are actually easier to solve by backdoor approaches. The two techniques that follow are terrific ways to solve multiple-choice word problems that you don't know how to solve with a straightforward approach. The first technique, *nice numbers*, is useful when there are unknowns (like x) in the text of the word problem, making the problem too abstract for you. The second technique, *working backwards*, presents a quick way to substitute numeric answer choices back into the problem to see which one works.

Nice Numbers

1. When a question contains unknowns, like x, plug nice numbers in for the unknowns. A nice number is easy to calculate with and makes sense in the problem.

2. Read the question with the nice numbers in place. Then solve it.

3. If the answer choices are all numbers, the choice that matches your answer is the right one.

4. If the answer choices contain unknowns, substitute the same nice numbers into **all** the answer choices. The choice that matches your answer is the right one. If more than one answer matches, do the problem again with different nice numbers. You'll only have to check the answer choices that have already matched.

> **Example:** Judi went shopping with p dollars in her pocket. If the price of shirts was s shirts for d dollars, what is the maximum number of shirts Judi could buy with the money in her pocket?

> **a.** psd **b.** $\frac{ps}{d}$ **c.** $\frac{pd}{s}$ **d.** $\frac{ds}{p}$

To solve this problem, let's try these nice numbers: $p = \$100$, $s = 2$; $d = \$25$. Now reread it with the numbers in place:

> Judi went shopping with **$100** in her pocket. If the price of shirts was **2** shirts for **$25**, what is the maximum number of shirts Judi could buy with the money in her pocket?

Since 2 shirts cost $25, that means that 4 shirts cost $50, and 8 shirts cost $100. So our answer is **8**. Let's substitute the nice numbers into all 4 answers:

> **a.** $100 \times 2 \times 25 = 5000$ **b.** $\frac{100 \times 2}{25} = 8$ **c.** $\frac{100 \times 25}{2} = 1250$ **d.** $\frac{25 \times 2}{100} = \frac{1}{2}$

The answer is **b** because it is the only one that matches our answer of **8**.

Working Backwards

You can frequently solve a word problem by plugging the answer choices back into the text of the problem to see which one fits all the facts stated in the problem. The process is faster than you think because you'll probably only have to substitute one or two answers to find the right one.

This approach works only when:

- All of the answer choices are numbers.
- You're asked to find a simple number, not a sum, product, difference, or ratio.

Here's what to do:

1. Look at all the answer choices and begin with the one in the middle of the range. For example, if the answers are 14, 8, 2, 20, and 25, begin by plugging 14 into the problem.

2. If your choice doesn't work, eliminate it. Determine if you need a bigger or smaller answer.

3. Plug in one of the remaining choices.

4. If none of the answers work, you may have made a careless error. Begin again or look for your mistake.

> **Example:** Juan ate $\frac{1}{3}$ of the jellybeans. Maria then ate $\frac{3}{4}$ of the remaining jellybeans, which left 10 jellybeans. How many jellybeans were there to begin with?

> **a.** 60   **b.** 80   **c.** 90   **d.** 120   **e.** 140

Starting with the middle answer, let's assume there were **90** jellybeans to begin with:

Since Juan ate $\frac{1}{3}$ of them, that means he ate 30 ($\frac{1}{3} \times 90 = 30$), leaving 60 of them ($90 - 30 = 60$). Maria then ate $\frac{3}{4}$ of the 60 jellybeans, or 45 of them ($\frac{3}{4} \times 60 = 45$). That leaves 15 jellybeans ($60 - 45 = 15$).

The problem states that there were **10** jellybeans left, and we wound up with **15** of them. That indicates that we started with too big a number. Thus, 90, 120, and 140 are all wrong! With only two choices left, let's use common sense to decide which one to try. The next lower answer is only a little smaller than 90 and may not be small enough. So, let's try **60**:

Since Juan ate $\frac{1}{3}$ of them, that means he ate 20 ($\frac{1}{3} \times 60 = 20$), leaving 40 of them ($60 - 20 = 40$). Maria then ate $\frac{3}{4}$ of the 40 jellybeans, or 30 of them ($\frac{3}{4} \times 40 = 30$). That leaves 10 jellybeans ($40 - 30 = 10$).

Because this result of **10** jellybeans left agrees with the problem, the right answer is **a.**

WORD PROBLEMS

Many of the math problems on tests are word problems. A word problem can include any kind of math, including simple arithmetic, fractions, decimals, percentages, even algebra and geometry.

The hardest part of any word problem is translating English into math. When you read a problem, you can frequently translate it *word for word* from English statements into mathematical statements. At other times, however, a key word in the word problem hints at the mathematical operation to be performed. Here are the translation rules:

EQUALS   key words: is, are, has

English	Math
Bob **is** 18 years old.	B = 18
There **are** 7 hats.	H = 7
Judi **has** 5 books.	J = 5

ADDITION   key words: sum; more, greater, or older than; total; altogether

English	Math
The **sum** of two numbers is 10.	X + Y = 10
Karen has $5 **more than** Sam.	K = 5 + S
The base is 3″ **greater than** the height.	B = 3 + H
Judi is 2 years **older than** Tony.	J = 2 + T
The **total** of three numbers is 25.	A + B + C = 25
How much do Joan and Tom have **altogether**?	J + T = ?

SUBTRACTION   key words: difference, less or younger than, remain, left over

English	Math
The **difference** between two numbers is 17.	X − Y = 17
Mike has 5 **less** cats **than** twice the number Jan has.	M = 2J − 5
Jay is 2 years **younger than** Brett.	J = B − 2
After Carol ate 3 apples, R apples **remained.**	R = A − 3

MULTIPLICATION   key words: of, product, times

English	Math
20% **of** Matthew's baseball caps	$.20 \times M$
Half **of** the boys	$\frac{1}{2} \times B$
The **product** of two numbers is 12	$A \times B = 12$

DIVISION   key word: per

English	Math
15 drops **per** teaspoon	$\frac{15 \text{ drops}}{\text{teaspoon}}$
22 miles **per** gallon	$\frac{22 \text{ miles}}{\text{gallon}}$

DISTANCE FORMULA: DISTANCE = RATE × TIME

The key words are movement words like: plane, train, boat, car, walk, run, climb, swim

- How far did the **plane** travel in 4 hours if it averaged 300 miles per hour?

    $D = 300 \times 4$

    $D = 1200$ miles

- Ben **walked** 20 miles in 4 hours. What was his average speed?

    $20 = r \times 4$

    5 miles per hour $= r$

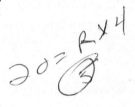

SOLVING A WORD PROBLEM USING THE TRANSLATION TABLE

Remember the problem at the beginning of this chapter about the jellybeans?

> Juan ate $\frac{1}{3}$ of the jellybeans. Maria then ate $\frac{3}{4}$ of the remaining jellybeans, which left 10 jellybeans.
> How many jellybeans were there to begin with?

a. 60	**b.** 80	**c.** 90	**d.** 120	**e.** 140

We solved it by working backwards. Now let's solve it using our translation rules.

Assume Juan started with J jellybeans. Eating $\frac{1}{3}$ **of** them means eating $\frac{1}{3} \times J$ jellybeans. Maria ate a fraction of the **remaining** jellybeans, which means we must **subtract** to find out how many are left: $J - \frac{1}{3} \times J = \frac{2}{3} \times J$. Maria then ate $\frac{3}{4}$, leaving $\frac{1}{4}$ **of** the $\frac{2}{3} \times J$ jellybeans, or $\frac{1}{4} \times \frac{2}{3} \times J$ jellybeans. Multiplying out $\frac{1}{4} \times \frac{2}{3} \times J$ gives $\frac{1}{6}J$ as the number of jellybeans left. The problem states that there were **10 jellybeans left**, meaning that we set $\frac{1}{6} \times J$ **equal to** 10:

$$\frac{1}{6} \times J = 60$$

Solving this equation for J gives $J = 60$. Thus, the right answer is **a** (the same answer we got when we worked backwards). As you can see, both methods—working backwards and translating from English to math—work. You should use whichever method is more comfortable for you.

PRACTICE WORD PROBLEMS

You will find word problems using fractions, decimals, and percentages in those sections of this chapter. For now, practice using the translation table on problems that just require you to work with basic arithmetic. Answers are at the end of the chapter.

_____ **1.** Joan went shopping with $100 and returned home with only $18.42. How much money did she spend?

    a. $81.58   **b.** $72.68   **c.** $72.58   **d.** $71.68   **e.** $71.58

_____ **2.** Mark invited 10 friends to a party. Each friend brought 3 guests. How many people came to the party, excluding Mark?

    a. 3   **b.** 10   **c.** 30   **d.** 40   **e.** 41

_____ **3.** The office secretary can type 80 words per minute on his word processor. How many minutes will it take him to type a report containing 760 words?

    a. 8   **b.** $8\frac{1}{2}$ **c.** 9   **d.** $9\frac{1}{2}$ **e.** 10

_____ **4.** Mr. Wallace is writing a budget request to upgrade his personal computer system. He wants to purchase 4 mb of RAM, which will cost $100, two new software programs at $350 each, a tape backup system for $249, and an additional tape for $25. What is the total amount Mr. Wallace should write on his budget request?

    a. $724   **b.** $974   **c.** $1049   **d.** $1064   **e.** $1074

FRACTION REVIEW

Problems involving fractions may be straightforward calculation questions, or they may be word problems. Typically, they ask you to add, subtract, multiply, divide, or compare fractions.

WORKING WITH FRACTIONS

A fraction is a part of something.

Example: Let's say that a pizza was cut into 8 equal slices and you ate 3 of them. The fraction $\frac{3}{8}$ tells you what part of the pizza you ate. The pizza below shows this: 3 of the 8 pieces (the ones you ate) are shaded.

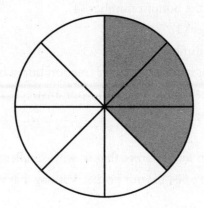

Three Kinds of Fractions

Proper fraction: The top number is less than the bottom number:

$\frac{1}{2}$; $\frac{2}{3}$; $\frac{4}{9}$; $\frac{8}{13}$

The value of a proper fraction is less than 1.

Improper fraction: The top number is greater than or equal to the bottom number:

$\frac{3}{2}$; $\frac{5}{3}$; $\frac{14}{9}$; $\frac{12}{12}$

The value of an improper fraction is 1 or more.

Mixed number: A fraction written to the right of a whole number:

$3\frac{1}{2}$; $4\frac{2}{3}$; $12\frac{3}{4}$; $24\frac{3}{4}$

The value of a mixed number is more than 1: it is the sum of the whole number plus the fraction.

Changing Improper Fractions into Mixed or Whole Numbers

It's easier to add and subtract fractions that are mixed numbers rather than improper fractions. To change an improper fraction, say $\frac{13}{2}$, into a mixed number, follow these steps:

1. Divide the bottom number (2) into the top number (13) to get the whole number portion (6) of the mixed number:

$$\begin{array}{r} 6 \\ 2\overline{)13} \\ \underline{12} \\ 1 \end{array}$$

2. Write the remainder of the division (1) over the old bottom number (2):

$6\frac{1}{2}$

3. Check: Change the mixed number back into an improper fraction (see steps below).

Changing Mixed Numbers into Improper Fractions

It's easier multiply and divide fractions when you're working with improper fractions rather than mixed numbers. To change a mixed number, say $2\frac{3}{4}$, into an improper fraction, follow these steps:

1. Multiply the whole number (2) by the bottom number (4). $2 \times 4 = 8$
2. Add the result (8) to the top number (3). $8 + 3 = 11$
3. Put the total (11) over the bottom number (4). $\frac{11}{4}$
4. Check: Reverse the process by changing the improper fraction into a mixed
   number. If you get back the number you started with, your answer is right.

Reducing Fractions

Reducing a fraction means writing it in *lowest terms*, that is, with smaller numbers. For instance, 50¢ is $\frac{50}{100}$ of a dollar, or $\frac{1}{2}$ of a dollar. In fact, if you have 50¢ in your pocket, you say that you have half a dollar. Reducing a fraction does not change its value.

   Follow these steps to reduce a fraction:

1. Find a whole number that divides *evenly* into both numbers that make up the fraction.
2. Divide that number into the top of the fraction, and replace the top of the fraction with the quotient (the answer you got when you divided).
3. Do the same thing to the bottom number.
4. Repeat the first 3 steps until you can't find a number that divides evenly into both numbers of the fraction.

   For example, let's reduce $\frac{8}{24}$. We could do it in 2 steps: $\frac{8 \div 4}{24 \div 4} = \frac{2}{6}$; then $\frac{2 \div 2}{6 \div 2} = \frac{1}{3}$. Or we could do it in a single step: $\frac{8 \div 8}{24 \div 8} = \frac{1}{3}$.

   Shortcut: When the top and bottom numbers both end in zeroes, cross out the same number of zeroes in both numbers to begin the reducing process. For example, $\frac{300}{4000}$ reduces to $\frac{3}{40}$ when you cross out 2 zeroes in both numbers.

   Whenever you do arithmetic with fractions, reduce your answer. On a multiple-choice test, don't panic if your answer isn't listed. Try to reduce it and then compare it to the choices.

   Reduce these fractions to lowest terms:

_____ **5.** $\frac{3}{12}$

_____ **6.** $\frac{14}{35}$

_____ **7.** $\frac{27}{72}$

Raising Fractions to Higher Terms

Before you can add and subtract fractions, you have to know how to raise a fraction to higher terms. This is actually the opposite of reducing a fraction.

Follow these steps to raise $\frac{2}{3}$ to 24ths:

1. Divide the old bottom number (3) into the new one (24): $3\overline{)24} = 8$
2. Multiply the answer (8) by the old top number (2): $2 \times 8 = 16$
3. Put the answer (16) over the new bottom number (24): $\frac{16}{24}$
4. Check: Reduce the new fraction to see if you get back the original one: $\frac{16 \div 8}{24 \div 8} = \frac{2}{3}$

Raise these fractions to higher terms:

_____ **8.** $\frac{5}{12} = \frac{}{24}$

_____ **9.** $\frac{2}{9} = \frac{}{27}$

_____ **10.** $\frac{2}{5} = \frac{}{500}$

ADDING FRACTIONS

If the fractions have the same bottom numbers, just add the top numbers together and write the total over the bottom number.

Examples: $\frac{2}{9} + \frac{4}{9} = \frac{2+4}{9} = \frac{6}{9}$ Reduce the sum: $\frac{2}{3}$

              $\frac{5}{8} + \frac{7}{8} = \frac{12}{8}$ Change the sum to a mixed number: $1\frac{4}{8}$; then reduce: $1\frac{1}{2}$

There are a few extra steps to add mixed numbers with the same bottom numbers, say $2\frac{3}{5} + 1\frac{4}{5}$:

1. Add the fractions: $\frac{3}{5} + \frac{4}{5} = \frac{7}{5}$
2. Change the improper fraction into a mixed number: $\frac{7}{5} = 1\frac{2}{5}$
3. Add the whole numbers: $2 + 1 = 3$
4. Add the results of steps 2 and 3: $1\frac{2}{5} + 3 = 4\frac{2}{5}$

Finding the Least Common Denominator

If the fractions you want to add don't have the same bottom number, you'll have to raise some or all of the fractions to higher terms so that they all have the same bottom number, called the **common denominator**. All of the original bottom numbers divide evenly into the common denominator. If it is the smallest number that they all divide evenly into, it is called the **least common denominator (LCD)**.

Here are a few tips for finding the LCD, the smallest number that all the bottom numbers evenly divide into:

- See if all the bottom numbers divide evenly into the biggest bottom number.
- Check out the multiplication table of the largest bottom number until you find a number that all the other bottom numbers evenly divide into.

- When all else fails, multiply all the bottom numbers together.

    Example: $\frac{2}{3} + \frac{4}{5}$

1. Find the LCD. Multiply the bottom numbers: $3 \times 5 = 15$

2. Raise each fraction to 15ths:

$$\frac{2}{3} = \frac{10}{15}$$
$$+\frac{4}{5} = \frac{12}{15}$$
$$\overline{\frac{22}{15}}$$

3. Add as usual:

Try these addition problems:

_____**11.** $\frac{3}{4} + \frac{1}{6}$

_____**12.** $\frac{7}{8} + \frac{2}{3} + \frac{3}{4}$

_____**13.** $4\frac{1}{3} + 2\frac{3}{4} + \frac{1}{6}$

SUBTRACTING FRACTIONS

If the fractions have the same bottom numbers, just subtract the top numbers and write the difference over the bottom number.

    Example: $\frac{4}{9} - \frac{3}{9} = \frac{4-3}{9} = \frac{1}{9}$

    If the fractions you want to subtract don't have the same bottom number, you'll have to raise some or all of the fractions to higher terms so that they all have the same bottom number, or LCD. If you forgot how to find the LCD, just read the section on adding fractions with different bottom numbers.

    Example: $\frac{5}{6} - \frac{3}{4}$

1. Raise each fraction to 12ths because 12 is the LCD, the smallest number
    that 6 and 4 both divide into evenly:

$$\frac{5}{6} = \frac{10}{12}$$
$$-\frac{3}{4} = \frac{9}{12}$$
$$\overline{\frac{1}{12}}$$

2. Subtract as usual:

    Subtracting mixed numbers with the same bottom number is similar to adding mixed numbers.

    Example: $4\frac{3}{5} - 1\frac{2}{5}$

1. Subtract the fractions: $\frac{3}{5} - \frac{2}{5} = \frac{1}{5}$

2. Subtract the whole numbers: $4 - 1 = 3$

3. Add the results of steps 1 and 2: $\frac{1}{5} + 3 = 3\frac{1}{5}$

    Sometimes there is an extra "borrowing" step when you subtract mixed numbers with the same bottom numbers, say $7\frac{3}{5} - 2\frac{4}{5}$:

1. You can't subtract the fractions the way they are because $\frac{4}{5}$ is bigger than $\frac{3}{5}$.

So you borrow 1 from the 7, making it 6, and change that 1 to $\frac{5}{5}$ because

5 is the bottom number: $\qquad$ $7\frac{3}{5} = 6\frac{5}{5} + \frac{3}{5}$

2. Add the numbers from step 1: $\qquad$ $6\frac{5}{5} + \frac{3}{5} = 6\frac{8}{5}$

3. Now you have a different version of the original problem: $\qquad$ $6\frac{8}{5} - 2\frac{4}{5}$

4. Subtract the fractional parts of the two mixed numbers: $\qquad$ $\frac{8}{5} - \frac{4}{5} = \frac{4}{5}$

5. Subtract the whole number parts of the two mixed numbers: $\qquad$ $6 - 2 = 4$

6. Add the results of the last 2 steps together: $\qquad$ $4 + \frac{4}{5} = 4\frac{4}{5}$

Try these subtraction problems:

_____**14.** $\frac{4}{5} - \frac{2}{3}$

_____**15.** $\frac{7}{8} - \frac{1}{4} - \frac{1}{2}$

_____**16.** $4\frac{1}{3} - 2\frac{3}{4}$

Now let's put what you've learned about adding and subtracting fractions to work in some real-life problems.

_____**17.** Patrolman Peterson drove $3\frac{1}{2}$ miles to the police station. Then he drove $4\frac{3}{4}$ miles to his first assignment. When he left there, he drove 2 miles to his next assignment. Then he drove $3\frac{2}{3}$ miles back to the police station for a meeting. Finally, he drove $3\frac{1}{2}$ miles home. How many miles did he travel in total?

    a. $17\frac{5}{12}$ **b.** $16\frac{5}{12}$ **c.** $15\frac{7}{12}$ **d.** $15\frac{5}{12}$ **e.** $13\frac{11}{12}$

_____**18.** Before leaving the fire station, Firefighter Sorensen noted that the mileage gauge on Engine 2 registered $4{,}357\frac{4}{10}$ miles. When he arrived at the scene of the fire, the mileage gauge then registered $4{,}400\frac{1}{10}$ miles. How many miles did he drive from the station to the fire scene?

    a. $42\frac{3}{10}$ **b.** $42\frac{7}{10}$ **c.** $43\frac{7}{10}$ **d.** $47\frac{2}{10}$ **e.** $57\frac{3}{10}$

MULTIPLYING FRACTIONS

Multiplying fractions is actually easier than adding them. All you do is multiply the top numbers and then multiply the bottom numbers.

    Examples: $\frac{2}{3} \times \frac{5}{7} = \frac{2 \times 5}{3 \times 7} = \frac{10}{21}$ $\frac{1}{2} \times \frac{3}{5} \times \frac{7}{4} = \frac{1 \times 3 \times 7}{2 \times 5 \times 4} = \frac{21}{40}$

Sometimes you can *cancel* before multiplying. Cancelling is a shortcut that makes the multiplication go faster because you're multiplying with smaller numbers. It's very similar to reducing: if there is a number that divides evenly into a top number and bottom number, do that division before multiplying. If you forget to cancel, you'll still get the right answer, but you'll have to reduce it.

Example: $\frac{5}{6} \times \frac{9}{20}$

1. Cancel the 6 and the 9 by dividing 3 into both of them: $6 \div 3 = 2$ and $9 \div 3 = 3$. Cross out the 6 and the 9.

$$\frac{5}{\cancel{6}_2} \times \frac{\cancel{9}^3}{20}$$

2. Cancel the 5 and the 20 by dividing 5 into both of them: $5 \div 5 = 1$ and $20 \div 5 = 4$. Cross out the 5 and the 20.

$$\frac{\cancel{5}^1}{\cancel{6}_2} \times \frac{\cancel{9}^3}{\cancel{20}_4}$$

3. Multiply across the new top numbers and the new bottom numbers:

$$\frac{1 \times 3}{2 \times 4} = \frac{3}{8}$$

Try these multiplication problems:

_____19. $\frac{1}{5} \times \frac{2}{3}$

_____20. $\frac{2}{3} \times \frac{4}{7} \times \frac{3}{5}$

_____21. $\frac{3}{4} \times \frac{8}{9}$

To multiply a fraction by a whole number, first rewrite the whole number as a fraction with a bottom number of 1:

Example: $5 \times \frac{2}{3} = \frac{5}{1} \times \frac{2}{3} = \frac{10}{3}$ (Optional: convert $\frac{10}{3}$ to a mixed number: $3\frac{1}{3}$)

To multiply with mixed numbers, it's easier to change them to improper fractions before multiplying.

Example: $4\frac{2}{3} \times 5\frac{1}{2}$

1. Convert $4\frac{2}{3}$ to an improper fraction:

$$4\frac{2}{3} = \frac{4 \times 3 + 2}{3} = \frac{14}{3}$$

2. Convert $5\frac{1}{2}$ to an improper fraction:

$$5\frac{1}{2} = \frac{5 \times 2 + 1}{2} = \frac{11}{2}$$

3. Cancel and multiply the fractions:

$$\frac{\cancel{14}^7}{3} \times \frac{11}{\cancel{2}_1} = \frac{77}{3}$$

4. Optional: convert the improper fraction to a mixed number:

$$\frac{77}{3} = 25\frac{2}{3}$$

Now try these multiplication problems with mixed numbers and whole numbers:

_____22. $4\frac{1}{3} \times \frac{2}{5}$

_____23. $2\frac{1}{2} \times 6$

_____24. $3\frac{3}{4} \times 4\frac{2}{5}$

Here are a few more real-life problems to test your skills:

_____**25.** After driving $\frac{2}{3}$ of the 15 miles to work, Mr. Stone stopped to make a phone call. How many miles had he driven when he made his call?
   a. 5   **b.** $7\frac{1}{2}$ **c.** 10   **d.** 12   **e.** $15\frac{2}{3}$

_____**26.** If Henry worked $\frac{3}{4}$ of a 40-hour week, how many hours did he work?
   a. $7\frac{1}{2}$ **b.** 10   **c.** 20   **d.** 25   **e.** 30

_____**27.** Technician Chin makes $14.00 an hour. When she works more than 8 hours a day, she gets over-time pay of $1\frac{1}{2}$ times her regular hourly wage for the extra hours. How much did she earn for working 11 hours in one day?
   a. $77   **b.** $154   **c.** $175   **d.** $210   **e.** $231

DIVIDING FRACTIONS

To divide one fraction by a second fraction, invert the second fraction (that is, flip the top and bottom numbers) and then multiply. That's all there is to it!

   Example: $\frac{1}{2} \div \frac{3}{5}$

1. Invert the second fraction ($\frac{3}{5}$): $\frac{5}{3}$
2. Change the division sign ($\div$) to a multiplication sign ($\times$)
3. Multiply the first fraction by the new second fraction: $\frac{1}{2} \times \frac{5}{3} = \frac{1 \times 5}{2 \times 3} = \frac{5}{6}$

   To divide a fraction by a whole number, first change the whole number to a fraction by putting it over 1. Then follow the division steps above.

   Example: $\frac{3}{5} \div 2 = \frac{3}{5} \div \frac{2}{1} = \frac{3}{5} \times \frac{1}{2} = \frac{3 \times 1}{5 \times 2} = \frac{3}{10}$

   When the division problem has a mixed number, convert it to an improper fraction and then divide as usual.

   Example: $2\frac{3}{4} \div \frac{1}{6}$

1. Convert $2\frac{3}{4}$ to an improper fraction: $2\frac{3}{4} = \frac{2 \times 4 + 3}{4} = \frac{11}{4}$
2. Divide $\frac{11}{4}$ by $\frac{1}{6}$: $\frac{11}{4} \div \frac{1}{6} = \frac{11}{4} \times \frac{6}{1}$
3. Flip $\frac{1}{6}$ to $\frac{6}{1}$, change $\div$ to $\times$, cancel and multiply: $\frac{11}{\underset{2}{4}} \times \frac{\overset{3}{6}}{1} = \frac{11 \times 3}{2 \times 1} = \frac{33}{2}$

Here are a few division problems to try:

_____**28.** $\frac{1}{3} \div \frac{2}{3}$

_____**29.** $2\frac{3}{4} \div \frac{1}{2}$

_____**30.** $\frac{3}{5} \div 3$

_____**31.** $3\frac{3}{4} \div 2\frac{1}{3}$

Let's wrap this up with some real-life problems.

_____**32.** If four friends evenly split $6\frac{1}{2}$ pounds of candy, how many pounds of candy does each friend get?

        a. $\frac{8}{13}$ **b.** $1\frac{5}{8}$ **c.** $1\frac{1}{2}$ **d.** $1\frac{5}{13}$ **e.** 4

_____**33.** How many $2\frac{1}{2}$-pound chunks of cheese can be cut from a single 20-pound piece of cheese?

        a. 2   **b.** 4   **c.** 6   **d.** 8   **e.** 10

_____**34.** Ms. Goldbaum earned \$36.75 for working $3\frac{1}{2}$ hours. What was her hourly wage?

        a. \$10.00   **b.** \$10.50   **c.** \$10.75   **d.** \$12.00   **e.** \$12.25

DECIMALS

WHAT IS A DECIMAL?

A decimal is a special kind of fraction. You use decimals every day when you deal with money—\$10.35 is a decimal that represents 10 dollars and 35 cents. The decimal point separates the dollars from the cents. Because there are 100 cents in one dollar, 1¢ is $\frac{1}{100}$ of a dollar, or \$.01.

Each decimal digit to the right of the decimal point has a name:

    Example: .1 = 1 tenth = $\frac{1}{10}$

                     .02 = 2 hundredths = $\frac{2}{100}$

                     .003 = 3 thousandths = $\frac{3}{1000}$

                     .0004 = 4 ten-thousandths = $\frac{4}{10,000}$

When you add zeroes after the rightmost decimal place, you don't change the value of the decimal. For example, 6.17 is the same as all of these:

6.170

6.1700

6.17000000000000000

If there are digits on both sides of the decimal point (like 10.35), the number is called a mixed decimal. If there are digits only to the right of the decimal point (like .53), the number is called a decimal. A whole number (like 15) is understood to have a decimal point at its right (15.). Thus, 15 is the same as 15.0, 15.00, 15.000, and so on.

CHANGING FRACTIONS TO DECIMALS

To change a fraction to a decimal, divide the bottom number into the top number after you put a decimal point and a few zeroes on the right of the top number. When you divide, bring the decimal point up into your answer.

Example: Change $\frac{3}{4}$ to a decimal.

1. Add a decimal point and 2 zeroes to the top number (3): 3.00

2. Divide the bottom number (4) into 3.00:
Bring the decimal point up into the answer:

$$
\begin{array}{r}
.75 \\
4\overline{)3.00} \\
\underline{2\,8} \\
20 \\
\underline{20} \\
0
\end{array}
$$

3. The quotient (result of the division) is the answer: .75

Some fractions may require you to add many decimal zeroes in order for the division to come out evenly. In fact, when you convert a fraction like $\frac{2}{3}$ to a decimal, you can keep adding decimal zeroes to the top number forever because the division will never come out evenly! As you divide 3 into 2, you'll keep getting 6's:

$$2 \div 3 = .6666666666 \text{ etc}$$

This is called a *repeating decimal* and it can be written as $.66\overline{6}$ or as $.66\frac{2}{3}$. You can approximate it as .67, .667, .6667, and so on.

CHANGING DECIMALS TO FRACTIONS

To change a decimal to a fraction, write the digits of the decimal as the top number of a fraction and write the decimal's name as the bottom number of the fraction. Then reduce the fraction, if possible.

Example: .018

1. Write 18 as the top of the fraction: $\frac{18}{}$

2. Three places to the right of the decimal means *thousandths,* so write 1000 as the bottom number: $\frac{18}{1000}$

3. Reduce by dividing 2 into the top and bottom numbers: $\frac{18 \div 2}{1000 \div 2} = \frac{9}{500}$

Change these decimals or mixed decimals to fractions:

_____ **35.** .005

_____ **36.** 3.48

_____ **37.** 123.456

COMPARING DECIMALS

Because decimals are easier to compare when they have the same number of digits after the decimal point, tack zeroes onto the end of the shorter decimals. Then all you have to do is compare the numbers as if the decimal points weren't there:

> **Example:** Compare .08 and .1

1. Tack one zero at the end of .1: .10

2. To compare .10 to .08, just compare 10 to 8.

3. Since 10 is larger than 8, .1 is larger than .08.

ADDING AND SUBTRACTING DECIMALS

To add or subtract decimals, line them up so their decimal points are even. You may want to tack on zeroes at the end of shorter decimals so you can keep all your digits lined up evenly. Remember, if a number doesn't have a decimal point, then put one at the right end of the number.

> **Example:** 1.23 + 57 + .038

1. Line up the numbers like this:

$$
\begin{array}{r}
1.230 \\
57.000 \\
+\quad .038 \\
\hline
\end{array}
$$

2. Add:

$$58.268$$

> **Example:** 1.23 − .038

1. Line up the numbers like this:

$$
\begin{array}{r}
1.230 \\
-\quad .038 \\
\hline
\end{array}
$$

2. Subtract:

$$1.192$$

Try these addition and subtraction problems:

_____**38.** .905 + .02 + 3.075

_____**39.** .005 + 8 + .3

_____**40.** 3.48 − 2.573

_____**41.** 123.456 − 122

[handwritten: 1 / 3.7 / 2.75 / 2.00 / 8.45]

_____ **42.** Officer Peterson drove 3.7 miles to the state park. He then walked 1.6 miles around the park to make sure everything was all right. He got back into the car, drove 2.75 miles to check on a broken traffic light and then drove 2 miles back to the police station. How many miles did he drive in total?

a. 8.05   **b. 8.45**   c. 8.8   d. 10   e. 10.05

_____ **43.** The average number of emergency room visits at City Hospital fell from 486.4 per week to 402.5 per week. By how many emergency room visits per week did the average fall?

a. 73.9   b. 83   c. 83.1   **d. 83.9**   e. 84.9

[handwritten: 486.4 / 402.5 / 83.9]

MULTIPLYING DECIMALS

To multiply decimals, ignore the decimal points and just multiply the numbers. Then count the total number of decimal digits (the digits to the *right* of the decimal point) in the numbers you're multiplying. Count off that number of digits in your answer beginning at the right side and put the decimal point to the *left* of those digits.

Example: 215.7×2.4

1. Multiply 2157 times 24:

$$
\begin{array}{r}
2157 \\
\times\ 24 \\
\hline
8628 \\
4314 \\
\hline
51768
\end{array}
$$

2. Because there are a total of 2 decimal digits in 215.7 and 2.4, count off 2 places from the right in 51768, placing the decimal point to the *left* of the last 2 digits: 517.68

If your answer doesn't have enough digits, tack zeroes on to the left of the answer.

Example: $.03 \times .006$

1. Multiply 3 times 6: $3 \times 6 = 18$

2. You need 5 decimal digits in your answer, so tack on 3 zeroes: 00018

3. Put the decimal point at the front of the number (which is 5 digits in from the right):   .00018

You can practice multiplying decimals with these:

_____ **44.** $.05 \times .6$ *[handwritten: .030]*

_____ **45.** $.053 \times 6.4$ *[handwritten: 53 / 64 / 212 / 318 / .3392]*

_____ **46.** $38.1 \times .0184$

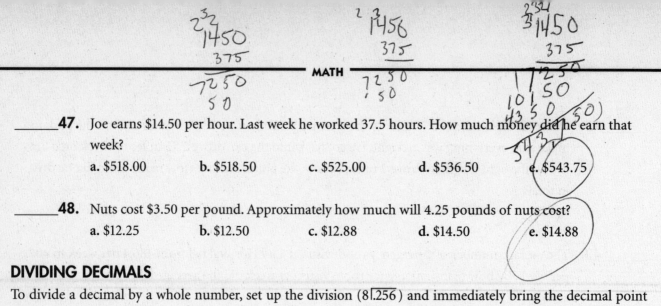

_____**47.** Joe earns $14.50 per hour. Last week he worked 37.5 hours. How much money did he earn that week?

    a. $518.00   **b.** $518.50   **c.** $525.00   **d.** $536.50   **e.** $543.75

_____**48.** Nuts cost $3.50 per pound. Approximately how much will 4.25 pounds of nuts cost?

    a. $12.25   **b.** $12.50   **c.** $12.88   **d.** $14.50   **e.** $14.88

DIVIDING DECIMALS

To divide a decimal by a whole number, set up the division ($8\overline{).256}$) and immediately bring the decimal point straight up into the answer ($8\overline{).256}$). Then divide as you would normally divide whole numbers:

Example:

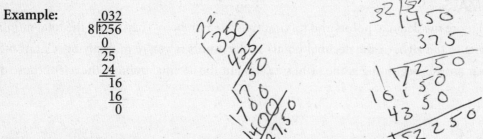

$$
\begin{array}{r}
.032 \\
8\overline{).256} \\
0 \\
\hline
25 \\
24 \\
\hline
16 \\
16 \\
\hline
0
\end{array}
$$

To divide any number by a decimal, there is an extra step to perform before you can divide. Move the decimal point to the very right of the number you're dividing by, counting the number of places you're moving it. Then move the decimal point the same number of places to the right in the number you're dividing into. In other words, first change the problem to one in which you're dividing by a whole number.

Example: $.06\overline{)1.218}$

1. Because there are 2 decimal digits in .06, move the decimal point 2 places to the right in both numbers and move the decimal point straight up into the answer: $.06.\overline{)1.21.8}$

2. Divide using the new numbers:

$$
\begin{array}{r}
20.3 \\
6\overline{)121.8} \\
12 \\
\hline
01 \\
00 \\
\hline
18 \\
18 \\
\hline
0
\end{array}
$$

Under certain conditions, you have to tack on zeroes to the right of the last decimal digit in number you're dividing into:

- If there aren't enough digits for you to move the decimal point to the right, or
- If the answer doesn't come out evenly when you do the division, or
- If you're dividing a whole number by a decimal. Then you'll have to tack on the decimal point as well as some zeroes.

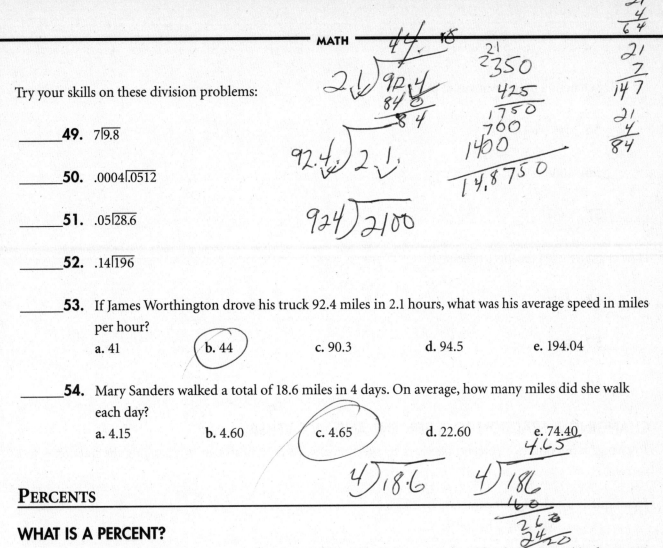

Try your skills on these division problems:

_____ **49.** 7$\overline{)9.8}$

_____ **50.** .0004$\overline{).0512}$

_____ **51.** .05$\overline{)28.6}$

_____ **52.** .14$\overline{)196}$

_____ **53.** If James Worthington drove his truck 92.4 miles in 2.1 hours, what was his average speed in miles per hour?

     a. 41   **b.** 44   **c.** 90.3   **d.** 94.5   **e.** 194.04

_____ **54.** Mary Sanders walked a total of 18.6 miles in 4 days. On average, how many miles did she walk each day?

     a. 4.15   **b.** 4.60   **c.** 4.65   **d.** 22.60   **e.** 74.40

PERCENTS

WHAT IS A PERCENT?

A percent is a special kind of fraction or part of something. The bottom number (the *denominator*) is always 100. For example, 17% is the same as $\frac{17}{100}$. Literally, the word *percent* means *per 100 parts*. The root *cent* means 100: a *cent*ury is 100 years, there are 100 *cent*s in a dollar, etc. Thus, 17% means 17 parts out of 100. Because fractions can also be expressed as decimals, 17% is also equivalent to .17, which is 17 hundredths.

You come into contact with percents every day. Sales tax, interest, and discounts are just a few common examples.

If you're shaky on fractions, you may want to review the fraction section before reading further.

CHANGING A DECIMAL TO A PERCENT AND VICE VERSA

To change a decimal to a percent, move the decimal point two places to the **right** and tack on a percent sign (%) at the end. If the decimal point moves to the very right of the number, you don't have to write the decimal point. If there aren't enough places to move the decimal point, add zeroes on the **right** before moving the decimal point.

To change a percent to a decimal, drop off the percent sign and move the decimal point two places to the **left**. If there aren't enough places to move the decimal point, add zeroes on the **left** before moving the decimal point.

Try changing these decimals to percents:

_____**55.** .45 %

_____**56.** .008

_____**57.** .16$\frac{2}{3}$

Now change these percents to decimals:

_____**58.** 12%

_____**59.** 87$\frac{1}{2}$%

_____**60.** 250%

CHANGING A FRACTION TO A PERCENT AND VICE VERSA

To change a fraction to a percent, there are two techniques. Each is illustrated by changing the fraction $\frac{1}{4}$ to a percent:

Technique 1:   Multiply the fraction by 100%.

Multiply $\frac{1}{4}$ by 100%:

$$\frac{1}{\underset{1}{4}} \times \frac{\overset{25}{\cancel{100}}\%}{1} = 25\%$$

Technique 2:   Divide the fraction's bottom number into the top number; then move the decimal point two places to the **right** and tack on a percent sign (%).

Divide 4 into 1 and move the decimal point 2 places to the right:

$$4\overline{)1.00}^{.25} \qquad .25 = 25\%$$

To change a percent to a fraction, remove the percent sign and write the number over 100. Then reduce if possible.

Example: Change 4% to a fraction

1. Remove the % and write the fraction 4 over 100: $\frac{4}{100}$

2. Reduce: $\frac{4 \div 4}{100 \div 4} = \frac{1}{25}$

Here's a more complicated example: Change 16$\frac{2}{3}$% to a fraction $\frac{16\frac{2}{3}}{100}$

1. Remove the % and write the fraction 16$\frac{2}{3}$ over 100:

2. Since a fraction means "top number divided by bottom number," rewrite the fraction as a division problem:

$$16\tfrac{2}{3} \div 100$$

3. Change the mixed number ($16\tfrac{2}{3}$) to an improper fraction ($\tfrac{50}{3}$):

$$\tfrac{50}{3} \div \tfrac{100}{1}$$

4. Flip the second fraction ($\tfrac{100}{1}$) and multiply:

$$\overset{1}{\underset{}{\tfrac{\cancel{50}}{3}}} \times \tfrac{1}{\underset{2}{\cancel{100}}} = \tfrac{1}{6}$$

Try changing these fractions to percents:

_____**61.** $\tfrac{1}{8}$

_____**62.** $\tfrac{13}{25}$

_____**63.** $\tfrac{7}{12}$

Now change these percents to fractions:

_____**64.** 95%

_____**65.** $37\tfrac{1}{2}\%$

_____**66.** 125%

Sometimes it is more convenient to work with a percentage as a fraction or a decimal. Rather than have to *calculate* the equivalent fraction or decimal, consider memorizing the equivalence table below. Not only will this increase your efficiency on the math test, but it will also be practical for real life situations.

CONVERSION TABLE

Decimal	%	Fraction
.25	25%	$\tfrac{1}{4}$
.50	50%	$\tfrac{1}{2}$
.75	75%	$\tfrac{3}{4}$
.10	10%	$\tfrac{1}{10}$
.20	20%	$\tfrac{1}{5}$
.40	40%	$\tfrac{2}{5}$
.60	60%	$\tfrac{3}{5}$
.80	80%	$\tfrac{4}{5}$
.33$\overline{3}$	$33\tfrac{1}{3}\%$	$\tfrac{1}{3}$
.66$\overline{6}$	$66\tfrac{2}{3}\%$	$\tfrac{2}{3}$

PERCENT WORD PROBLEMS

Word problems involving percents come in three main varieties:

- Find a percent of a whole.

    Example: What is 30% of 40?

- Find what percent one number is of another number.

    Example: 12 is what percent of 40?

- Find the whole when the percent of it is given.

    Example: 12 is 30% of what number?

While each variety has its own approach, there is a single shortcut formula you can use to solve each of these:

$$\frac{is}{of} = \frac{\%}{100}$$

The *is* is the number that usually follows or is just before the word *is* in the question.

The *of* is the number that usually follows the word *of* in the question.

The *%* is the number that in front of the % or *percent* in the question.

Or you may think of the shortcut formula as:

$$\frac{part}{whole} = \frac{\%}{100}$$

To solve each of the three varieties, we're going to use the fact that the **cross-products** are equal. The cross-products are the products of the numbers diagonally across from each other. Remembering that *product* means *multiply*, here's how to create the cross-products for the percent shortcut:

$$\frac{part}{whole} = \frac{\%}{100}$$
$$part \times 100 = whole \times \%$$

Here's how to use the shortcut with cross-products:

- Find a percent of a whole.

    What is 30% of 40?

    30 is the % and 40 is the *of* number: $\frac{is}{40} = \frac{30}{100}$

    Cross-multiply and solve for *is*: $is \times 100 = 40 \times 30$

    $is \times 100 = 1200$

    $12 \times 100 = 1200$

    Thus, **12** *is* 30% of 40.

- Find what percent one number is of another number.

    12 is what percent of 40?

    12 is the *is* number and 40 is the *of* number: $\frac{12}{40} = \frac{\%}{100}$

    Cross-multiply and solve for %: $12 \times 100 = 40 \times \%$

    $1200 = 40 \times \%$

    $1200 = 40 \times 30$

    Thus, 12 is **30%** of 40.

- Find the whole when the percent of it is given.
  12 is 30% of what number?
  12 is the *is* number and 30 is the %:
  Cross-multiply and solve for the *of* number:

$$\frac{12}{of} = \frac{30}{100}$$
$$12 \times 100 = of \times 30$$
$$1200 = of \times 30$$
$$1200 = \mathbf{40} \times 30$$

Thus 12 is 30% *of* **40**.

You can use the same technique to find the percent increase or decrease. The *is* number is the actual increase or decrease, and the *of* number is the original amount.

Example: If a merchant puts his $20 hats on sale for $15, by what percent does he decrease the selling price?

1. Calculate the decrease, the *is* number: $20 − $15 = $5

2. The *of* number is the original amount, $20

3. Set up the equation and solve for *of* by cross-multiplying:

$$\frac{5}{20} = \frac{\%}{100}$$
$$5 \times 100 = 20 \times \%$$
$$500 = 20 \times \%$$
$$500 = 20 \times 25$$

4. Thus, the selling price is decreased by **25%**.

If the merchant later raises the price of the hats from $15 back to $20, don't be fooled into thinking that the percent increase is also 25%! It's actually more, because the increase amount of $5 is now based on a lower original price of only $15:

$$\frac{5}{15} = \frac{\%}{100}$$
$$5 \times 100 = 15 \times \%$$
$$500 = 15 \times \%$$
$$500 = 15 \times 33\frac{1}{3}$$

Thus, the selling price is increased by **33%**.

Find a percent of a whole:

_____**67.** 1% of 25

_____**68.** 18.2% of 50

_____**69.** $37\frac{1}{2}$% of 100

_____**70.** 125% of 60

Find what percent one number is of another number.

_____**71.** 10 is what % of 20?

_____**72.** 4 is what % of 12?

_____**73.** 12 is what % of 4?

Find the whole when the percent of it is given.

_____**74.** 15% of what number is 15?

_____**75.** $37\frac{1}{2}$% of what number is 3?

_____**76.** 200% of what number is 20?

Now try your percent skills on some real life problems.

_____**77.** Last Monday, 20% of the 140-member nursing staff was absent. How many nurses were absent that day?
    a. 14   **b.** 20   **c.** 28   **d.** 112   **e.** 126

_____**78.** 40% of Vero's postal service employees are women. If there are 80 women in Vero's postal service, how many men are employed there?
    a. 32   **b.** 112   **c.** 120   **d.** 160   **e.** 200

_____**79.** Of the 840 crimes committed last month, 42 involved petty theft. What percent of the crimes involved petty theft?
    a. .5%   **b.** 2%   **c.** 5%   **d.** 20%   **e.** 50%

_____**80.** Sam's Shoe Store put all of its merchandise on sale for 20% off. If Jason saved $10 by purchasing one pair of shoes during the sale, what was the original price of the shoes before the sale?
    a. $12   **b.** $20   **c.** $40   **d.** $50   **e.** $70

LENGTH, WEIGHT, AND TIME UNITS

The questions involving length, weight, and time on the math test will ask you either to convert between different measurement units or to add or subtract measurement values.

CONVERTING

You may encounter questions that ask you to convert between units of measurement in length, weight, or time. To convert from a smaller unit (like inches) to a larger unit (like feet), divide the smaller unit by the number of those units necessary to equal the larger unit. To convert from a larger unit to a smaller unit, multiply the larger unit by the conversion number.

> **Example:** Convert 36 inches to feet.

- Since 1 ft = 12 in, divide 36 by 12: $36 ÷ 12 = 3$ ft

> **Example:** Convert 4 feet to inches.

- Since 1 ft = 12 in, multiply 4 by 12: $4 × 12 = 48$ in

> **Example:** Convert 32 ounces to pounds.

- Since 1 lb = 16 oz, divide 32 by 16: $32 ÷ 16 = 2$ lb

> **Example:** Convert 2 pounds to ounces.

- Since 1 lb = 16 oz, multiply 2 by 16: $2 × 16 = 32$ oz

> **Example:** Convert 180 minutes to hours.

- Since 1 hr = 60 min, divide 180 by 60: $180 ÷ 60 = 3$ hr

> **Example:** Convert 4 hours to minutes.

- Since 1 hr = 60 min, multiply 4 by 60: $4 × 60 = 240$ min

Now try some on your own. Convert as indicated. Answers are at the end of the chapter.

_____**81.** 2 ft = _____ in

_____**82.** 2 hr = _____ min

_____**83.** 3 lb = _____ oz

_____**84.** 120 min = _____ hr

CALCULATING WITH LENGTH, WEIGHT, AND TIME UNITS

You may be asked on the test to add or subtract length, weight, and time units. The only trick to doing this correctly is to remember to convert the smaller units to larger units and vice versa, if need be.

Example: find the perimeter of the figure:

To add the lengths, add each column of length units separately:

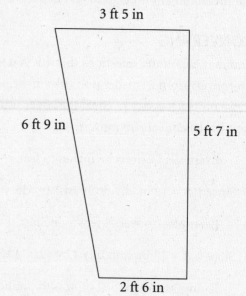
3 ft 5 in
6 ft 9 in
5 ft 7 in
2 ft 6 in

```
      5 ft    7 in
      2 ft    6 in
      6 ft    9 in
   +  3 ft    5 in
     16 ft   27 in
```

Since 27 inches is more than 1 foot, the total of 16 ft 27 in must be simplified:

- Convert 27 inches to feet and inches:

$$27\ in \times \frac{1ft}{12\ in} = \frac{27}{12}\ ft = 2\frac{3}{12}\ ft = 2\ ft\ 3\ in$$

- Add:
```
     16 ft
   +  2 ft   3 in
     18 ft   3 in
```
Thus, the perimeter is **18 feet 3 inches.**

Finding the length of a line segment may require subtracting lengths of different units. For example, find the length of line segment $\overline{AB}$ below:

To subtract the lengths, subtract each column of length units separately, starting with the rightmost column.

```
     9 ft   3 in
   - 3 ft   8 in
```

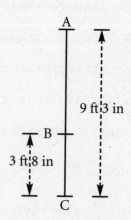
A
B
C
9 ft 3 in
3 ft 8 in

Warning: You can't subtract 8 inches from 3 inches because 8 is larger than 3! As in regular subtraction, you have to *borrow* 1 from the column on the left. However, borrowing *1 ft* is the same as borrowing *12 inches;* adding the borrowed 12 inches to the 3 inches gives 15 inches. Thus:

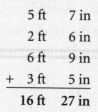
```
     8   12/15
     9 ft   3 in
   - 3 ft   8 in
     5 ft   7 in
```
Thus, the length of $\overline{AB}$ is **5 feet 7 inches.**

Add and simplify. Answers are at the end of this chapter.

85.   5 ft 3 in
        +   2 ft 9 in

86.   7 lb 12 oz
        +   5 lb 14 oz

Subtract and simplify.

87.   1 ft 1 in
        −   2 ft 9 in

88.   5 hr 38 min
        −   3 hr 45 min

Now try these time word problems.

_____**89.** During finals week, Jan took three tests that each required 45 minutes. If she then took one last test, and all fourt tests required a total of $3\frac{1}{4}$ hours, how long did the last test take?

a. $\frac{1}{2}$ hour   b. $\frac{2}{3}$ hour   c. $\frac{3}{4}$ hour   d. 1 hour   e. $1\frac{1}{4}$ hours

_____**90.** If each of eight biology classrooms is in use for 5 hours and 15 minutes per day, and a total of 84 student experiments are done, how long does each experiment take on average?

a. 20 minutes   b. 30 minutes   c. 40 minutes   d. 50 minutes   e. 1 hour

ANSWERS TO MATH PROBLEMS

WORD PROBLEMS

1. a
2. d
3. d
4. e

FRACTIONS

5. $\frac{1}{4}$
6. $\frac{2}{5}$
7. $\frac{3}{8}$
8. 10
9. 6
10. 200
11. $\frac{11}{12}$
12. $\frac{55}{24}$ or $2\frac{7}{24}$
13. $7\frac{1}{4}$
14. $\frac{2}{15}$
15. $\frac{1}{8}$
16. $\frac{19}{12}$ or $1\frac{7}{12}$
17. a
18. b
19. $\frac{2}{15}$
20. $\frac{8}{35}$
21. $\frac{2}{3}$
22. $\frac{26}{15}$ or $1\frac{11}{15}$
23. 15
24. $\frac{33}{2}$ or $16\frac{1}{2}$
25. c
26. e
27. c
28. $\frac{1}{2}$
29. $5\frac{1}{2}$
30. $\frac{1}{5}$
31. $\frac{45}{28}$ or $1\frac{17}{28}$
32. b
33. d
34. b

DECIMALS

35. $\frac{5}{1000}$ or $\frac{1}{200}$
36. $3\frac{12}{25}$
37. $123\frac{456}{1000}$ or $123\frac{57}{125}$
38. 4
39. 8.305
40. .907
41. 1.456
42. b
43. d
44. .03
45. .3392
46. .70104
47. e
48. e
49. 1.4
50. 128
51. 572
52. 1400
53. b
54. c

PERCENTS

55. 45%
56. .8%
57. 16.67% or $16\frac{2}{3}$%
58. .12
59. .875
60. 2.5
61. 12.5% or $12\frac{1}{2}$%
62. 52%
63. 58.33% or $58\frac{1}{3}$%
64. $\frac{19}{20}$
65. $\frac{3}{8}$
66. $\frac{5}{4}$ or $1\frac{1}{4}$
67. $\frac{1}{4}$ or .25
68. 9.1
69. $37\frac{1}{2}$ or 37.5
70. 75
71. 50%
72. $33\frac{1}{3}$%
73. 300%
74. 100
75. 8
76. 10
77. c
78. c
79. c
80. d

LENGTH, WEIGHT, AND TIME

81. 24
82. 120
83. 48
84. 2
85. 8 ft
86. 13 lb 10 oz
87. 1 ft 4 in
88. 1 hr 53 min
89. d
90. b

JUDGMENT AND REASONING

CHAPTER SUMMARY

This chapter will familiarize you with questions on the firefighter exam that test your judgment and reasoning ability. It shows you a systematic approach to answering these questions, using sample questions as examples.

Firefighters have to be able to make sound judgments under pressure. Lives can and do depend on it. Firefighters who react without thinking endanger themselves, their fellow firefighters, and the people they are trying to protect. Judgment and reasoning questions on a firefighter exam are designed to measure your ability to use reason in firefighting situations. Judgment and reasoning questions ask you to play the game "what if?" If you were a firefighter in a given situation, what would you do? The fire department wants to know whether, given a certain set of job-related conditions, you can think on your feet, follow directions, take orders from superiors, and interact with the public. To arrive at the correct answer to this kind of question, you have to analyze a situation and to use good judgment and common sense to arrive at a course of action.

WHAT JUDGMENT AND REASONING QUESTIONS ARE LIKE

Judgment and reasoning questions may be based on any number of different situations and are presented in varying formats. The following are examples of various kinds of judgment and reasoning questions as they may appear on the test.

- **Firefighting operations.** After a fire is extinguished, the water in the hose lines must be removed before the hose lines are reloaded onto the fire truck. The best place to remove this water is. . . .
- **Firehouse routines.** Each shift, on arriving at the firehouse, performs a thorough inspection of the tools and equipment. Which of the following best expresses the reason for this procedure?
- **Public relations.** A man enters the firehouse and tells you he has locked his keys in the car with the ignition running. His puppy is in the car, and it's a very hot day. Which of the following should you do?
- **Interpersonal skills.** Your superior officer has asked you to give a car a summons for parking in a fire zone at a local shopping mall. When you get to the car, you recognize that it belongs to your neighbor. The best course of action for you to take is to. . . .

There may also be questions that test your ability to follow directions. You might, for instance, be given a list of procedures to follow in ventilating the roof of a fire building. You would then be given a situation in which a roof needs to be ventilated and be asked which step is the next step you should take, according to the procedure you read.

A SYSTEMATIC APPROACH TO JUDGMENT QUESTIONS

To answer judgment and reasoning questions, use decision-making techniques to help you think through the best course of action. Use a systematic approach:

1. **Read the question carefully.** You may want to read it twice. Be sure you understand what is being asked. Look for and underline key words such as *all, always, every, never, except, not.*

2. **Read all the answer choices.** Eliminate answers intelligently. Use common sense to rule out the choices that cannot possibly be correct. Try to use the information from the question to select the correct answer. When faced with two answers that both seem correct, try to select the one that is *always* correct rather than the one which is only *sometimes* correct. Look for answers that are opposite; there's a good chance that one of these is correct.

3. **Make a decision.** After careful consideration select the best possible choice.

4. **Reread the question.** Make absolutely certain that the answer you have chosen satisfies all conditions of the question.

Watch for Tricky Wording

Use caution! There's more than one way to ask the same question, and the correct answer may depend on the way the question is worded. You might be asked to choose the *best* possible answer, but on the other hand you might instead be asked which choice is *not* correct or what would *not* be the best course of action. Each of the questions below is based on the same situation, but choosing the correct answer depends on a careful reading of the wording of the question itself:

- While you are on your way to work, you see a gasoline truck with fluid apparently leaking from the rear tank. You suspect that the leak is gasoline but are not certain. **Which of the following actions is the most appropriate for you to take?**
- While you are on your way to work, you see a gasoline truck with fluid apparently leaking from the rear tank. You suspect that the leak is gasoline but are not certain. **You would be correct in doing all of the following EXCEPT. . . .**
- While you are on your way to work, you see a gasoline truck with fluid apparently leaking from the rear tank. You suspect that the leak is gasoline but are not certain. **Which of the following would NOT be the best course of action for you to take?**

In the first version of this question, you are simply being asked to choose the best course of action. In the other two versions, however, you must choose the *least appropriate* action. In these cases, three out of four answer choices are likely to be actions that would be more or less appropriate, while another—the correct answer—will be an inappropriate, perhaps dangerous or careless, thing you might do.

Example: How to Use the Systematic Approach

This first sample question is followed by a step-by-step analysis that shows you how to use common sense and a systematic problem solving approach to select the best possible answer. You might want to try working through to the answer yourself before you read the explanation that follows.

1. While on your way to work, you see flames shooting out a second-floor window of a six-story apartment building. What should you do?
   a. Immediately evacuate the building.
   b. Proceed to work and report the fire as soon as you get there.
   c. Ignore the fire because you are not yet on duty.
   d. Report the fire at the nearest phone and then try to evacuate the building.

Here's how to use the systematic approach outlined above to answer the question.

1. **Read the question carefully.** What is the question asking? Stated simply, the question is asking, "What would you do if you saw a building on fire?"

2. **Read all the answer choices.** Read and evaluate *each* answer choice, eliminating choices that are clearly wrong.
   a. "Immediately evacuate the building." Common sense tells you that getting the people out of a burning building is a good course of action. Your reaction may save the lives of the people inside the building. This sounds like a possible answer.
   b. "Proceed to work and report the fire as soon as you get there." It is never a good idea to delay reporting a fire. There may be people who need help. Obviously this is not a good option, so eliminate it.
   c. "Ignore the fire because you are not yet on duty." A building fire should never be ignored. The fact that you are not on duty is not relevant: as a firefighter, on or off duty, you are

sworn to protect the public. Discard this option as well.

d. "Report the fire at the nearest phone and then try to evacuate the building." Reporting the fire would bring help from other firefighters, as well as equipment for rescuing the occupants. After that, evacuating the building will save lives, due to your quick response and sure knowledge. This appears to be a very good choice.

3. **Make a decision.** You eliminated options **b** and **c**. Now you should review choices **a** and **d**. They are very similar to each other, but choice **d** is the better answer because you are getting the proper help and equipment to the scene of the fire as well as trying to remove the residents from the fire building.

4. **Reread the question.** Once you've made a decision, review the question to make sure the answer you've chosen meets the conditions set out in the situation. Sure enough, choice **d** represents the best course of action for an off-duty firefighter who sees a building fire.

You'll get more practice in using this kind of systematic approach as you read the sections that follow on the types of situations and questions you might encounter in a judgment and reasoning section of the firefighter exam.

QUESTIONS ON FIREFIGHTING OPERATIONS

The most frequently asked questions require candidates to place themselves in the position of a firefighter at the scene of a fire or emergency. In answering a question of this type, you must consider a firefighter's priorities:

saving lives, preserving property, and extinguishing the fire. Overall safety, both for firefighters and civilians, and observing proper authority and the chain of command are also important priorities.

Keep these priorities in mind as you try to answer the sample questions below on firefighting operations.

2. Your company responds to a report of a multi-vehicle accident. When you arrive on the scene, you see that one car is turned upside-down with at least two civilians trapped inside. The other car seems to have less damage; however, it is leaking what appears to be gasoline. What should you do?
   a. Bring a hose to wash away the gasoline before beginning to extract the trapped civilians.
   b. Immediately remove the trapped civilians from their car.
   c. Disregard the gasoline, since nothing is currently on fire.
   d. Call for a tow truck.

Good judgment and common sense should enable you to eliminate choice **c**. You should also reject choice **d**, since it does not address the urgency of the situation. Choice **b** may be appealing at first; however, you should consider the whole situation. A gasoline leak always raises the possibility of a fire or an explosion, which could injure not only the people trapped in the car but also you and your fellow firefighters. The safety of all concerned should be your first priority. Keeping this principle in mind, you should eliminate choice **b** and pick **a** instead. If you washed down the gasoline, you would reduce the risk of a fire or explosion and ensure the safety of everyone around you.

Now try another question, this time one based on more routine operations. Remember, safety is still a firefighter's first concern.

3. Firefighters must do inspections of any buildings, hospitals, factories, and schools in their area. They check the premises for any violations of fire safety regulations. All of the following should be checked for violations EXCEPT the
   a. automatic sprinkler system
   b. electrical wires and outlets
   c. fire extinguishers
   d. television and stereo

The first thing you should notice when you read the question is that word *EXCEPT*. It tells you to look for something that the firefighters will *not* check for violations as the answer.

The correct answer is choice **d**. The firefighters would check all of the other choices when they do an inspection, keeping in mind that people's safety can depend on the proper functioning of sprinkler systems, electrical wires and outlets, and fire extinguishers.

QUESTIONS ON FIREHOUSE ROUTINE

If equipment that is used in fighting fires does not work properly, lives may be lost. Thus, firefighters have to check and maintain their equipment and apparatus, usually at the firehouse at the beginning of each shift. Some questions on the firefighter exam may ask questions about the routine of examining and maintaining equipment.

Even though the operations described in these questions are routine, the firefighter's priorities of life, property, and extinguishment, as well as safety and authority, are still paramount. For this reason, fire-fighters follow specific procedures in maintaining equipment and always replace damaged equipment or bring it to the attention of superior officers. Keeping that in mind, try to answer the sample questions below.

4. At the beginning of each shift, the power saw must be filled with gasoline and tested to make sure it works properly. The best reason for this requirement is that it
   a. gives the firefighters something to do every day
   b. makes the firefighters' job easier than if they waited until the tank was empty
   c. ensures that the power saw is ready for maximum use if needed at a fire
   d. ensures that the power saw is always ready for inspection by the fire chief

You can eliminate choices **a** and **b** because they do not give good common sense reasons for this procedure. And while it is true that the chief may order an inspection of equipment at any time, choice **d** is not the *best* reason, either. That leaves choice **c** as the best answer. If a tool is not ready to be used on arrival at the scene of an emergency, people's lives may be at risk.

Try your hand at another question based on routine procedures.

5. When a fire truck is leaving or returning to the firehouse, firefighters are required to stand on the street, one on the sidewalk and one inside the station. Which of the following is the most important reason for following this procedure?

a. to let the neighbors know that the firefighters are leaving so that the neighbors will watch the station while they are gone

b. to let pedestrians and automobiles know the truck is moving and to guide the truck's driver

c. to test the truck's lights and sirens before leaving the station to make sure they work efficiently

d. to give the firefighters time to get dressed and to show the neighborhood how their tax money is being used

You can eliminate choices **a** and **d** pretty quickly, because they do not use good judgment or common sense. Choice **c** looks a little better, but common sense should tell you that the moment the truck is leaving for a fire is not a good time to run an equipment check; anyway, the lights and siren shouldn't have to be checked every time the truck leaves or enters.

Choice **b** is the best answer. For their safety and the safety of others, firefighters stand outside in the street and on the sidewalk to warn motorists and pedestrians that the truck is in motion. The firefighter standing inside the firehouse helps to guide the truck's driver as the truck backs into the station.

PUBLIC RELATIONS QUESTIONS

Another part of exercising good jugment and common sense involves dealing with the public. Firefighters hold a position of public trust and must act in a manner con-

sistent with such a position. People must feel they can call on firefighters for help. Children should be able to look up to firefighters as role models and protectors. While firefighters cannot be expected to know and do all, they can be and are expected to treat civilians with respect at all times. Keep these ideas in mind as you try some sample questions.

6. A neighborhood woman enters the firehouse and asks you to cut down a tree in her yard because it is too close to the utility lines. She claims that this is a fire hazard and that therefore you should handle it. You should

a. get the ax and chop the tree down

b. tell her to call her utility company so that they can handle the problem properly

c. refuse her request but tell her your brother will do it for $50.00

d. tell her to stop bothering the fire department unless there is a fire

Good judgment and common sense, not to mention common courtesy, should lead you to eliminate choices **c** and **d** as inappropriate responses. The problem-solving approach should help you to reason that choice **a** is not appropriate. If you chop down a tree near utility lines, the tree or the lines may cause injury to yourself or others. Since this choice does not show concern for safety, it can also be eliminated.

The best possible answer is thus choice **b**. A firefighter must always be polite and courteous to the public. An explanation of why the utility company is best suited to help her allows the citizen to understand your actions. Though it would be unsafe for you to do as the citizen asks, you have still taken responsibility for the request and helped in the best way possible.

Using what you know about firefighters' priorities and concern for the public, try another question:

7. Your company arrives at the scene of a house fire with a response time of approximately five minutes. The owner of the house, however, begins to yell that his house and possessions are burning and that it has been half an hour since he called the fire department. The best response for you to give would be to

a. tell the man to get control of himself; he is getting hysterical

b. explain that your response time was only five minutes and assure the man that you will do the best you can to save his house and possessions

c. ignore the man and begin working on putting out the fire

d. tell the man he should not have been so careless in the first place, so you would not have to be there putting out this fire

The best answer is choice **b**. You need to explain to the citizen the procedures for receiving and responding to a call, as well as reassuring him that you want to prevent as much damage as possible. Your explanation will help the man understand that you are really doing all you can to help him, so that he may feel better and respect the job you are doing. Choices **a, c,** and **d** are not acceptable answers because they do not treat the citizen with respect. A firefighter must always be courteous and polite to the public, especially in a crisis situation when people may react inappropriately because of the stress they are under.

QUESTIONS ON INTERPERSONAL RELATIONS

The firefighters in a station house consider themselves one big family. They work as a dedicated team, entrusting their lives to one another. They also operate within a hierarchical structure. In this structure, they treat their superiors with the utmost respect, valuing their experience and knowledge. Judgment and reasoning questions that deal with interpersonal relations stress respect for authority, dedication to all firefighters, and responsibility for one's actions.

8. While replacing the hose on the fire engine toward the end of your shift, you drop the nozzle and think it may be damaged. You should

a. do nothing, because you know the nozzle is expensive to replace

b. report the damage to your superior officer so he or she can get a new one

c. choose not to worry about it, since your shift is almost over

d. try to blame it on someone else so you will not get in trouble

Keeping safety and the well-being of other firefighters in mind should enable you to eliminate choices **a, c,** and **d** immediately. Firefighters should never allow damaged equipment to be used, since injury can result. Firefighters must also be honest, responsible, and concerned for the safety of their fellow firefighters. Choice **b** is the only choice that shows these characteristics.

9. A firefighter enters an apartment to search for victims. While she is in the apartment, the fire spreads and blocks the stairs. The apartment is on the fifth floor and has no fire escape. What should the firefighter do?
   a. She should call for other firefighters to assist her.
   b. She should jump from the window and hope she lands on something soft.
   c. She should take the stairs one flight up to the next floor.
   d. She should wait for the fire to die down, so then she can use the stairs.

Choice a is the best answer. All firefighters work as a team. Each firefighter who goes into a fire building knows that he or she can count on the other members to come to his or her aid. Choice b does not use good judgment. Choice c is not possible because the question clearly states that the stairs are blocked by the fire. Choice d is not an intelligent choice and also shows lack of teamwork.

QUESTIONS ON FOLLOWING PROCEDURES

A good firefighter has the ability to follow directions. Firefighters must follow detailed written procedures for everything from operating at building fires to equipment maintenance. Therefore, some firefighter exams include another kind of judgment question, one that tests your ability to follow a set of written procedures to the letter.

In this kind of question, the examiners provide you with a set of directions for completing a typical firehouse assignment or operating at a fire scene. The directions might, for instance, provide step-by-step instructions for loading hoses on the apparatus or specify the uses and location of tools.

The list of procedures is then followed by one or more questions that ask you something about the order of the steps in the list. The answers to these questions rely less on your judgment, as in the previous types, than on your ability to read and understand the procedures. So it's important to read the procedure carefully. There may be certain conditions that have to be met before you would take a particular step; if they are not met, you would have to skip that step and go to the next. Key words to look for in this type of question are:

- "What would you do *next*?" In this case, you have to find the answer that is the next step in the procedure.
- "What did you do *before . . .*?" In this case, you have to find the last step completed *before* the step you're on now in the list of procedures.

The most important thing to remember in answering this kind of question is not to make assumptions. Instead, follow the procedure to the letter. You will see how this process works as you go through the sample questions that follow.

Questions 10–12 refer to the following procedure. Firefighters must often move injured or unconscious victims in order to get them out of danger and to a location where they can receive proper medical attention. As a firefighter, you should carry out the following steps in the order listed in order to move a victim.

1. Check to make sure there is no immediate danger to you or the victim.

2. Provide support for the victim's neck and spine.

3. Avoid bending or twisting the victim's body.

4. Lift the victim to a sitting position, using your knees, not your back.

5. If you are alone, drag the victim to safety, keeping the victim's body straight.

6. If there are two people, use a two-handed seat carry.

10. You are searching an apartment that is smoky but apparently not on fire. You find an unconscious woman on the floor in the kitchen. You have supported the woman's neck and spine. What would you do next?
    a. Drag the woman to safety, keeping her body straight.
    b. Avoid bending or twisting the woman's body.
    c. Lift the woman to a sitting position, using your knees, not your back.
    d. Use a two-handed seat carry to remove the woman from the apartment.

    The key word in the question is *next*. Reviewing the procedure, you should see that the next step after supporting the woman's neck and spine is to keep the woman's body from bending or twisting, choice **b**. The other choices do not immediately follow supporting the neck and spine.

    Use the same process to arrive at the answer to another question based on the same procedure.

11. Your company responds to an apartment fire. You are alone when you find a man unconscious on the floor. Seeing that the fire is under control, you support the man's neck and spine

and then lift him to a sitting position without twisting his body. What would you do next?
    a. Use a two-handed seat carry.
    b. Check to make sure there is no immediate danger to you or the victim.
    c. Provide support for the man's neck and spine.
    d. Drag the man, keeping his body straight.

    The correct choice is **d**. The procedure tells you that when you are alone you should drag the victim to safety, keeping the body straight. The two-handed seat carry (choice **a**) is used when there are two rescuers. The other two choices are steps that you have already accomplished, according to the situation described in the question.

12. A fellow firefighter has injured his ankle while climbing the stairs in a house fire. As there is no immediate danger, you call another firefighter to help you. How would you remove the injured firefighter?
    a. Use a two-handed seat carry to remove the firefighter from the house.
    b. Avoid bending or twisting the firefighter's body.
    c. Provide support for the firefighter's neck and spine.
    d. Lift the firefighter to a sitting position and drag him to safety.

    The correct answer is **a** because the procedure states that when there are two people, you should use a two-handed seat carry. The other choices are steps in the procedure that are not necessary in the given situation.

Now try your hand at another set of questions based on a different procedure.

Questions 13–15 refer to the following procedure.

Firefighters inspect buildings for any violations of the fire safety laws. There are specific steps to conducting an inspection. They are listed below.

1. Locate the building manager and inform him that you are here to inspect the premises.

2. Inspect the exits. Make sure that all doors are working properly and are not blocked. Make sure that exit signs are posted above each door.

3. Check the public hallway. Ensure that it is free from accumulations of rubbish.

4. Fire extinguishers should be fully charged and properly placed.

5. Test the fire escape. It should be sturdy and in good repair.

6. Check the automatic sprinkler systems.

7. Check for the storage of flammable materials.

8. Visually examine the premises for improper wiring.

13. On arriving at a building to inspect it, you inform the building manager that you are here for your annual fire safety inspection. What should you do next?
   a. Make sure there is no trash blocking the public hallway.
   b. Check for the storage of flammable materials.
   c. Check the doors to ensure that they work properly.
   d. Make sure the fire escape is sturdy and in good repair.

Read the question, and then return to the building inspection procedure. The question states that you have met with the building manager and asks what you will do next. The key word is *next*. According to the question, you have accomplished step 1. Step 2 is to inspect the exits, so choice **c** is the answer.

14. Your inspection of a building is almost complete. What is the last thing you will do before leaving the premises?
   a. Look at the wiring.
   b. Check the automatic sprinkler systems.
   c. Ensure that the fire extinguishers are fully charged.
   d. Tell the building manager that you are here to inspect the premises.

This time you have been asked what the last step in the inspection is. The key word is *last*. The last step given in the procedure is to visually examine the premises for improper wiring. Thus, the answer is choice **a**.

15. In your building inspection, you have found that the doors are satisfactory and exit signs are properly posted. What should you check next?
   a. the automatic sprinkler
   b. the public hallway
   c. the roof
   d. the fire escape

The key word, once again, is *next*. You have accomplished step 2 and should go on to step 3, the public hallway, which is choice **b**. Notice that choice **c**, the roof, does not appear anywhere in the inspection procedure, so it should have been easy to eliminate that choice immediately.

LOGICAL REASONING QUESTIONS

Firefighters have the ability to analyze and reason. A good firefighter must use analytical and logical reasoning skills when making important decisions. Therefore, firefighter exams sometimes include questions that test critical thinking.

Analytical and logical reasoning questions take many different forms: number series, sequences, analogies, and logic problems are just some of them.

SERIES AND SEQUENCES

Use your reasoning abilities as you try to answer the following sample questions.

16. Look at this series: 1, 1, 5, __, 9, 9, 13,... What number should fill the blank?
   a. 3
   b. 5
   c. 9
   d. 17

Number series, letter series, and sequence questions measure your ability to reason without words. To answer these questions you must determine the pattern in each one. In each number series, look for the degree and direction of change between the numbers. In other words, do the numbers increase or decrease, and by how much? In question 16 above, the numbers repeat once and then increase by 4. Notice also that this question asks you to fill in the blank, not to add to the end of the series. Since the number 5 is repeated once, the answer is choice **b**.

ANALOGIES

Another type of logical reasoning question is the verbal analogy. In an analogy, two sets of words are related to each other in a specific similar way. Verbal analogies will test your ability to see these word relationships.

17. Aspirin is to headache as bandage is to
   a. injection
   b. fracture
   c. accident
   d. wound

The correct answer is choice **d**, *wound*. This is a "use or function" analogy; in both sets of words—*aspirin* and *headache*, *bandage* and *wound*—something is used for something else. *Aspirin* is used to treat a *headache*, a *bandage* is used to treat a *wound*. All the other choices in this question are loosely associated with injury, but the best answer is clearly choice **d**.

A good way to figure out the relationship in a given analogy question is to make up a sentence. You must first read each question carefully, as it is easy to mistake one kind of analogy for another. Formulating a sentence that expresses the relationship is the best way to avoid this mistake. Take question 17 above as an example. Following are sentences you might make when approaching this analogy:

- *Aspirin* is used to treat a *headache*. A *bandage* is used to treat an *injection*? No. As soon as you say the sentence, you know that choice **a** is wrong. So you must try again.
- A *bandage* is used to treat a *fracture*. Again, no. A fracture requires a cast, a bandage won't help.
- A *bandage* is used to treat an *accident*. No, once again. A bandage might treat a person who has been in an accident, but it will not treat the accident itself.
- A *bandage* is used to treat a *wound*. Yes, of course. Your sentence tells you this is the right choice.

LOGIC

Next, try this logic problem:

18. During the past year, Zoe read more books than Heather.

Jane read fewer books than Heather.

Jane read more books than Zoe.

If the first two statements are true, the third statement is
a. true
b. false
c. uncertain

Logic problems may appear daunting at first. However, solving these problems can be done in the most straightforward way. Simply "translate" the abstract relationships in the questions into real-world relationships, so you can see the facts more clearly. For the problem above, make a chart and list the names of the people and the possible number of books they have read, according to the information given.

Z = 10 books
H = 8 books
J = 6 books

Using this list, you can quickly see that the third statement, *Jane read more books than Zoe,* is false. The answer, then, is choice **b.**

Another way to solve this type of problem is to set up a chart using terms like "more than" or "less than":

Z more than H; H less than J; or, Z > H > J

Either way, you can see that Zoe read the most books, Heather was next, and Jane read the fewest.

How To Answer Judgment and Reasoning Questions

Judgment and reasoning questions are used to see how you would approach situations you may face as a firefighter on a day-to-day basis. Potential firefighters are expected to be sharp, safety conscious, respectful, and professional. When answering judgment and reasoning questions:

- Read slowly, so that you will understand what the question is asking as well as the scenario given to you.
- Look for key words that direct you to the correct answers.
- Read each answer carefully. Use common sense to eliminate answers that are clearly wrong.
- When faced with more than one answer you haven't been able to eliminate, choose the best answer by reasoning out the situation.
- Reread the question to be sure the answer you chose uses sound judgment.

C·H·A·P·T·E·R

MECHANICAL APTITUDE

10

CHAPTER SUMMARY

Mechanical aptitude is tested on many firefighter exams. This chapter will familiarize you with commonly tested concepts by presenting definitions, study tips, and sample test questions for basic mechanical devices and systems.

F irefighters use mechanical devices every day: simple hand tools such as axes and wrenches, as well as more complex systems such as pumps and internal combustion engines. The ability to understand and use mechanical concepts is critical to a firefighter's job.

If your exam includes a section on mechanical aptitude, it may cover topics with which you are very familiar, as well as some that are new. Regardless of your background, understanding the concepts in this chapter will benefit you both for the exam and in your career as a firefighter. After an introduction to mechanical aptitude questions, this chapter summarizes the most commonly tested mechanical devices and mechanical systems. It also suggests ways in which you can further improve your knowledge of mechanical devices and related scientific and mathematical knowledge. Finally, it gives you an opportunity to review what you've learned by presenting a sample mechanical aptitude section like those found on firefighter exams.

WHAT MECHANICAL APTITUDE QUESTIONS ARE LIKE

Mechanical aptitude questions tend to cover a wide range of topics. The questions will usually be multiple choice with four or five possible answers. Some questions may require previous knowledge of the topic—so it is a good idea to study this chapter well!—and other questions will include all of the information you will need.

Some questions will require the identification of various mechanical tools or devices. Some of the types of mechanical devices that may appear on the exam—and are covered in this chapter—include hand tools, gears, pulleys, levers, fasteners, springs, valves, gauges, and pumps. In addition to individual mechanical devices, the exam may test your knowledge of various *systems*, or combinations of mechanical devices. A common example of a mechanical system is the internal combustion engine of an automobile.

A typical mechanical aptitude question will look something like this:

> Which of the following is a common component of an internal combustion engine?
> a. a piston
> b. a compass
> c. a hammer
> d. a hydraulic jack

The answer is **a**, a piston. A compass is used to determine a direction on a map. A hammer is used to drive nails. A hydraulic jack is used to lift heavy items.

DEFINITION: WHAT IS A MECHANICAL DEVICE?

A mechanical device is a tool invented to make a given task easier. For example, you could drive a nail into a piece of wood with a rock. However, a long time ago, someone who spent most of his time building things with wood figured out that it would be a lot more efficient if he had something easier to hold on to than a rock. He thought that a long slender handle might be nice and that a hard piece of metal for striking the nail would provide more accuracy and would not damage the wood as easily. Thus was born the hammer.

Most mechanical devices were invented in the same manner: people looking for easier ways to perform their everyday jobs. Some mechanical devices are thousands of years old, such as the lever, the wheel, and many hand tools. Other more complex devices, such as pumps and valves, were invented more recently. Many times the idea of a new mechanical device exists but the technology to actually make it does not. For example, many years before the pump was invented, people probably discussed the need for an easier way to move water from the river to the town on the hill. However, the technologies of the electric motor and casting of metal had not yet been invented, so the modern pump could not possibly have been invented at that time.

Mechanical devices cover a wide range of types of tools. In general, they are tools that relate to physical work and are governed by mechanical forces and movements. You can usually see what they do and how they work—as opposed to, say, a light switch or a battery, which are electrical devices. Some tools are used to directly accomplish a specific task, as when you use a hand saw to cut a piece of wood. Others, such as pulleys and gears, may be used indirectly to accomplish certain tasks that would be possible without the device but are easier with the device. Still others, such as gauges, only provide feedback information on the operation of other mechanical devices. You see and use mechanical devices many times each day, so there's no reason to be intimidated by a mechanical aptitude section on the exam.

COMMONLY TESTED MECHANICAL DEVICES

The sections below review some of the mechanical devices that are most likely to appear on firefighter exams.

Hand Tools

Hand tools are defined as tools operated not by motors but rather by human power. There are many different types of hand tools including carpentry tools, automotive hand tools, and hand tools used specifically by firefighters. This chapter cannot cover every conceivable hand tool, so it will be limited to tools used in everyday situations and those specific to firefighting—the ones you are most likely to be tested on.

Some of the hand tools used by carpenters and other workers, including firefighters, are listed in the table on the next page, along with their most common uses and some examples of each kind.

Some of the hand tools used in the automotive industry are listed below.

- **Wrenches** are used to tighten and loosen nuts and bolts. Examples include vice grips and box end, ratchet, crescent, and pipe wrenches.
- **Mechanical jacks** are used to lift cars so that tires can be changed. The jack in the trunk of your car is an example.

In addition to the tools above, some hand tools are used specifically by firefighters (and sometimes by other workers as well):

- **Ladders** are used to access high areas. Firefighters use different kinds of ladders, including extension ladders and aerial ladders.
- **Axes** are used by firefighters to break down doors and walls and as prying tools. This tool is very similar to an ax used to chop firewood.

Gears

A gear is generally a toothed wheel or cylinder that meshes with another toothed element to transmit motion or to change speed or direction. Gears are typically attached to a rotating shaft turned by an outside energy source such as an electric motor or an internal combustion engine. Gears are used in many mechanical devices including automotive transmissions, carpenter's hand drills, elevator lifting mechanisms, bicycles, and carnival rides such as Ferris wheels and merry-go-rounds.

Gears can be used in several different configurations. Two gears may be connected by directly touching each other, as in an automotive transmission. In this arrangement, one gear spins clockwise and the other rotates counterclockwise. Another possible configuration is to have two gears connected by a loop of chain, as on a bicycle. In this arrangement, the first gear rotates in one direction, causing the chain to move. Since the chain is directly connected to the second gear, the second gear will immediately begin to rotate in the same direction as the first gear.

Many times a system will use two gears of different sizes, as on a ten-speed bicycle. This will allow changes in speed of the bicycle or machine.

Problems about gears will always involve rotation, or spinning. The easiest way to approach test questions

(continued on page 5)

CARPENTER'S TOOLS

Tool	Description/Function	Examples
hammer	used primarily to drive and remove nails, as well as to pound on devices such as chisels	claw hammer, rubber mallet, ball-peen hammer
saw	thin metal blade with a sharp-toothed edge used to cut wood or metal	hand saw, hacksaw, jigsaw
screwdriver	used to tighten and loosen screws and bolts	slotted (regular) head, Phillips head
level	two- to four-foot long piece of metal or plastic that contains calibrated air bubble tubes, used to ensure that things are vertically plumb or horizontally level	hand level, laser level
square	used primarily to aid in drawing a cut line on a board to insure a straight, ninety-degree cut	L-square, T-square
plane	metal tool with a handle and an adjustable blade, used to shave off thin strips of wood for the purpose of smoothing or leveling	block plane, varous sizes of carpenter's planes
chisel	metal tool with a sharp, beveled edge that is struck with a hammer in order to cut and shape stone, metal, or wood	scoop chisel, beveled chisel, masonry chisel, cold chisel
protractor	half circle with tick marks around the edge spaced at one-degree intervals, used to measure angles	only one type, made of metal or plastic
C-clamp	C-shaped metallic instrument with a threaded stop that can be adjusted to clamp together pieces of material of different thicknesses	furniture clamps, many types and sizes of metallic C-clamps
compass	V-shaped metallic instrument with a sharp point on the end of one leg and a pencil or pen on the end of the other leg, used to draw circles	only one type exists

that involve gears is to draw a diagram of what the question is describing, if one is not already provided. Use arrows next to each gear to indicate which direction (clockwise or counterclockwise) it is rotating.

Pulleys

A pulley consists of a wheel with a grooved rim in which a pulled rope or cable is run. Pulleys are commonly used with ropes or steel cable to change the direction of a pulling force.

Pulleys are often used to lift things. For instance, a pulley could be attached to the ceiling of a room. A rope could be run from the floor, up through the pulley, and back down to a box sitting on the floor. The pulley would allow you to pull *down* on the rope and cause the box to go *up.* That is, the pulley caused a change in direction of the pulling force.

Another common use for a pulley is to connect an electric motor to a mechanical device such as a pump. One pulley is placed on the shaft of the motor, and a second pulley is placed on the shaft of the pump. A belt is used to connect the two pulleys. When the motor is turned on, the first pulley rotates and causes the belt to rotate, which in turn causes the second pulley to rotate and turn the pump. This arrangement is very similar to the previous example of a bicycle chain and gears.

You may have seen pulleys used in a warehouse to lift heavy loads. Another use for a pulley is on a large construction crane. The cable extends from the object being lifted up to the top of the crane boom, across a pulley, and back down to the electric winch that is used to pull on the cable. In this situation the pulley again causes a change in direction of the pulling force, from the downward force of the winch that pulls the cable to the upward movement of the object being lifted.

Levers

A lever is a very old mechanical device. A lever typically consists of a metal or wooden bar that pivots on a fixed point. The object of using a lever is to gain a *mechanical advantage.* Mechanical advantage results when you use a mechanical device in order to make a task easier; that is, you gain an *advantage* by using a *mechanical* device. A lever allows you to complete a task, typically lifting, that would be more difficult or impossible without the lever.

The most common example of a lever is a playground seesaw. A force (a person's weight) is applied to one side of the lever, which causes the weight on the other side (the other person) to be lifted. However, since the pivot point on a seesaw is in the center, each person must weigh the same or things do not work well. You see, a seesaw is a lever with no mechanical advantage. If you push down on one side with a weight of 10 pounds you can only lift a maximum of 10 pounds on the other side. This is no great advantage.

This brings us to the secret of the lever: in order to lift an object that is heavier than the force you want to apply to the other side of the lever, you must locate the pivot point closer to the object you want to lift. If two 50-pound children sit close to the center of the seesaw, one 50-pound child close to the end of the board on the other side will be able to lift them both.

Test questions about levers will typically require a bit of math (multiplication and division) to solve the problem. There is one simple concept which you must understand in order to solve lever problems: the product of the weight to be lifted times the distance from the weight to the pivot point must be equal to the product of the lifting force times the distance from the force to the pivot point. Stated as an equation, $w \times d_1 = f \times d_2$.

For example, Bill has a 15-foot long lever and he wants to lift a 100-pound box. If he locates the pivot point 5 feet from the box, leaving 10 feet between the pivot point and the other end of the lever where he will apply the lifting force, how hard must he press on the lever to lift the box?

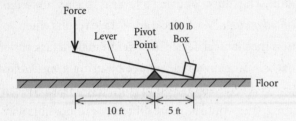

Use the lever formula, $w \times d_1 = f \times d_2$. The weight of 100 pounds times 5 feet must equal 10 feet times the force: $100 \times 5 = 10 \times force$. Using multiplication and division to solve for the force, you get 50 pounds of force that Bill must apply to the lever to lift the box.

Fasteners

A mechanical fastener is as any mechanical device or process used to connect two or more items together. Typical examples of fastening *devices* are bolts, screws, nails, and rivets. *Processes* can be used to mechanically join items together including gluing and welding. There are also unique mechanical fasteners such as "hook and loop," which consist of two tapes of material with many small plastic hooks and loops that stick together. Children's sneakers often use such fastening tape instead of laces.

Springs

A spring is an elastic mechanical device, normally a coil of wire, that returns to its original shape after being compressed or extended. There are many types of springs including the compression coil, spiral coil, flat spiral, extension coil, leaf spring, and torsional spring.

Springs are used for many applications such as car suspensions (compression coil and leaf springs), garage doors (extension coil and torsion springs), wind-up clocks (flat spiral and torsion springs), and some styles of ballpoint pens (compression coil).

In the kinds of questions you're likely to be asked on the firefighter exam, you can assume that springs behave linearly. That is, if an extension spring stretches one inch under a pull of ten pounds, then it will stretch two inches under a pull of twenty pounds. In real life, if you pull too hard on a spring, it will not return to its original shape. This is called exceeding the spring's elastic limit. Your exam is not likely to deal with this type of spring behavior.

If several springs are used for one application, they can be arranged in one of two ways: in series or in parallel. The easiest way to remember the difference is that if the springs are all hooked together, end to end, then you have a *series* of springs. The other option is for the springs not to be hooked together but to be lined up side by side, *parallel* to each other. If two springs are arranged in *series*, they will stretch much farther than the same two springs arranged in *parallel* under the same pulling force. This is because in series, the total pulling force passes through both springs. If the same springs are arranged in parallel, the pulling force is divided equally with half going through each spring.

Springs in Series:

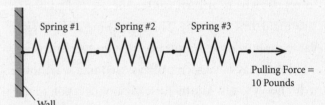

Springs in Parallel:

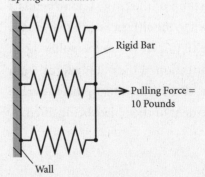

The key to solving spring problems is to draw a diagram of the arrangement, if one isn't already provided, and follow the pulling force through the system.

Valves

A valve is a mechanical device that controls the flow of liquids, gases, or loose material through piping systems. There are many types of valves including butterfly valves, gate valves, plug valves, ball valves, and check valves.

A valve is basically a gate that can be closed or opened in order to permit the fluid or gas to travel in a particular direction. The type of exam question you are likely to see that involves valves will be one in which you must follow a piping flow diagram through several sets of valves. These problems are best approached by taking your time and methodically following each branch of the piping system from start to finish.

Gauges

Gauges are used to monitor various conditions and performance of mechanical machines such as pumps and internal combustion engines, as well as to monitor the surrounding atmospheric conditions which could indirectly affect a particular machine.

Gauges are usually marked with the *units* they are measuring. A few examples of different types of units are:

- Degrees Celsius or Fahrenheit for temperature gauges
- Pounds per square inch (psi) for pressure gauges
- Meters (or sometimes feet) for elevation gauges

You must be very careful to recognize and understand the units of a gauge that appears in a test question. For instance, a temperature gauge (commonly called a thermometer) could use either degrees Fahrenheit or degrees Celsius. Mistakes on units can cause major problems, so be careful! The table on the next page shows some common types of gauges, what they measure, and the kind of units they use.

Gauges are sometimes marked with warnings about limits of safe operation. For instance, an oil pressure gauge on an internal combustion engine may show a maximum safe working pressure of 15 psi. If you're asked about the safe operation of a device with a gauge on it, you should pay careful attention to any markings that show such a limit.

Pumps

A pump is a device used to transfer a liquid or a gas from one location, through a piping system, to another location. There are many different types of pumps, including centrifugal pumps, positive displacement pumps, metering pumps, diaphragm pumps, and progressive cavity pumps.

Generally speaking, a working pump consists of the pump itself (case, bearings, impeller, seals, shaft, base, and other components) and an outside energy source. The outside energy source could be an electric motor, internal combustion engine, or battery to provide mechanical energy to the pump. This energy causes the inner workings of the pump to propel the liquid or gas through the piping system. The flow rate at which the liquid or gas is pushed through the piping system is typically measured by a flow meter in units of gallons per minute (gpm) or cubic feet per minute (cfm).

Pumps are used for many purposes. Some examples include gasoline pumps used to pump the gasoline from a holding tank into your car, water pumps to transfer drinking water from a reservoir to your house or business, and industrial pumps used to move industrial fluids such as chemicals or waste products from

ATMOSPHERIC GAUGES		
Gauge	**What It Measures**	**Units**
Thermometer	temperature	degrees Fahrenheit or Celsius
Barometer	atmospheric pressure	inches or millimeters of mercury
Hygrometer	relative humidity	percentage of water in air
MACHINE PERFORMANCE GAUGES		
Gauge	**What It Measures**	**Units**
Speedometer	velocity	miles per hour (mph) or kilometers per hour (kph)
Tachometer	speed of rotation for equipment such as pumps, internal combustion engines, or fans	revolutions per minute (rpm)
Pressure gauge	internal pressure	pounds per square inch (psi) or inches of water
Flow meter	volume of flow in a piping system	cubic feet per minute (cfm) or gallons per minute (gpm)

one tank to another inside a plant. A car also uses pumps to pump fuel from the gas tank to the engine and to pump coolant from the radiator to the engine block.

SYSTEMS THAT USE MECHANICAL DEVICES

Many mechanical devices are actually a combination of several simple devices that work in conjunction to form a group of interacting mechanical and electrical components called a system. Some of the systems most likely to appear on the exam are discussed below.

INTERNAL COMBUSTION ENGINES

Internal combustion engines (ICEs) are commonly used to drive many mechanical devices. However, they are very complex mechanical devices themselves. ICEs are used in cars, trucks, construction equipment, and many other devices. They can be fueled by gasoline,

diesel fuel, natural gas, or other combustible fossil fuels.

An ICE is a system composed of dozens of individual mechanical (as well as electrical) systems. A few of the major systems within an ICE are discussed below.

The Cooling System

The purpose of the cooling system is to dissipate the heat generated by the engine. The system consists of a pump that moves the coolant, antifreeze, from the radiator through piping to the engine block, where it becomes hot, and then back out to the radiator where the liquid coolant is cooled.

The Pistons, Tie Rods, and Crankshaft

The pistons, tie rods, and crankshaft are all parts of the inner workings of an ICE. When the spark plug inside the engine cylinder ignites the fuel, the piston is forced downward. The piston is mechanically fastened to the tie rod, which is therefore also driven downward. The tie rod is attached to the crankshaft and applies a rotation to the crankshaft. The crankshaft has gears attached to it that are connected to other gears on the transmission. Eventually the power is transferred to the wheels of the car, the inner workings of the pump, or whatever device the ICE is driving.

The Fuel Pump

Fuel, typically gasoline or diesel fuel, is transferred from the tank to the engine by the engine's mechanical fuel pump.

The Throttle Governor

The throttle governor is a device in an ICE that uses a spring to reduce the flow of gas back to idle level when you take your foot off of the gas pedal.

AUTOMOBILES AND OTHER VEHICLES

An automobile is one of the most complex assemblies of mechanical devices in existence. The ICE is only one of many subsystems of mechanical devices on an automobile. A few of the other devices and systems are discussed below.

The Brakes

Automobile brakes are activated by pressing the brake pedal, which compresses a piston that forces hydraulic fluid through the brake line piping. The brake fluid presses against a set of mechanical calipers that squeeze the brake pads against the rotors. The rotation of the wheels is slowed by friction. Several springs are used to return the brake pedal and the calipers to their neutral position.

The Steering Assembly

The steering wheel is attached to a shaft with gears on it. The gears turn to rotate a series of levers that are connected by bolted connections. The levers then cause the wheels to turn.

The Exhaust System

The exhaust system includes a system of piping connected to the engine with welded joints. Several brackets are used to suspend the piping beneath the automobile. The engine's exhaust passes through the piping to the muffler, which is an acoustical chamber that reduces the engine noise.

BICYCLES

A bicycle is not nearly as complex as an automobile. However, it too uses several mechanical devices.

- **The chain drive.** The pedals are connected to the drive gear. A chain is used to connect the drive gear to the gears on the rear wheel.
- **The frame.** Many welded joints are used to hold the frame together.
- **The suspension system.** These days many bikes have suspension systems. The front wheel may use a hydraulic shock absorber. The rear wheel may use two springs in parallel to reduce shock to the rider.

BRUSHING UP ON RELATED TOPICS

Some mechanical aptitude questions may require the use of math or science to determine the correct answer. This chapter cannot cover all the possible questions you might be asked on the firefighter exam, but here are suggestions for ways to increase your knowledge of math, science, and general mechanical aptitude.

Math

The required mathematical skills are primarily arithmetic (addition, subtraction, multiplication, and division) and geometry (angles and shapes). The arithmetic involved is almost always fairly simple. If you had trouble with arithmetic or geometry in your past schooling, you can brush up by reading the math chapter of this book. If you still want more help, pull out your old high school math book or check out a math book from the library.

Science

Science subjects such as physics, materials science, thermodynamics, and chemistry are confusing for some people, but they needn't be. Science is real, everyday life. You see science in action dozens of times every day. A car is stopped by brakes, which use friction (physics). A magnet adheres to the refrigerator due to the properties of the magnet and carbon steel of which the door is made (materials science). A pot of water boils when you set it on the stove and turn on the burner (thermodynamics). A tomato plant grows through the chemical reaction of sunlight, water, and food (chemistry). This chapter has reviewed many of the scientific concepts that are involved in mechanical devices. Again, as with math, you may have science books from previous schooling that you can use to help you solidify your scientific knowledge. If not, the library is full of scientific resources.

General Mechanical Aptitude

Mechanical devices are such an integral part of everyday life that there are many real-life sources you can investigate to gain more knowledge of their design and use. A construction site is a great place to visit for a day to learn more about hand tools, cranes, pumps, and other devices. Ask the construction supervisor if you can take a tour.

Another alternative would be to hang out at an automotive repair shop. Internal combustion engines, lifts, levers, and hand tools are only a few of the types of mechanical devices you could see in use. Yet another possibility would be to visit a local manufacturer in your town. Examples include a foundry, a sheet metal fabricator, an automotive manufacturer, or a pump manufacturer. Look in the yellow pages under "manufacturing" for possibilities.

SAMPLE MECHANICAL APTITUDE QUESTIONS

Now use what you've learned by reading this chapter by answering the following mechanical aptitude questions. Answers are at the end of the chapter.

1. Which of the following tools is used to smooth or level a piece of wood?
   a. a wrench
   b. a screwdriver
   c. a plane
   d. a hammer

2. A compass is used for what purpose?
   a. to measure angles
   b. to tighten and loosen nuts and bolts
   c. to drive and remove nails
   d. to draw circles of various sizes

3. Which of the following is NOT a carpenter's hand tool?
   a. a winch
   b. a level
   c. a compass
   d. a chisel

4. Vice grips are a type of
   a. ax
   b. wrench
   c. ladder
   d. mechanical jack

5. How can gears be used to change the speed of a machine?
   a. use more gears
   b. use two gears of the same size
   c. use two gears of different sizes
   d. use two large gears

6. What is the main function of a pulley?
   a. to increase the strength of a construction crane
   b. to override the power of an electric motor
   c. to add energy to a system
   d. to change the direction of a pulling force

7. Steve has a lever whose pivot point is 3 feet from the 50-pound box he wants to lift. Steve is standing at the other end of the lever, 6 feet from the pivot point. How much force must he apply to lift the box?

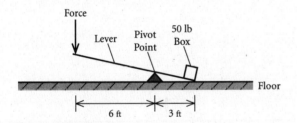

   a. 50 pounds
   b. 25 pounds
   c. 100 pounds
   d. 6 pounds

8. Which of the following is NOT a mechanical process for fastening?
   a. welding
   b. buttoning
   c. bolting
   d. covalent bonding

9. When three identical springs are arranged in series and a pulling force of 10 pounds is applied, the total stretch is 9 inches. If these same three springs were arranged in parallel and the same 10-pound force is applied to the new arrangement, what will be the total distance of stretch?

Springs in Series:

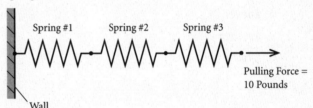

Springs in Parallel:

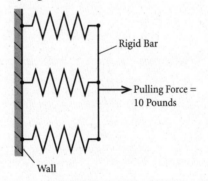

   a. 3 inches
   b. 4.5 inches
   c. 9 inches
   d. 18 inches

10. What type of gauge uses units of rpm?
a. a pressure gauge
b. a tachometer
c. a speedometer
d. a thermometer

11. What type of outside energy source could be used to operate a pump?
a. a battery
b. an internal combustion engine
c. an electric motor
d. all of the above

12. What type of mechanical device is used to aid in cooling of an internal combustion engine?
a. a pump
b. a lever
c. a gauge
d. a hammer

13. Of the following mechanical devices on an automobile, which one uses friction to accomplish its purpose?
a. the steering system
b. the exhaust system
c. the braking system
d. the internal combustion engine

14. The suspension system on a bicycle is likely to use which of the following mechanical devices?
a. a chain
b. a pulley
c. a gear
d. a spring

How to Answer Mechanical Aptitude Questions

- Read each problem carefully. Questions may contain words such as *not, all,* or *mostly,* which can be tricky unless you pay attention.
- Read the entire question once or even a few times before trying to pick an answer. Decide exactly what the question is asking. Take notes and draw pictures on scratch paper. That way you won't waste time by going in the wrong direction.
- Some questions will require the use of math (typically addition, subtraction, multiplication, and division) and science. In these situations, think about what you have learned previously in school.
- Use your common sense. Some mechanical devices can seem intimidating at first but are really a combination of a few simple items. Try to break complicated questions down into smaller, manageable pieces.
- Answer the questions that are easiest for you first. You do not have to go in order from start to finish. Read each question and, if you are not sure what to do, move on to the next question. You can go back to harder questions if you have time at the end.
- Many mechanical devices are commonly used in everyday life. You do not have to be a mechanic or an engineer to use these devices. If something seems unfamiliar, try to think of items around your house that might be similar.
- Don't be intimidated by unfamiliar terms. In most instances, there are clues in the question that will point you towards the correct answer, and some of the answers can be ruled out by common sense.

ANSWERS TO SAMPLE QUESTIONS

1. **c.** See the table under "Carpenter's Tools" earlier in this chapter for the functions of the items listed.

2. **d.** As defined under "Carpenter's Tools," a compass is used to draw circles.

3. **a.** A level, a compass, and a chisel are all carpenter's hand tools.

4. **b.** Vice grips are a kind of wrench.

5. **c.** Changing gears on a ten-speed bicycle is a good example of using different size gears to change speed.

6. **d.** Pulleys are used to change not the strength of a force but its direction.

7. **b.** Apply the distance formula, $w \times d_1 = f \times d_2$, to come up with the equation $50 \times 3 = f \times 6$. Solve for the unknown f by multiplying 3 times 50 to get 150 and then dividing by 6 to get 25 pounds.

8. **d.** A covalent bond is a chemical bond. Welding, buttoning, and bolting are all mechanical fastening processes.

9. **a.** The total pulling force will be divided equally, with each spring experiencing one-third of the total force. Since the force is divided by 3, the amount of movement will be divided by 3 also. The original configuration stretched 9 inches, so the new arrangement will stretch only 3 inches.

10. **b.** A tachometer measures rotation in units of revolutions per minute or rpm.

11. **d.** Any of the energy sources listed could be used to operate a pump.

12. **a.** As discussed in the section "Internal Combustion Engines" earlier in this chapter, a pump is used to help cool an ICE.

13. **c.** The braking system uses friction to slow or stop the rotation of the wheels.

14. **d.** Springs are commonly used in suspension systems.

C·H·A·P·T·E·R 11

SPATIAL RELATIONS

CHAPTER SUMMARY

Firefighter exams often include questions that test your ability to read maps, floor plans, and pictures. This chapter shows you how to tackle such questions on spatial relationships.

magine you are shopping in a local mall. You look at the store directory to find the closest restaurant. You locate the arrow that says "You Are Here." Do you know where you are? Do you know which way to go to find the restaurant?

The store directory has just asked a typical spatial relations question. Spatial relations is the ability to visualize in three dimensions. As the store directory example suggests, everyone needs to be able to translate a two-dimensional representation into a three-dimensional sense of where they are and where they want to go. But this ability is particularly important for firefighters, who must read maps and floor plans in order to get to the people who need their help.

Spatial relations questions on a firefighter exam are based on a map, a building floor plan, or a picture, usually accompanied by a short explanation of the scene. The examiners may give you a picture of a street with apartment buildings, houses, and stores, possibly including a fire scene containing apparatus and personnel. The questions require you to locate certain points or give details on objects shown in the picture. The answers to the questions can all be found in the diagram; however you must read each question carefully and pay close attention to the details.

READING A MAP

Many spatial relations questions are based on maps. Map reading skills are essential to the work of a firefighter. Firefighters are expected to be able to figure out the quickest route to the scene of an emergency without hesitation. They are frequently stopped by lost motorists trying to find their way. Pedestrians often come into the firehouse to ask directions.

QUESTIONS ON THE MOST DIRECT ROUTE

Map-based questions typically ask for the most direct route between two points. As you answer such questions, keep in mind that you must choose the best legal route, observing one-way streets and traffic rules. When giving directions to pedestrians, you don't have to consider the flow of traffic, so providing them with the shortest route may be easier to do. Take a systematic approach to answering this type of question, using the following procedure:

1. **Look at the map.** Take a moment to scan the buildings and streets. Locate the legend, if any; it tells you which way is north and explains any special symbols, such as those indicating one-way streets.

2. **Read the question.** Read carefully and be sure you understand what is being asked. Do not read the answer choices at this time. Read only the question so that you can plot the route yourself. That way, you're less likely to be con-

fused by incorrect choices purposely included to distract you.

3. **Return to the map.** Locate the information asked for in the question. Look at the street names and traffic patterns.

4. **Prepare your answer by tracing your route.** Remember to observe any traffic rules that are necessary. Write down the route you have selected. Read the question again. Have you understood what was asked, and have you answered correctly?

5. **Read the answer choices.** Be very observant, as the choices may be very similar to each other. Does one of the choices match your route *exactly*? Some answers may *almost* match your route but contain one wrong direction, for example, using north when you are supposed to go south. If you do not find an answer choice that matches yours exactly, reread the question and try again. Carefully review the question to see what is being asked. Do you understand the question? Have you mapped out the correct directions in selecting this route?

A street map is on the next page. Following the map are questions that ask you to find the best route based on the map. After each question is a detailed explanation of how to use the procedure outlined above to find the correct answer.

A firefighter is often required to assist civilians who seek travel directions or referral to city agencies and facilities. The accompanying map shows a section of the city where some public buildings are located. Each of the squares represent one city block. Street names are as shown. If there is an arrow next to the street name, it means the street traffic is one way in the direction of the arrow. If there is no arrow next to the street name, two-way traffic is allowed. Answer questions 1–4 on the basis of this map.

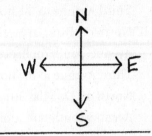

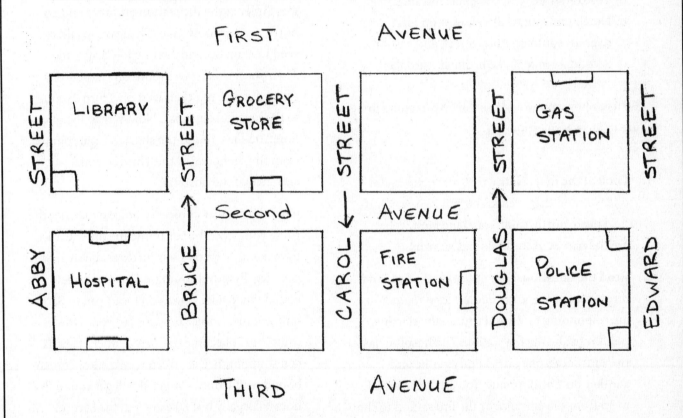

1. Your company must respond to a reported fire at the Third Avenue entrance of the hospital. What is the shortest legal route the engine can take?
   a. South on Douglas Street, west on Second Avenue, north on Carol Street, and west on Third Avenue to the hospital entrance.
   b. North on Douglas Street, west on Second Avenue, south on Bruce Street, and west on Third Avenue to the hospital entrance.
   c. North on Douglas Street, west on Second Avenue, south on Carol Street, and west on Third Avenue to the hospital entrance.
   d. North on Douglas Street, west on First Avenue, south on Abby Street, and east on Second Avenue to the hospital entrance.

Here's how you would use the map-reading procedure to answer question 1:

1. **Look at the map.** Notice that some streets are one way and that avenues permit two-way traffic. Locate north, south, east, and west. What are the names of the buildings shown?

2. **Read the question.** Take note of key words and directions, in this case, *shortest legal route*. You are responding to a fire alarm, so the starting point must be the fire station. The hospital has two entrances, one on Second Avenue and another on Third Avenue. You are being asked to go from the entrance of the fire station to the Third Avenue entrance of the hospital using the shortest legal route.

3. **Return to the map.** Locate the fire station entrance. It is on Douglas Street between Second Avenue and Third Avenue. Douglas Street is one way going north. The hospital entrance you are asked to report to is on Third Avenue between Abby Street and Bruce Street. Avenues allow two-way traffic, but Bruce Street is one way going north. You need to go south in order to get to Third Avenue. Abby Street is a two-way street but you would have to go past the hospital to use it. Carol Street, which is one-way going south, is the better option.

4. **Prepare your answer by tracing your route.** After careful consideration, you find that the shortest legal route would be to start on Douglas Street at the fire station entrance and go north to Second Avenue. Then you would proceed west on Second Avenue to Carol Street. Then you would travel south on Carol Street to Third Avenue and then west on Third Avenue to the hospital entrance. Now, reread the question. You have found the shortest legal route from the firehouse to the Third Avenue entrance of the hospital.

5. **Read the answer choices.** Choice **c** matches the route you chose, but examine the other choices to make sure. Choice **a** is incorrect because you can't legally travel south on Douglas Street, and, if you could, it wouldn't lead you to Second Avenue. Choice **b** is close to your chosen route, but it becomes incorrect when it sends you south on Bruce Street, which allows northbound traffic only. Choice **d** will get you to the hospital legally but takes you to the Second Avenue entrance of the hospital instead of the Third Avenue entrance. It also takes you out of the way by traveling on First Avenue to Abby Street.

Use the same procedure to answer the next question.

2. The delivery boy from the grocery store calls to ask directions to the firehouse so that he can walk over with the order. You should direct him to walk
   a. west on Second Avenue to Douglas Street, make a left, and go half a block to the firehouse
   b. east on Second Avenue to Douglas Street, make a right, and go half a block to the firehouse
   c. west on Second Avenue to Douglas Street, make a right, and go half a block to the firehouse
   d. east on First Avenue to Douglas Street, make a left, and go half a block to the firehouse

The delivery boy needs to walk from the grocery store to the firehouse. First, locate the grocery store and the firehouse. The grocery store is on Second Avenue between Bruce Street and Carol Street. The firehouse is on Douglas Street between Second and Third Avenues. Since the delivery boy is walking, you can ignore the one-way streets. Trace a route: beginning at the grocery store, the delivery boy should walk east on Second Avenue to Douglas Street, turn right, and go half a block to the firehouse.

Now read the answer choices. Choice **b** is the route you would have directed the delivery boy to use to get from the grocery store to the firehouse. Choices **a** and **c** have him walking west on Second Avenue, which is not the correct direction from the grocery store to the firehouse. Choice **d** has the delivery boy walking on First Avenue, which is not where the entrance to the grocery store is located, and left on Douglas Street, which will not take him to the firehouse.

QUESTIONS ON FINDING YOUR LOCATION OR DIRECTION

Map questions may also ask you for your location after following a series of directions. These questions, while worded differently, should be answered using the same procedure:

1. Look at the map.

2. Read the question.

3. Return to the map and follow the directions given.

4. Go back to the question and examine the answer choices to see which one matches the direction or location you found in step 3.

Try this procedure on the questions that follow, using the same map given previously.

3. You are on the corner of First Avenue and Abby Street. Drive east two blocks, south one block, and west half a block. You are in front of the
   a. hospital
   b. library
   c. fire station
   d. grocery store

Trace the steps given in the question on the map, paying careful attention to the specific directions, north, south, east, and west. Turn the map as you go to help you keep track of where you are. You have arrived in front of the grocery store, choice **d**.

4. You are walking north on Bruce Street. You turn right on Second Avenue, walk two blocks to Douglas Street, and turn right. What direction are you now facing?

   a. north

   b. south

   c. east

   d. west

The answer to this question is also found by tracing the steps given in the question. Again, turn the map as you are reading the directions indicated. If you are facing north on Bruce Street, a right turn will leave you walking east. Turning right onto Douglas Street, leaves you facing south, choice **b**.

READING A FLOOR PLAN

A floor plan is a map of the interior of a building, apartment, or house. The ability to read floor plans and visualize your position is critical if you want to be a firefighter. Firefighters sometimes find themselves crawling down dark and smoky hallways. Knowing the location of doors, windows, and rooms in an apartment on fire may mean the difference between life and death. If fire conditions in the apartment worsen, you do not want to crawl into a closet while trying to find the exit. Firefighters also need to know the location of fire apparatus and personnel, the fire itself, and victims; furthermore, they have to be aware of the risk of the fire spreading to adjoining buildings or apartments.

In questions based on floor plans, your ability to observe and judge location and potential hazards are being challenged to see if you have what it takes to become a firefighter. The floor plan or fire scene may be accompanied by a brief explanation of what the picture shows. The questions may ask the number of exits, windows, bedrooms, or smoke detectors. You may be asked where you would position a ladder to attempt a rescue or which room you are in based on a set of directions.

Handle floor-plan questions in the same manner as those on maps. Before attempting to answer any questions, look at the diagram. Familiarize yourself with such features as doors, windows, doorways, patio doors, fire extinguishers, and smoke detectors. Read each question carefully. Then return to the diagram to find the answer. After you've determined your answer, try to match it to the choices. The correct answer should be apparent, but read each choice carefully to avoid making unnecessary errors. Never jump at one option without carefully reading all the others.

A floor plan is on the next page. Apply the procedure outlined above to answer the questions that come after it.

Office buildings and apartment buildings may post floor plans at the front entrance or by the elevators to assist visitors. Firefighters arriving at the scene of a fire must be able to read a floor plan quickly and develop a mental picture of the interior. When there is a fire, the smoke can be very thick, so firefighters need to know their way in and out without seeing where they are. The diagram on the next page shows two apartments on the first floor of a building. Answer questions 5–8 based on this diagram.

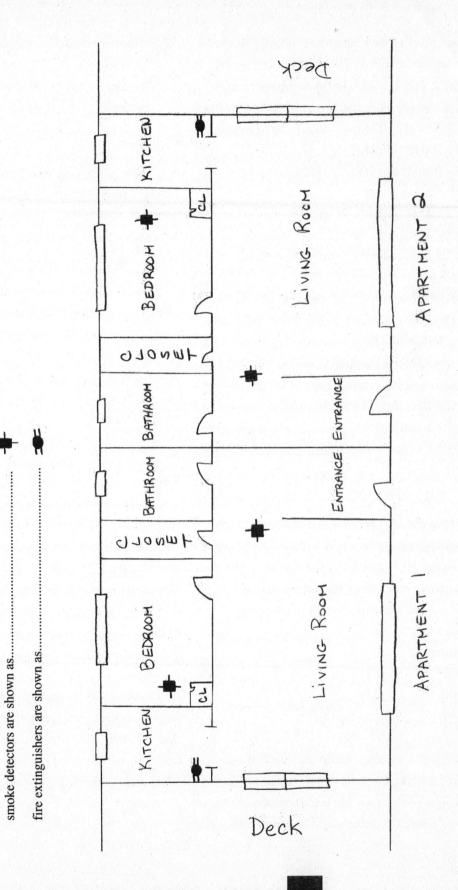

doors are shown as..............

windows are shown as..............

doorways are shown as..............

patio doors are shown as..............

smoke detectors are shown as..............

fire extinguishers are shown as..............

5. Firefighters arrive at the scene to find that there is a woman trapped in the bedroom of apartment 2. There is a fire in the living room, and the entrance to the apartment is blocked by fire. What would be the most direct way to rescue the trapped woman?

    a. Go into the apartment through the patio doors.

    b. Climb through the kitchen window.

    c. Climb through the bedroom window.

    d. Climb through the bathroom window.

The question asks for an alternate way to reach the bedroom of apartment 2, since the entrance is blocked. A look at the floor plan shows that choices **a, b,** and **d** would bring the firefighters through the living room, where the fire is located. Choice **c,** which brings you directly into the bedroom, is the fastest and safest means of entering the apartment and rescuing the woman with the least risk of injuring either her or the rescuers.

6. A fire in the kitchen has filled apartment 1 with smoke. You must reach the bedroom to search for sleeping occupants. Visibility is near zero as you are crawling down the entry hall. How many doors will you encounter before you reach the bedroom?

    a. none

    b. six

    c. four

    d. two

To answer this question, locate the entrance to apartment 1 and trace a route down the hall and to the bedroom. You would pass the bathroom door and a closet door before the bedroom: two doors, choice **d.**

7. How many bathrooms are there in apartment 1?

    a. one

    b. two

    c. three

    d. four

Review the diagram. Two apartments are shown, labeled 1 and 2. The question asks for the number of bathrooms in apartment 1. Apartment 1 contains one bathroom, choice **a.** If you counted all the bathrooms shown on the diagram, you would incorrectly choose **b.**

8. How many smoke detectors and fire extinguishers are there in apartments 1 and 2?

    a. six

    b. ten

    c. four

    d. three

The answer is **a.** You must read the question carefully to see that it asks you to look at *both* apartments and to find *two* items, the smoke detectors and the fire extinguishers. There are two smoke detectors and one fire extinguisher in each apartment. If you counted the smoke detectors (but not the fire extinguishers) in both apartments, you would have chosen **c.** On the other hand, if you counted both smoke detectors and fire extinguishers, but only in one apartment, you would have thought choice **d** was correct.

The ability to understand spatial relations is an important firefighting tool. Can you apply what you see and mentally navigate yourself through the city or a building, while paying close attention to detail? That's what these questions try to assess.

How to Answer Spatial Relations Questions

- First, familiarize yourself with the map or diagram.
- Next, read the question carefully to determine what you are being asked to do.
- Return to the diagram and find your own answer before reading the choices given.
- Reread the question and the answer choices. Don't rush; read all the possible choices. Misleading answers are placed on the test to see if you can be caught not paying attention.
- If the answer you found does not match the choices, look at the question thoroughly, return to the diagram, and go over your options to see what you missed.
- Remember, the answers to the questions are right there in the map or diagram. Take your time, read to understand and think through your answers.

C · H · A · P · T · E · R
VERBAL EXPRESSION

CHAPTER SUMMARY

This chapter will help you brush up your vocabulary and grammar skills so that you'll be able to do well on exam questions that test your ability to express yourself in writing.

Some questions on the firefighter exam test how well you can use words to express yourself. Basically, there are two different kinds of questions: **vocabulary** questions ask you to identify the meanings of words, while **clarity** questions ask you which is the best way to express the information given in the question.

Here's an example of a **vocabulary** question:

Choose the word that most nearly means the same as the *italicized* word.

1. The mechanic inspected the faulty hydraulic system and discovered that it was *defective*.
   a. efficient
   b. offensive
   c. flawed
   d. powerful

The answer is **c**. Something that is *defective* contains a *flaw* that keeps it from working or looking as it should.

The context clue in this sentence is the word *faulty.* Hydraulic systems may be *efficient* (choice **a**) or *powerful* (choice **d**), but these choices don't fit the context of the sentence. Choice **b** can be ruled out because *flawed* is clearly a better choice than *offensive.*

Clarity questions ask you to choose the sentence that states an idea most clearly and accurately.

Here's one type of clarity question:

2. A firefighter notices a leaking fire hydrant near 612 36th Street. This is between Woodland Avenue and Grand Avenue. Which of the following states the problem most clearly and accurately?
   a. The hydrant was leaking between Woodland and Grand Avenue. It's all wet and needs to be fixed.
   b. There's a leaking hydrant near 612 on 36th Street. That's between Grand and Woodland.
   c. At 612 between Grand and Woodland is a leaking hydrant.
   d. There's a leaking hydrant at Grand and Woodland at 36th Street. It's near 612.

The best answer is **b**. This answer choice states the problem and gives the exact location in the first sentence. It further identifies the location by mentioning the nearest cross streets.

This chapter explains in detail how to handle both vocabulary and clarity questions.

VOCABULARY

Many firefighter exams test vocabulary. There are two basic kinds of questions.

■ **Synonyms:** Identifying words that mean the same as the given words

■ **Context:** Determining the meaning of a word or phrase by noting how it is used in a sentence or paragraph

SYNONYM QUESTIONS

A word is a *synonym* of another word if it has the same or nearly the same meaning as the other word. Test questions often ask you to find the synonym or antonym of a word. If you're lucky, the word will be surrounded by a sentence that helps you guess what the word means. If you're less lucky, you'll just get the word, and then you have to figure out what the word means without any help.

Questions that ask for synonyms can be tricky because they require you to recognize the meaning of several words that may be unfamiliar—not only the words in the questions but also the answer choices. Usually the best strategy is to *look* at the structure of the word and to *listen* for its sound. See if a part of a word looks familiar. Think of other words you know that have similar key elements. How could those words be related?

Synonym Practice

Try your hand at identifying the word parts and related words in these sample synonym questions. Circle the word that means the same or about the same as the italicized word. Answers and explanations appear right after the questions.

3. *incoherent* answer
   a. not understandable
   b. not likely
   c. undeniable
   d. challenging

4. *ambiguous* questions
   a. meaningless
   b. difficult
   c. simple
   d. vague

5. covered with *debris*
   a. good excuses
   b. transparent material
   c. scattered rubble
   d. protective material

6. *inadvertently* left
   a. mistakenly
   b. purposely
   c. cautiously
   d. carefully

7. *exorbitant* prices
   a. bargain
   b. unexpected
   c. reasonable
   d. outrageous

8. *compatible* workers
   a. gifted
   b. competitive
   c. harmonious
   d. experienced

9. *belligerent* attitude
   a. hostile
   b. reasonable
   c. instinctive
   d. friendly

Answers to Synonym Questions

The explanations are just as important as the answers, because they show you how to go about choosing a synonym if you don't know the word.

3. **a.** *Incoherent* means *not understandable*. To *cohere* means *to connect*. A coherent answer connects or makes sense. The prefix *in-* means *not*.

4. **d.** *Ambiguous* questions are *vague* or uncertain. The key part of this word is *ambi-*, which means *two* or *both*. An ambiguous question can be taken two ways.

5. **c.** *Debris* is scattered fragments and trash.

6. **a.** *Inadvertently* means *by mistake*. The key element in this word is the prefix *in-*, which usually means *not, the opposite of.*

7. **d.** The key element here is *ex-*, which means *out of* or *away from*. Exorbitant literally means "out of orbit." An *exorbitant* price would be an *outrageous* one.

8. **c.** *Compatible* means *harmonious*.

9. **a.** The key element in this word is the root *belli-*, which means *warlike*. The synonym choice, then, is *hostile*.

CONTEXT QUESTIONS

Context is the surrounding text in which a word is used. Most people use context to help them determine the meaning of an unknown word. A vocabulary question that gives you a sentence around the vocabulary word is usually easier to answer than one with little or no context. The surrounding text can help you as you look for synonyms for the specified words in the sentences.

The best way to take meaning from context is to look for key words in sentences or paragraphs that convey the meaning of the text. If nothing else, the context will give you a means to eliminate wrong answer choices that clearly don't fit. The process of elimination will often leave you with the correct answer.

Context Practice

Try these sample questions. Choose the word that most nearly means the same as the italicized word in the sentence.

10. The maintenance workers were *appalled* by the filthy, cluttered condition of the building.
  a. horrified
  b. amused
  c. surprised
  d. dismayed

11. Even though he seemed rich, the defendent claimed to be *destitute*.
  a. wealthy
  b. ambitious
  c. solvent
  d. poor

12. Though she was *distraught* over the disappearance of her child, the woman was calm enough to give the officer her description.
  a. punished
  b. distracted
  c. composed
  d. anguished

13. The evil criminal expressed no *remorse* for his actions.
  a. sympathy
  b. regret
  c. reward
  d. complacency

Some tests may ask you to fill in the blank by choosing a word that fits the context. In the following questions, choose the word that best completes the sentence.

14. Professor Washington was a very_____ man known for his reputation as a scholar.
  a. stubborn
  b. knowledgeable
  c. illiterate
  d. disciplined

15. His_____was demonstrated by his willingness to donate large amounts of money to worthy causes.
  a. honesty
  b. loyalty
  c. selfishness
  d. altruism

Answers to Context Questions

Check to see whether you were able to pick out the key words that help you define the target word, as well as whether you got the right answer.

10. a. The key words *filthy* and *cluttered* signify horror rather than the milder emotions described by the other choices.

11. d. The key word here is *rich*, but this is a clue by contrast. The introductory *Even though* signals that you should look for the opposite of the idea of having financial resources.

12. d. The key words here are *though* and *disappearance of her child*, signalling that you are looking for an opposite of *calm* in describing how the mother spoke to the officer. The only word strong enough to match the situation is *anguish*.

13. b. *Remorse* means *regret* for one's action. The part of the word here to beware of is the prefix *re-*. It doesn't signify anything in this word, though it often means again or back. Don't be confused by the two choices that also contain the prefix *re-*. The strategy here is to see which word sounds better in the sentence. The key words are *evil* and *no*, indicating that you're looking for something that shows no repentance.

14. b. The key words here are *professor* and *scholarly*.

15. d. The key words here are *large amounts of money to worthy causes*. They give you a definition of the word you're looking for. Even if you don't know the word *altruism*, the other choices seem inappropriate to describe someone so generous.

For Non-Native Speakers of English
Be very careful not to be confused by the *sound* of words that may mislead you. Be sure to look at the word carefully, and pay attention to the structure and appearance of the word as well as its sound. You may be used to hearing English words spoken with an accent. The sounds of those words may be misleading in choosing a correct answer.

WORD PARTS

The best way to improve your vocabulary is to learn word parts: roots, which are the main part of the word; prefixes, which go before the root word; or suffixes, which go after. Any of these elements can carry meaning or change the use of a word in a sentence. For instance, the suffix *-s* or *-es* can change the meaning of a noun from singular to plural: *boy, boys*. The prefix *un-* can change the meaning of a root word to its opposite: *necessary, unnecessary*.

On the next page are some of the word elements seen most often in vocabulary tests. Simply reading them and their examples five to ten minutes a day will give you the quick recognition you need to make a good association with the meaning of an unfamiliar word.

word element	meaning	example
ama	love	amateur
ambi	both	ambivalent, ambidextrous
aud	hear	audition
bell	war	belligerent, bellicose
bene	good	benefactor
cid/cis	cut	homicide, scissor
cogn/gno	know	knowledge, recognize
curr	run	current
flu/flux	flow	fluid, fluctuate
gress	to go	congress, congregation
in	not, in	ingenious
ject	throw	inject, reject
luc/lux	light	lucid, translucent
neo	new	neophyte
omni	all	omnivorous
pel/puls	push	impulse, propeller
pro	forward	project
pseudo	false	pseudonym
rog	ask	interrogate
sub	under	subjugate
spec/spic	look, see	spectator
super	over	superfluous
temp	time	contemporary, temporal
un	not, opposite	uncoordinated
viv	live	vivid

MORE VOCABULARY PRACTICE

Here is another set of practice exercises with samples of each kind of question covered in this chapter. Answers are at the end of the exercise.

Choose the word that means the same or nearly the same as the italicized word.

16. *congenial* company
   a. friendly
   b. dull
   c. tiresome
   d. angry

17. *conspicuous* mess
   a. secret
   b. notable
   c. visible
   d. boorish

18. *meticulous* record-keeping
   a. dishonest
   b. casual
   c. painstaking
   d. careless

19. *superficial* wounds
   a. life-threatening
   b. bloody
   c. severe
   d. surface

20. *impulsive* actions
   a. cautious
   b. sudden
   c. courageous
   d. cowardly

21. *tactful* comments
   a. polite
   b. rude
   c. angry
   d. confused

Using the context, choose the word that means the same or nearly the same as the italicized word.

22. Though flexible about homework, the teacher was *adamant* that papers be in on time.
   a. liberal
   b. casual
   c. strict
   d. pliable

23. The condition of the room after the party was *deplorable*.
   a. regrettable
   b. pristine
   c. festive
   d. tidy

Choose the word that best completes the following sentences.

24. Her position as a(n) _____ teacher took her all over the city.
   a. primary
   b. secondary
   c. itinerant
   d. permanent

25. Despite her promise to stay in touch, she remained _____ and difficult to locate.
   a. steadfast
   b. stubborn
   c. dishonest
   d. elusive

How to Answer Vocabulary Questions

- The key to answering vocabulary questions is to **notice and connect** what you do know to what you may not recognize.
- **Know your word parts.** You can recognize or make a good guess at the meanings of words when you see some suggested meaning in a root word, prefix, or suffix.
- **Use a process of elimination.** Think of how the word makes sense in the sentence.
- **Don't be confused by words that sound like other words,** but may have no relation to the word you need.

Answers to Practice Vocabulary Questions

16. a.
17. c.
18. c.
19. d.
20. b.
21. a.
22. c.
23. a.
24. c.
25. d.

CLARITY

Your communication skills may be tested in another way, by seeing how well you can express a given idea orally or in writing. You may be asked to read two or more versions of the same information and then choose the one that most clearly and accurately presents the given information, the **best** option. The **best** option should be:

- Accurate
- Clear
- Logical
- Grammatically correct

Imagine this situation:

It is 2:30 on Tuesday, August 22. You are driving Vehicle #25, heading west on NW 91st Street. Your coworker Alex Thorp is riding on the platform at the back of the truck. Just as you round the corner to head north on Park Place, he loses his grip and falls from the truck. You stop immediately to see if he is hurt. He says he's fine, but about an hour later his wrist hurts badly enough that he asks you to take him to the hospital. You go to the Mercy Medical Center. The doctor who examines him says the wrist is mildly fractured.

The information above can be expressed accurately or inaccurately, clearly or unclearly, logically or illogically, grammatically or ungrammatically. The examples below will show you how this works.

ACCURATE

Check the facts for accuracy first. If the facts are wrong or confused in a particular answer choice, that choice is wrong, no matter how well written it is.

Inaccurate

Alex Thorp was in #25 on NE 91st when he fell off onto Park Place because he broke his wrist. I stopped, but he wasn't hurt. Later the doctor said he had a fractured wrist. It was 3:30 on Tuesday, August 22.

Accurate

Around 2:30 on Tuesday, August 22, Alex Thorp fell from the back platform of #25 while I was turning the corner from the west lane of NW 91st to go north on Park Place. About an hour later he asked to go to the hospital. The doctor said his wrist was fractured.

CLEAR

The **best** answer is written in plain English in such a way that most readers can understand it the first time through. If you read through an answer choice and then need to reread it to know what it means, look for a better option.

Garbled

On or about 2:30 on Tuesday, August 22, my coworker Alex Thorp and I were headed westbound on NW 91st Street. As I proceeded around the corner to head northbound on Park Place, he lost his grip and suffered an unknown injury. Later we went to Mercy Medical Center to seek a doctor's attention, who said it was fractured wrist, only mildly.

Clear

Around 2:30 on Tuesday, August 22, I was driving Vehicle #25, and Alex Thorp was riding on the back platform. He lost his grip and fell as I

rounded a corner from NW 91st west onto Park Place north. He thought he was all right at first, but about an hour later he asked to go to the hospital. The doctor who saw him at Mercy Medical Center said he had a mildly fractured wrist.

LOGICAL

The **best** answer will present information in logical order, usually time order. If the information seems disorganized, look for a better option.

Illogical Order

The doctor said Alex's wrist was mildly fractured. It happened when he fell off the back of Vehicle #25. He went to the doctor later at Mercy Medical Center. It didn't hurt at first. He lost his grip. I turned from NW 91st west onto Park Place north. This was Tuesday, August 22, at around 2:30.

Logical Order

Around 2:30 on Tuesday, August 22, Alex Thorp lost his grip while riding on the back platform of Vehicle #25 as I was driving around the corner from NW 91st west onto Park Place north. He didn't realize he was hurt until about an hour later. I took him to Mercy Medical Center where a doctor examined him and said he had a mildly fractured wrist.

In addition to accuracy, clarity, and logic, below are some other characteristics of well-written, grammatically correct sentences that you can look for.

MATCHING PRONOUNS

The **best** answer contains clearly identified pronouns (*he, she, him, her, them,* etc.) that match the number of nouns they represent. First, the pronouns should be clearly identified.

Unclear

Ann Dorr and the supervisor went to the central office, where she made her report.

Bob reminded his father that he had an appointment.

Clear

Ann Dorr and the supervisor went to the central office, where the supervisor made her report.

Bob reminded his father that Bob had an appointment.

An answer choice with clearly identified pronouns is a better choice than one with uncertain pronoun references. Sometimes the noun must be repeated to make the meaning clear.

In addition, the pronoun must match the noun it represents. If the noun is singular, the pronoun must be singular. Similarly, if the noun is plural, the pronoun must match.

Mismatch

I stopped the driver to tell them a headlight was burned out.

Match

I stopped the driver to tell him a headlight was burned out.

In the first example, *driver* is singular but the pronoun *them* is plural. In the second, the singular pronoun *him* matches the word it refers to.

CONSISTENT VERBS

The **best** option is one in which the verb tense is consistent. Look for answer choices that describe the action as though it has already happened, using past tense verbs (mostly *-ed* forms). The verb tense must remain consistent throughout the passage.

Inconsistent

I searched the cell and find nothing unusual.

Consistent

I searched the cell and found nothing unusual.

The verbs *opened* and *found* are both in the past tense in the second version. In the first, *find,* in the present tense, is inconsistent with *opened.*

It's easy to distinguish present tense from past tense by simply fitting the verb into a sentence.

VERB TENSE	
Present tense (Today, I ___ ...)	**Past Tense (Yesterday, I ___ ...)**
drive	drove
think	thought
rise	rose
catch	caught

The important thing to remember about verb tense is to keep it consistent. If a passage begins in the present tense, keep it in the present tense unless there is a specific reason to change—to indicate that some action occurred in the past, for instance. If a passage begins in the past tense, it should remain in the past tense.

Check yourself with these sample questions. Choose the option that uses verb tense correctly. The answers are right after the questions.

26. a. When I cry, I always get what I want.

    b. When I cry, I always got what I want.

    c. When I cried, I always got what I want.

    d. When I cried, I always get what I wanted.

27. a. It all started after I came home and am in my room studying for a big test.

    b. It all started after I came home and was in my room studying for a big test.

    c. It all starts after I come home and was in my room studying for a big test.

    d. It all starts after I came home and am in my room studying for a big test.

28. a. The child became excited and dashes into the house and slams the door.

    b. The child becomes excited and dashed into the house and slammed the door.

    c. The child becomes excited and dashes into the house and slammed the door.

    d. The child became excited and dashed into the house and slammed the door.

Answers

26. a.

27. b.

28. d.

CLEAR MODIFIERS

The **best** option will use words clearly. Watch for unclear modifying words or phrases such as the ones in the following sentences. Misplaced and dangling modifiers can be hard to spot because your brain tries to make sense of things as it reads. In the case of misplaced or dangling modifiers, you may make a logical connection that is not present in the words.

Dangling Modifiers

Nailed to the tree, Cedric saw a "No Hunting" sign.

Waddling down the road, we saw a skunk.

Clear Modifiers

Cedric saw a "No Hunting" sign nailed to a tree.

We saw a skunk waddling down the road.

In the first version of the sentences, it sounds like *Cedric* was nailed to a tree and *we* were waddling down the road. The second version probably represents the writer's intentions: the *sign* was nailed to a tree and the *skunk* was waddling.

Misplaced Modifier

A dog followed the boy who was growling and barking.

George told us about safe sex in the kitchen.

Clear Modifiers

A dog who was growling and barking followed the boy.

In the kitchen, George told us about safe sex.

Do you think the boy was growling and barking? Did George discuss avoiding sharp knives and household poisons? The second version of each sentence represents the real situation.

EFFICIENT LANGUAGE

Finally, the **best** option will use words efficiently. Avoid answer choices that are redundant (repeat unnecessarily) or wordy. Extra words take up valuable time and increase the chances that facts will be misunderstood. In the following examples, the italicized words are redundant or unnecessary. Try reading the sentences without the italicized words.

Redundant

They refunded our money *back to us*.

We can proceed *ahead* with the plan we made *ahead of time*.

The car was red *in color*.

Wordy

The reason we left *was* because the job was done.

We didn't know what *it was* we were doing.

There are many citizens *who* obey the law.

In each case, the sentence is simpler and easier to read without the italicized words. When you find an answer choice that uses unnecessary words, look for a better option.

COMPLETE

The best option will be written in complete sentences. Sentences are the basic unit of written language. Most writing is done using complete sentences, so it's important to distinguish sentences from fragments. A sentence expresses a complete thought, while a fragment requires something more to express a complete thought.

Look at the word groups in the next column.

Fragment

The dog walking down the street.

Exploding from the bat for a home run.

Complete Sentence

The dog was walking down the street.

The ball exploded from the bat for a home run.

These examples show that a sentence must have a subject and a verb to complete its meaning. The first fragment has a subject but not a verb. *Walking* looks like a verb, but it is actually an adjective describing *dog*. The second fragment has neither a subject nor a verb. *Exploding* looks like a verb, but it actually describes something not identified in the word group.

Now look at the next set of word groups. Mark those that are complete sentences.

29. a. We saw the tornado approaching.
    b. When we saw the tornado approaching.

30. a. Before the house was built in 1972.
    b. The house was built in 1972.

31. a. Since we are leaving in the morning.
    b. We are leaving in the morning.

If you chose **29. a.**, **30.b.**, and **31.b.**, you were correct. You may have noticed that the groups of words are the same, but the fragments have an extra word at the beginning. These words are called subordinating conjunctions. If a group of words that would normally be a complete sentence is preceded by a subordinating conjunction, something more is needed to complete the thought.

- When we saw the tornado approaching, we headed for cover.

- Before the house was built in 1972, the old house was demolished.
- Since we were leaving in the morning, we went to bed early.

Here is a list of words that can be used as subordinating conjunctions.

after	that
although	though
as	unless
because	until
before	when
if	whenever
once	where
since	wherever
than	while

SPECIFIC LANGUAGE

Language that is specific and detailed says more than language that is general and vague.

General

My sister and I enjoyed each other's company as we were growing up. We had a lot of fun, and I will always remember her. We did interesting things and played fun games.

Specific

As children, my sister and I built rafts out of old barrels and tires, then tried to float them on the pond behind our house. I'll never forget playing war or hide-and-seek in the grove beside the pond.

The idea behind both of these versions is similar, but the specific example is more interesting and memorable. Choose the option that uses specific language.

CORRECT WORDS

The best answer uses words correctly. The following word pairs are often misused in written language. By reading the explanations and looking at the examples, you can learn to spot the correct way of using these easily confused word pairs.

Its/it's

Its is a possessive pronoun that means "belonging to it." *It's* is a contraction for *it is* or *it has*. The only time you will ever use *it's* is when you can also substitute the words *it is* or *it has*.

Who/that

Who refers to people. *That* refers to things.

- There is the man *who* helped me find a new pet.
- The woman *who* invented the copper-bottomed kettle died in 1995.
- This is the house *that* Harold bought.
- The magazine *that* I needed was no longer in print.

There/their/they're

Their is a possessive pronoun that shows ownership. *There* is an adverb that tells where an action or item is located. *They're* is a contraction for the words *they are*. Here is an easy way to remember these words.

- *Their* means "belonging to them." Of the three words, *their* can be most easily transformed into the word *them*. Extend the *r* on the right side and connect the *i* and the *r* to turn *their* into *them*. This clue will help you remember that *their* means "belonging to them."
- If you examine the word *there*, you can see from the way it's written that it contains the word *here*. Whenever you use *there*, you should be able to

substitute *here*. The sentence should still make sense.

- Imagine that the apostrophe in *they're* is actually a very small letter *a*. Use *they're* in a sentence only when you can substitute *they are*.

Your/you're

Your is a possessive pronoun that means "belonging to you." *You're* is a contraction for the words *you are*. The only time you will ever use *you're* is when you can also substitute the words *you are*.

To/too/two

To is a preposition or an infinitive.

- As a preposition: to the mall, to the bottom, to my church, to our garage, to his school, to his hideout, to our disadvantage, to an open room, to a ballad, to the gymnasium
- As an infinitive (*to* followed by a verb, sometimes separated by adverbs): to walk, to leap, to see badly, to find, to advance, to read, to build, to sorely want, to badly misinterpret, to carefully peruse

Too means "also." Whenever you use the word *too*, substitute the word *also*. The sentence should still make sense.

Two is a number, as in one, two. If you give it any thought at all, you'll never misuse this form.

The key is to think consciously about these words when you see them in written language. Circle the correct form of these easily confused words in the following sentences. Answers are at the end of the exercise.

32. (Its, It's) (to, too, two) late (to, too, two) remedy the problem now.

33. This is the man (who, that) helped me find the book I needed.

34. (There, Their, They're) going (to, too, two) begin construction as soon as the plans are finished.

35. We left (there, their, they're) house after the storm subsided.

36. I think (your, you're) going (to, too, two) win at least (to, too, two) more times.

37. The corporation moved (its, it's) home office.

Answers

32. It's, too, to
33. who
34. They're, to
35. their
36. you're, to, two
37. its

Following are four sample multiple-choice questions. By applying the principles explained in this section, choose the best version of each of the four sets of sentences. The answers and a short explanation for each question follow the exercise.

38. a. Vanover caught the ball. This was after it had been thrown by the shortstop. Vanover was the first baseman who caught the double-play ball. The shortstop was Hennings. He caught a line drive.
  b. After the shortstop Hennings caught the line drive, he threw it to the first baseman Vanover for the double play.
  c. After the line drive was caught by Hennings, the shortstop, it was thrown to Vanover at first base for a double play.

d. Vanover the first baseman caught the flip from shortstop Hennings.

39. a. This writer attended the movie *Casino* starring Robert DeNiro.
b. The movie *Casino* starring Robert DeNiro was attended by me.
c. The movie *Casino* starring Robert DeNiro was attended by this writer.
d. I attended the movie *Casino* starring Robert DeNiro.

40. a. They gave cereal boxes with prizes inside to the children.
b. They gave cereal boxes to children with prizes inside.
c. Children were given boxes of cereal by them with prizes inside.
d. Inside the boxes of cereal were prizes. The children got them.

41. a. After playing an exciting drum solo, the crowd rose to its feet and then claps and yells until the band plays another cut from their new album.
b. After playing an exciting drum solo, the crowd rose to its feet and then clapped and yelled until the band played another cut from their new album.
c. After the drummer's exciting solo, the crowd rose to its feet and then claps and yells until the band plays another cut from their new album.
d. After the drummer's exciting solo, the crowd rose to its feet and then clapped and yelled until the band played another cut from their new album.

The BEST Option
■ Is accurate
■ Is written in plain English
■ Presents information in a logical order
■ Has clearly identified pronouns that match the number of the nouns they represent
■ Has a consistent verb tense
■ Uses modifiers clearly
■ Uses words efficiently
■ Is written using complete sentences
■ Is specific
■ Uses words correctly

Answers

38. b. Answer a is unnecessarily wordy and the order is not logical. Answer c is also wordy and unclear. Answer d omits a piece of important information.

39. d. Both answers a and c use the stuffy-sounding *this writer*. Answer d is best because it avoids the wordy phrase "was attended by."

40. a. In both answers b and c the modifying phrase *with prizes inside* is misplaced.

41. d. Both answers a and b contain a dangling modifier, stating that the crowd played an exciting drum solo. Both answers b and c mix past and present verb tense. Only answer d has clearly written modifiers and a consistent verb tense.

ADDITIONAL RESOURCES

One of the best resources for any adult student is the public library. Many libraries have sections for adult learners or for those preparing to enter or change careers. Those sections contain skill books and review books on a number of subjects, including vocabulary. Here are some books you might consult:

VOCABULARY

- *1001 Vocabulary & Spelling Questions* (LearningExpress, order information at the back of this book)
- *21st Century Guide to Building Your Vocabulary* by Elizabeth Read (Dell)
- *601 Words You Need to Know to Pass Your Exam* by Murray Bromberg et al. (Barrons)
- *How to Build a Better Vocabulary* by Morris Rosenblum et al. (Warner Books)
- *Merriam-Webster's Vocabulary Builder* by Mary Wood Cornog (Merriam-Webster)
- *Vocabulary and Spelling in 20 Minutes a Day* by Judith Meyers (LearningExpress, order information at the back of this book)

GRAMMAR AND WRITING

For more help with verbal expression, here are some books you can consult.

For Non-Native Speakers of English

- *English Made Simple* by Arthur Waldhorn and Arthur Ziegler (Made Simple Books)
- *Errors in English and How to Correct Them* by Harry Shaw (HarperCollins)
- *Living in English* by Betsy J. Blusser (National Textbook Company)

For Everyone

- *501 Grammar & Writing Questions* (LearningExpress, order information at the back of this book)
- *The American Heritage Book of English Usage* (Houghton Mifflin)
- *Cliffs Quick Review Writing: Grammar, Usage & Style* by Jean Eggenschwiler (Cliffs Notes)
- *The Handbook of Good English* by Edward D. Johnson (Washington Square Press)
- *Smart English* by Anne Francis (Signet)
- *Writing Skills in 20 Minutes a Day* by Judith Olson (LearningExpress, order information at the back of this book)
- *Writing Smart* by Marcia Lerner (Princeton Review)

C·H·A·P·T·E·R

13

FIREFIGHTER EXAM 3

CHAPTER SUMMARY

This is the third practice exam in this book based on the fire-fighter written exam. After working through the instructional material in the previous chapters, use this test to see how much your score has improved since you took the first exam.

Now that you've been introduced to the skills tested on the firefighter exam, you should be more confident taking this third practice exam. Like Firefighter Exam 1, this practice exam tests job-related skills.

The exam will test you in six areas: memory and observation, reading comprehension, verbal expression, spatial relations, judgment, and following procedures. Though the actual exam is likely to use different categories for some of these questions, the skills tested here are similar to those tested on previous firefighter exams.

For this third exam, simulate the actual test-taking experience as closely as possible. Find a quiet place to work where you won't be interrupted. Tear out the answer sheet on the next page and find some number 2 pencils. Set a timer or stopwatch, and give yourself three hours for the entire exam. When that time is up, stop, even if you haven't finished the entire test.

After the exam, use the answer key that follows to see how you did and to find out why the correct answers are correct. The answer key is followed by a section on how to score your exam.

1.	ⓐ	ⓑ	ⓒ	ⓓ		35.	ⓐ	ⓑ	ⓒ	ⓓ		69.	ⓐ	ⓑ	ⓒ	ⓓ
2.	ⓐ	ⓑ	ⓒ	ⓓ		36.	ⓐ	ⓑ	ⓒ	ⓓ		70.	ⓐ	ⓑ	ⓒ	ⓓ
3.	ⓐ	ⓑ	ⓒ	ⓓ		37.	ⓐ	ⓑ	ⓒ	ⓓ		71.	ⓐ	ⓑ	ⓒ	ⓓ
4.	ⓐ	ⓑ	ⓒ	ⓓ		38.	ⓐ	ⓑ	ⓒ	ⓓ		72.	ⓐ	ⓑ	ⓒ	ⓓ
5.	ⓐ	ⓑ	ⓒ	ⓓ		39.	ⓐ	ⓑ	ⓒ	ⓓ		73.	ⓐ	ⓑ	ⓒ	ⓓ
6.	ⓐ	ⓑ	ⓒ	ⓓ		40.	ⓐ	ⓑ	ⓒ	ⓓ		74.	ⓐ	ⓑ	ⓒ	ⓓ
7.	ⓐ	ⓑ	ⓒ	ⓓ		41.	ⓐ	ⓑ	ⓒ	ⓓ		75.	ⓐ	ⓑ	ⓒ	ⓓ
8.	ⓐ	ⓑ	ⓒ	ⓓ		42.	ⓐ	ⓑ	ⓒ	ⓓ		76.	ⓐ	ⓑ	ⓒ	ⓓ
9.	ⓐ	ⓑ	ⓒ	ⓓ		43.	ⓐ	ⓑ	ⓒ	ⓓ		77.	ⓐ	ⓑ	ⓒ	ⓓ
10.	ⓐ	ⓑ	ⓒ	ⓓ		44.	ⓐ	ⓑ	ⓒ	ⓓ		78.	ⓐ	ⓑ	ⓒ	ⓓ
11.	ⓐ	ⓑ	ⓒ	ⓓ		45.	ⓐ	ⓑ	ⓒ	ⓓ		79.	ⓐ	ⓑ	ⓒ	ⓓ
12.	ⓐ	ⓑ	ⓒ	ⓓ		46.	ⓐ	ⓑ	ⓒ	ⓓ		80.	ⓐ	ⓑ	ⓒ	ⓓ
13.	ⓐ	ⓑ	ⓒ	ⓓ		47.	ⓐ	ⓑ	ⓒ	ⓓ		81.	ⓐ	ⓑ	ⓒ	ⓓ
14.	ⓐ	ⓑ	ⓒ	ⓓ		48.	ⓐ	ⓑ	ⓒ	ⓓ		82.	ⓐ	ⓑ	ⓒ	ⓓ
15.	ⓐ	ⓑ	ⓒ	ⓓ		49.	ⓐ	ⓑ	ⓒ	ⓓ		83.	ⓐ	ⓑ	ⓒ	ⓓ
16.	ⓐ	ⓑ	ⓒ	ⓓ		50.	ⓐ	ⓑ	ⓒ	ⓓ		84.	ⓐ	ⓑ	ⓒ	ⓓ
17.	ⓐ	ⓑ	ⓒ	ⓓ		51.	ⓐ	ⓑ	ⓒ	ⓓ		85.	ⓐ	ⓑ	ⓒ	ⓓ
18.	ⓐ	ⓑ	ⓒ	ⓓ		52.	ⓐ	ⓑ	ⓒ	ⓓ		86.	ⓐ	ⓑ	ⓒ	ⓓ
19.	ⓐ	ⓑ	ⓒ	ⓓ		53.	ⓐ	ⓑ	ⓒ	ⓓ		87.	ⓐ	ⓑ	ⓒ	ⓓ
20.	ⓐ	ⓑ	ⓒ	ⓓ		54.	ⓐ	ⓑ	ⓒ	ⓓ		88.	ⓐ	ⓑ	ⓒ	ⓓ
21.	ⓐ	ⓑ	ⓒ	ⓓ		55.	ⓐ	ⓑ	ⓒ	ⓓ		89.	ⓐ	ⓑ	ⓒ	ⓓ
22.	ⓐ	ⓑ	ⓒ	ⓓ		56.	ⓐ	ⓑ	ⓒ	ⓓ		90.	ⓐ	ⓑ	ⓒ	ⓓ
23.	ⓐ	ⓑ	ⓒ	ⓓ		57.	ⓐ	ⓑ	ⓒ	ⓓ		91.	ⓐ	ⓑ	ⓒ	ⓓ
24.	ⓐ	ⓑ	ⓒ	ⓓ		58.	ⓐ	ⓑ	ⓒ	ⓓ		92.	ⓐ	ⓑ	ⓒ	ⓓ
25.	ⓐ	ⓑ	ⓒ	ⓓ		59.	ⓐ	ⓑ	ⓒ	ⓓ		93.	ⓐ	ⓑ	ⓒ	ⓓ
26.	ⓐ	ⓑ	ⓒ	ⓓ		60.	ⓐ	ⓑ	ⓒ	ⓓ		94.	ⓐ	ⓑ	ⓒ	ⓓ
27.	ⓐ	ⓑ	ⓒ	ⓓ		61.	ⓐ	ⓑ	ⓒ	ⓓ		95.	ⓐ	ⓑ	ⓒ	ⓓ
28.	ⓐ	ⓑ	ⓒ	ⓓ		62.	ⓐ	ⓑ	ⓒ	ⓓ		96.	ⓐ	ⓑ	ⓒ	ⓓ
29.	ⓐ	ⓑ	ⓒ	ⓓ		63.	ⓐ	ⓑ	ⓒ	ⓓ		97.	ⓐ	ⓑ	ⓒ	ⓓ
30.	ⓐ	ⓑ	ⓒ	ⓓ		64.	ⓐ	ⓑ	ⓒ	ⓓ		98.	ⓐ	ⓑ	ⓒ	ⓓ
31.	ⓐ	ⓑ	ⓒ	ⓓ		65.	ⓐ	ⓑ	ⓒ	ⓓ		99.	ⓐ	ⓑ	ⓒ	ⓓ
32.	ⓐ	ⓑ	ⓒ	ⓓ		66.	ⓐ	ⓑ	ⓒ	ⓓ		100.	ⓐ	ⓑ	ⓒ	ⓓ
33.	ⓐ	ⓑ	ⓒ	ⓓ		67.	ⓐ	ⓑ	ⓒ	ⓓ						
34.	ⓐ	ⓑ	ⓒ	ⓓ		68.	ⓐ	ⓑ	ⓒ	ⓓ						

You will have 5 minutes to study the diagram on the following page, after which you must turn the page and answer questions 1–7 from memory. You will not be permitted to look back at the diagram in order to answer the questions.

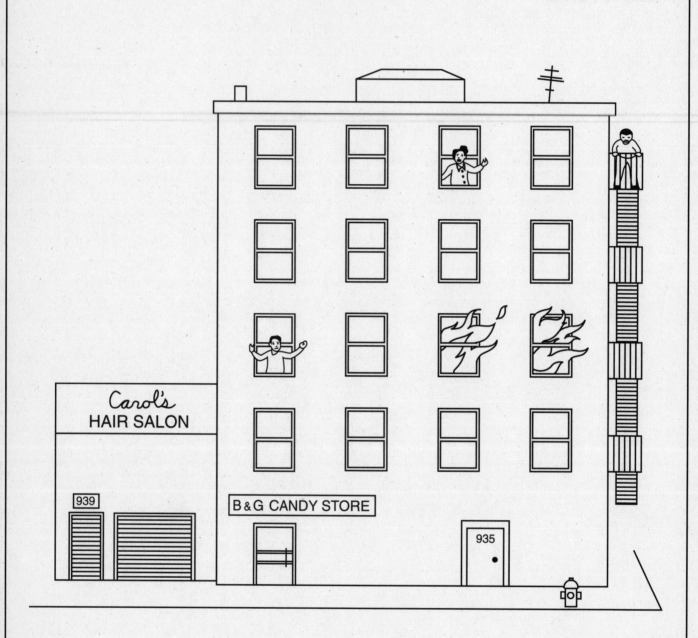

After you have spent 5 minutes studying the diagram on the previous page, answer questions 1–7 based on the diagram. DO NOT turn back to the diagram to answer these questions. When you have finished questions 1–7, you may go on to the next memory diagram.

1. The fire building has
   a. no fire escape or stairs on the sides of the building
   b. one set of stairs on the outside of the building
   c. a fire escape on the outside of the building
   d. a fire escape and a set of stairs on the outside of the building

2. Fire is showing at
   a. two windows in 935
   b. one window in 939
   c. two windows in 939
   d. one window in 935

3. There are three civilians in the drawing. They are located on
   a. the second, third, and fourth floors
   b. the fourth and fifth floors and the fire escape
   c. the third, fourth, and fifth floors
   d. the third and fifth floors and the fire escape

4. The closest fire hydrant can be found
   a. in front of the store
   b. in front of the apartment building
   c. on the side of the apartment building
   d. on the side of the store

5. The sign on the first floor of the fire building reads
   a. #939
   b. Carol's Hair Salon
   c. Apartment #935
   d. B & G Candy Store

6. The firefighters need to do a roof rescue. What obstacles may be in their way?
   a. a TV antenna, a clothes line, and a smoke stack
   b. a TV antenna, a smoke stack, and two civilians
   c. a TV antenna, a smoke stack, and an air shaft
   d. a TV antenna, a clothes line, and an air shaft

7. How many people most likely need to be evacuated from the Hair Salon?
   a. none
   b. one
   c. two
   d. three

You will have 5 minutes to study the diagram on the following page, after which you must turn the page and answer questions 8–15 from memory. You will not be permitted to look back at the diagram in order to answer the questions.

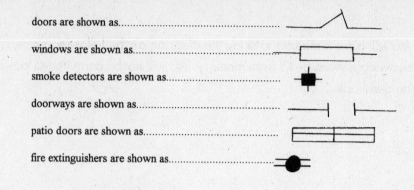

doors are shown as..

windows are shown as..

smoke detectors are shown as...

doorways are shown as...

patio doors are shown as..

fire extinguishers are shown as...

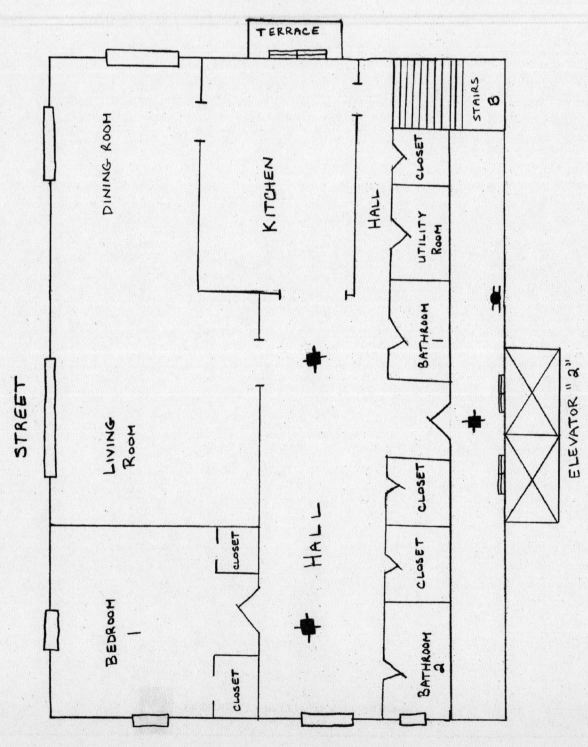

TERRACE

STREET

DINING ROOM

KITCHEN

HALL

LIVING ROOM

CLOSET

HALL

BEDROOM 1

CLOSET

CLOSET

CLOSET

CLOSET

BATHROOM 2

BATHROOM 1

UTILITY ROOM

CLOSET

STAIRS B

ELEVATOR "2"

After you have spent 5 minutes studying the diagram on the previous page, turn the page and answer questions 8–15 based on the diagram. DO NOT turn back to the diagram to answer these questions. When you have finished questions 8–15, you may go on with the rest of the test.

8. Which of the following rooms is NOT found in this apartment?
- a. a closet
- b. a basement
- c. a utility room
- d. a dining room

9. If a fire starts in the kitchen near the terrace, the room most affected by the spread of the fire would be
- a. the dining room
- b. the living room
- c. bedroom 1
- d. bathroom 2

10. How many smoke detectors are located in the apartment?
- a. none
- b. one
- c. two
- d. three

11. While you are searching the apartment for victims, you think you see a form by the terrace doors. What room are you in?
- a. the dining room
- b. the kitchen
- c. the living room
- d. the bedroom

12. You can see smoke and fire coming from the windows as you approach the apartment from the street. In which rooms could the fire be?
- a. bedroom, bathroom, and hall
- b. bedroom, hall, and living room
- c. hall, living room, and dining room
- d. dining room, living room, and bedroom

13. If you are walking through the hall, how many doors are there?
- a. eight
- b. nine
- c. ten
- d. eleven

14. A kitchen fire has spread into the stairway. Your superior officer tells you to search the bedroom for any occupants. Which of the following is the best way to enter the bedroom?
- a. Climb down the roof to the dining room window.
- b. Raise a ladder to one of the two bedroom windows.
- c. Raise a ladder to the terrace and enter the patio doors.
- d. Climb down from the roof to the terrace and enter the patio doors.

15. You think you hear someone moaning in the dining room and you need to go and check. You can enter the dining room from either
- a. the living room or the kitchen
- b. the street or bedroom 1
- c. bathroom 2 or bathroom 1
- d. the kitchen or the terrace

Answer questions 16–19 based on the following information.

A firefighter's self-contained breathing apparatus must be inspected at the beginning of each tour and after each use. The following procedure is used to ensure that a thorough inspection is completed.

1. Check the condition of the harness assembly. The harness assembly should be free of defects. If defects are found, the unit should be placed out of service.

2. Check the condition of the air cylinder, and read the cylinder gauge. If the cylinder is damaged or less than full, it must be replaced.

3. Turn the air cylinder on.

4. Examine the hoses and hose couplings. Check for cuts or air leaks. If any are found, the unit must be placed out of service.

5. Inspect the face piece and regulator. If either is found to be damaged, the unit must be placed out of service.

6. Test the system. Don the face piece, and inhale and exhale to verify that the system is functioning. Malfunctioning units must be placed out of service.

7. Shut down the unit.

16. The self-contained breathing apparatus must be inspected
a. weekly
b. only after use
c. before each tour and after it is used
d. before each use

17. The cylinder gauge on the breathing apparatus you are inspecting reads half full. You should
a. place the unit out of service
b. replace the cylinder with a full one
c. use the cylinder until it is empty
d. turn the air cylinder on

18. The air cylinder should be turned on
a. before the inspection is begun
b. after checking the condition of the hose coupling
c. after checking the cylinder gauge
d. after the inspection is complete

19. Which of these should be done before the face piece is inspected?
a. Check the hoses for air leaks.
b. Put on the face piece.
c. Inhale and exhale through the apparatus.
d. Turn the unit off.

Answer questions 20–22 based on your best judgment and common sense.

20. The driver or chauffeur of the fire truck is required to keep the gas tank full at all times. The reason for this requirement is that
a. the chauffeur can drive faster with a full tank
b. the truck must always be available for maximum use
c. the truck may stall if the tank is not full
d. the chauffeur may go on report if an inspection is called

21. Fires in vacant buildings can cause many problems for firefighters. Which of the following is LEAST likely to pose difficulty?
    a. The building is likely to be boarded up.
    b. The building's structure may be weak and unstable.
    c. There could be unknown combustible materials in the building.
    d. Probably no one lives in the building.

22. There has been a small fire in a first floor apartment. Your company has put the fire out, and you are cleaning up the debris. As you look around, you wonder where all the expensive items in the apartment came from. Then you discover a small box full of money. Now you believe that the money is drug money. In this situation you should
    a. give the money to your superior officer and report your suspicions
    b. keep the money since the drug dealers came by it illegally
    c. call the police, but tell no one else since this might interfere with police procedure
    d. split the money with the other firefighters since it belongs to no one in particular

Answer questions 23–26 solely on the basis of the information in the following passage.

One of the most hazardous conditions a firefighter will ever encounter is a backdraft (also known as a smoke explosion). A backdraft can occur in the hot-smoldering phase of a fire when burning is incomplete and there is not enough oxygen to sustain the fire. Unburned carbon particles and other flammable products, combined with the intense heat, may cause instantaneous combustion if more oxygen reaches the fire.

Firefighters should be aware of the conditions that indicate the possibility for a backdraft to occur. When there is a lack of oxygen during a fire, the smoke becomes filled with carbon dioxide or carbon monoxide and turns dense gray or black. Other warning signs of a potential backdraft are little or no visible flame, excessive heat, smoke leaving the building in puffs, muffled sounds, and smoke-stained windows.

Proper ventilation will make a backdraft less likely. Opening a room or building at the highest point allows heated gases and smoke to be released gradually. Suddenly breaking a window or opening a door allows oxygen to rush in, causing an explosion.

23. A backdraft is a dangerous condition for firefighters because
    a. there is not enough oxygen for breathing
    b. the heat is too intense
    c. the smoke is too thick
    d. an explosion occurs

24. Which of the following is NOT mentioned as a potential backdraft warning sign?
    a. windows stained with smoke
    b. flames shooting up from the building
    c. puffs of smoke leaving the building
    d. more intense heat than usual

25. To prevent the possibility of a backdraft, a firefighter should
    a. carry an oxygen tank
    b. open a door slowly to allow gases to escape
    c. make an opening at the top of the building
    d. break a window to release carbon particles

26. When compared with a hot, smoldering fire, a fire with visible, high-reaching flames
   a. has more oxygen available for combustion
   b. has more carbon dioxide available for consumption
   c. produces more dense gray smoke
   d. is more likely to cause a backdraft

Answer questions 27–31 solely on the basis of the map on the following page. The arrows indicate traffic flow; one arrow indicates a one-way street going in the direction of the arrow; no arrows represent a two-way street. You are not allowed to go the wrong way on a one-way street.

27. While you are on duty in the fire station, an elderly man asks you to help him find the Senior Citizens Center. You should tell him to
   a. walk across the street to the Senior Citizens Center
   b. ask a police officer how to get to the Senior Citizens Center
   c. walk north to Avenue B, west on Avenue B to the end of the park, make a right and go one block
   d. walk north to Avenue B, west on Avenue B to Lafayette Street, make a right and go one block

28. The head librarian needs gasoline for his automobile. He is leaving the Avenue D garage exit from the library. His quickest legal route to the gas station is to go
   a. north on Central Street to Avenue C and west on Avenue C to the gas station
   b. west on Brooklyn Street to Avenue B and north on Avenue B to the gas station
   c. west on Avenue D to Grand Street and north on Grand Street to the gas station

   d. west on Avenue D to Lafayette Street and north on Lafayette Street to the gas station

29. You are leaving the firehouse and are on your way to the high school to pick up your son. Which is the most direct, legal way to go?
   a. north to Avenue B, west to Grand Street, south to Avenue D, east to Greene Street, and then north to the entrance to the high school
   b. south on Brooklyn Street, west on Avenue D, and north on Greene Street to the entrance of the high school
   c. north to Avenue A, west to Lafayette Street, south on Lafayette Street, east on Avenue C, and south on Greene Street to the entrance of the high school
   d. south on Brooklyn Street, west on 1st Avenue, and north on Greene Street to the entrance of the high school

30. Your spouse is a nurse at the city hospital and goes to the public library every Monday as a volunteer. What would be the shortest legal route from the hospital to the library?
   a. west on Avenue A, south on Lafayette Street, east on Avenue C, and south on Central Street to the library entrance
   b. east on Avenue B and south on Central Street to the library entrance
   c. west on Avenue A, south on Lafayette Street, and east on Avenue D to the library entrance
   d. east on Avenue A and south on Central Street to the library entrance

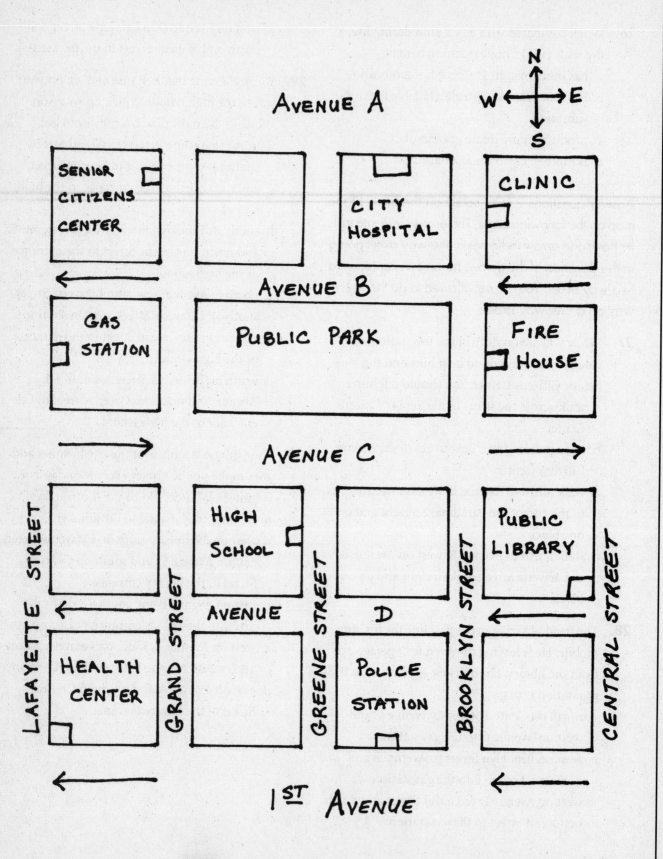

31. Your company receives a call reporting a fire at the police station. What is the engine's quickest legal route?

    a. south on Brooklyn Street and west on 1st Avenue to the police station

    b. north on Brooklyn Street, west on Avenue A, south on Lafayette Street, and east on 1st Avenue to the police station

    c. north on Brooklyn Street and east on 1st Avenue to the police station

    d. south on Brooklyn Street, west on Avenue C, south on Grand Street, and east on 1st Avenue to the police station

Answer questions 32–35 solely on the basis of the information in the following passage.

Heat reactions usually occur when large amounts of water and/or salt are lost through excessive sweating following strenuous exercise. When the body becomes overheated and cannot eliminate this excess heat, heat exhaustion and heat stroke are possible.

Heat exhaustion is generally characterized by clammy skin, fatigue, nausea, dizziness, profuse perspiration, and sometimes fainting, resulting from an inadequate intake of water and the loss of fluids. First aid treatment for this condition includes having the victim lie down, raising the feet 8–12 inches, applying cool, wet cloths to the skin, and giving the victim sips of salt water (1 teaspoon per glass, half a glass every 15 minutes), over the period of an hour.

Heat stroke is much more serious; it is an immediate life-threatening situation. The characteristics of heat stroke are a high body temperature (which may reach 106°F or more); a rapid pulse; hot, dry skin; and a blocked sweating mechanism. Victims of this condition may be unconscious, and first aid measures should be directed at cooling the body quickly. The victim should be placed in a tub of cold water or repeatedly sponged with cool water until his or her temperature is lowered sufficiently. Fans or air conditioners will also help with the cooling process. Care should be taken, however, not to overly chill the victim once the temperature is below 102°F.

32. The most immediate concern of a person tending a victim of heat stroke should be to

    a. get salt into the victim's body

    b. raise the victim's feet

    c. lower the victim's pulse

    d. lower the victim's temperature

33. Which of the following is a symptom of heat exhaustion?

    a. a rapid pulse

    b. profuse sweating

    c. hot, dry skin

    d. a weak pulse

34. Heat stroke is more serious than heat exhaustion because heat stroke victims

    a. have no salt in their bodies

    b. cannot take in water

    c. do not sweat

    d. have frequent fainting spells

35. Symptoms such as nausea and dizziness in a heat exhaustion victim indicate that the person most likely needs to

    a. be immediately taken to a hospital

    b. be given salt water

    c. be immersed in a tub of water

    d. sweat more

36. Choose the sentence that is most clearly written.

a. Less money for new fire trucks and other equipment mean the occurrence of budget cuts as well as the recession.

b. Budget cuts, as well as the recession, have meant less money for new fire trucks and other equipment.

c. Budget cuts, the recession as well, and there is less money for fire trucks and other equipment.

d. With less money, recessive budget cuts means fewer fire trucks and other equipment.

37. Choose the sentence that is most clearly written.

a. All day, the exhausted volunteers struggled through snake-ridden underbrush, but they still have not been found during this search.

b. The exhausted volunteers struggled all day as they searched for the teenagers through snake-ridden underbrush who still had not been found.

c. All day, the exhausted volunteers had struggled through snake-ridden underbrush in search of the missing teenagers, who still have not been found.

d. During their search, the teenagers still have not been found all day while the exhausted volunteers struggled through the snake-ridden underbrush.

Answer questions 38–41 solely on the basis of the information in the following passage.

In October of 1999, a disastrous wildfire swept across portions of Charlesburg. Five residents were killed, 320 homes destroyed, and 19,500 acres burned. A public safety task force was formed to review emergency response. The task force findings were as follows:

■ The water supply in the residential areas was insufficient, and some hydrants could not even be opened. The task force recommended a review of hydrant inspection policy.

■ Fire companies that responded had difficulty locating specific sites. Most came from other areas and were not familiar with Charlesburg. The available maps were outdated and did not reflect recent housing developments.

■ Evacuation procedures were inadequate. Residents reported being given conflicting and/or confusing information. Some residents of the Hilltop Estates subdivision ignored mandatory evacuation orders, yet others were praised for their cooperation.

■ Firefighters reported a number of items that contributed to the spread of the fires. Some homes were lost long after the fire had passed through, because dried undergrowth nearby caught fire and slowly spread.

■ Homeowners had not been sufficiently educated on emergency procedures. Many residents underestimated hazards such as shifting winds, poor visibility due to smoke, and the speed with which fire spreads.

38. According to the passage, why did some fire companies have difficulty adequately responding to the Charlesburg fire?
a. Visibility was poor, due to smoke.
b. They were given conflicting information.
c. They lacked knowledge about Charlesburg streets.
d. They could not locate water sources.

39. According to the passage, which of the following was a specific task force recommendation?
a. Evacuation shelters should be better supplied.
b. Residents of Hilltop Estates should be reprimanded.
c. Outdated maps should be destroyed.
d. Hydrant inspection procedures should be reexamined.

40. One reason for confusion among some homeowners was that
a. they lacked adequate guidance on emergency procedures
b. their subdivisions were not included on emergency maps
c. they could not locate emergency shelters
d. they misunderstood hydrant inspection policy

41. Which of the following is NOT included in this passage?
a. the reason some homes burned after the main fire had swept through
b. statistics based on the aftermath of the fire
c. the role played by wind direction
d. the location of other fire departments who responded

Answer questions 42 and 43 solely on the basis of the following map. The arrows indicate traffic flow; one arrow indicates a one-way street going in the direction of the arrow; two arrows represent a two-way street. You are not allowed to go the wrong way on a one-way street.

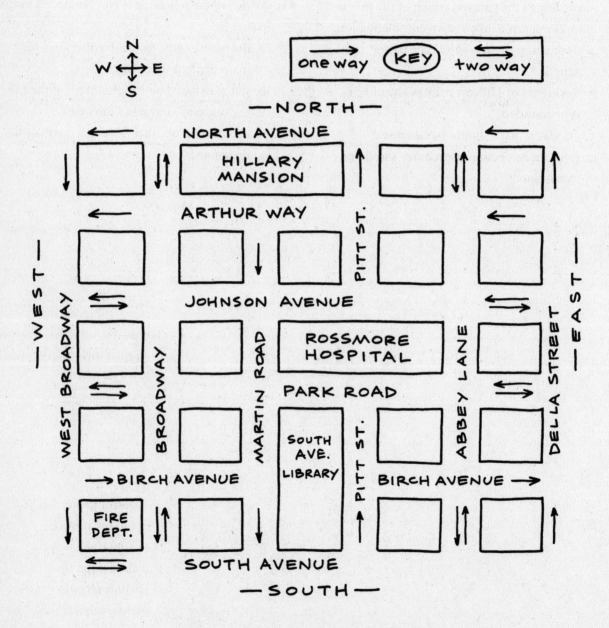

42. Firefighter Lazere has just had his lunch break at the South Avenue Library, which faces South Avenue. He now must go to a meeting at the Hillary Mansion, the entrance to which faces North Avenue. What is Firefighter Lazere's most direct route to the Hillary Mansion?

a. Go east on South Avenue, then turn north on Abbey Lane to North Avenue, then west on North Avenue to the Hillary Mansion.

b. Go east on South Avenue, then turn north on Pitt Street, then west on North Avenue to the Hillary Mansion.

c. Go west on South Avenue, then turn north on West Broadway, then east on North Avenue to the Hillary Mansion.

d. Go west on South Avenue, then turn north on Broadway to North Avenue, then east on North Avenue to the Hillary Mansion.

43. Firefighter Lew is just returning from lunch and is southbound on Martin Road. He has just crossed Park Road, when he receives a call for help at a fire in a residence at the corner of Arthur Way and Della Street. What is Officer Lew's most direct route to the residence?

a. Make a U-turn on Martin Road, then go north on Martin Road to Arthur Way, then east on Johnson Avenue to Della Street, then north on Della Street to the residence.

b. Continue south on Martin Road, then go east on South Avenue, then north on Pitt Street, then east on Park Road, then north on Abbey Lane, and then east on Arthur Way.

c. Continue south on Martin Road, then go east on South Avenue, then north on Della Street to the residence.

d. Continue south on Martin Road, then go north on Abbey Lane, then east on Arthur Way to the residence.

Answer questions 44–48 solely on the basis of the information in the following list of procedures.

Firefighters must learn the proper procedures for responding to residential carbon monoxide (CO) emergencies.

Upon arriving at the scene of the alarm, personnel shall put on protective clothing, then bring an operational, calibrated CO meter onto the premises.

Occupants of the premises shall then be examined. If they are experiencing CO poisoning symptoms—i.e., headaches, nausea, confusion, dizziness, and other flu-like symptoms—an emergency medical services (EMS) crew shall be notified immediately and the occupants evacuated and administered oxygen.

To test for CO contamination, meters must be held head high. Appliances should be operating for five to ten minutes before testing, and a check must be made near all gas appliances and vents. If vents are working properly, no CO emissions will enter the structure.

If the meters register unsafe levels—above 10 parts per million (ppm)—all occupants shall be evacuated and the source of the contamination investigated. Occupants shall be interviewed to ascertain the location of the CO detector (if any), the length of time the alarm has sounded, what the occupants were doing at the time of the alarm (cooking, etc.), and what electrical appliances were functioning. Occupants shall not re-enter the premises until the environment is deemed safe.

If the meters register levels lower than nine ppm, occupants shall be allowed to re-enter the building. They shall be notified of the recorded level and given a CO informational packet.

44. When arriving at a CO emergency, what is the first thing a firefighter should do?
   a. Take a CO meter reading.
   b. Put on protective clothing.
   c. Administer oxygen to the occupants of the premises.
   d. Interview the occupants of the premises.

45. If residents are experiencing carbon monoxide poisoning symptoms, which of the following steps should firefighters take immediately?
   a. allow the residents to lie down
   b. determine CO levels in the household
   c. summon an emergency services team
   d. investigate the source of contamination

46. Carbon monoxide levels under nine ppm are considered
   a. relatively safe
   b. very dangerous
   c. capable of causing illness
   d. cause for evacuation

47. According to the passage, all occupants of a residence should be evacuated when
   a. the investigators arrive
   b. an EMS crew arrives
   c. the source of contamination is discovered
   d. any occupant exhibits symptoms of CO poisoning

48. Which of the following is NOT included in this passage?
   a. potential sources of contamination
   b. indications of CO toxicity
   c. proper levels of oxygen for ailing occupants
   d. which pieces of equipment should be taken into homes

Answer questions 49–51 based on your best judgment and common sense.

49. You are on the fire department's softball team, and your team has advanced to the play-offs. In the bottom of the ninth inning with the bases loaded, you are up next. If you score for your team, the game will be tied and go into extra innings. You look at your watch and realize you have to be at work in 20 minutes. If the game does go into extra innings, you will be late. You should
   a. lose the game on purpose because getting to work on time is more important
   b. call your superior officer and tell him you will be late because of the game
   c. keep playing and explain the circumstances to your superior officer when you get to the firehouse
   d. ask someone to take your place so you can report for duty on time

50. You are driving your spouse home and are planning to go straight on to work; however, you have an accident. The other driver insists that you should exchange license information, which will make you late for work. You should
   a. leave without delay since the public and other firefighters depend on you, and you must not be late
   b. call your superior officer, explain what happened, and then proceed with exchanging licenses
   c. tell the driver of the other car that you will be in touch later, explaining how important it is for you to be on time
   d. leave the scene, but have your spouse stay and exchange license numbers

51. You have just gotten off duty and arrive back home. When you get out of your car, you hear your neighbors across the street yelling and see that the husband is on a ladder by an open window. You go over to find out if you can help. The wife explains that their two-year-old has locked herself in the bathroom. You can see that the ladder is not tall enough for the man to reach the child from the open window. Your best course of action would be to
   a. tell them to call the fire department, whose taller ladders will enable firefighters to rescue the child quickly and safely
   b. leave them to deal with the situation on their own, so they will learn to be more responsible in the future about their child's safety
   c. call the police and report them for child endangerment
   d. advise them that breaking down the bathroom door would be easier than climbing the ladder

Answer questions 52–55 solely on the basis of the information in the following passage.

Understanding the basics of fire extinguishers is a requirement for firefighters who teach fire safety to the public. Different types of fires require different types of extinguishers. Being able to clearly explain the differences can save lives and property.

Class A fires involve combustible materials such as paper, wood, and cloth. A water-filled extinguisher is the most effective in putting out these fires. Residents should direct the nozzle toward the base of the fire and spray until all involved material is wet. A dry chemical extinguisher can also be used on some Class A fires.

Fires that involve flammable liquids such as gasoline and paint are Class B fires. Dry chemical extinguishers are most effective on these types of fires. Residents should stand about ten feet from the fire and spray the chemical substance at the base of the fire. As the fire diminishes, they can slowly move closer. If there is no wind, carbon dioxide extinguishers, which decrease the amount of oxygen, can be used. Oxygen can accelerate the spread of fires.

Electrical fires are in the Class C category. Residents should attempt to shut off power before confronting this type of fire. If power is shut off, a water-filled unit is most effective and can be used safely. Otherwise, residents should use carbon dioxide or dry chemical units.

Fires involving combustible metals such as magnesium are Class D fires. Special foam compounds are needed to extinguish these fires.

Extinguishers should be kept in areas where they are easily accessible but safe from damage and out of the reach of children.

52. On which of the following types of fires should water-filled extinguishers be used?
   a. Class A and Class C
   b. Class B and Class D
   c. Class A and Class B
   d. Class B and Class C

53. If cotton sheets in a bedroom caught fire, the proper method of fighting the fire would be to
   a. use a carbon dioxide extinguisher
   b. spray toward the base until the materials are soaked
   c. spray toward the base, then gradually move closer
   d. direct foam compound toward the base of the fire

54. If an electrical fire caused a power outage, which of the following would be the ideal extinguisher to employ?
   a. water-filled unit
   b. carbon dioxide unit
   c. foam unit
   d. dry chemical unit

55. Which of the following is the main idea of the passage?
   a. Residents should learn how to operate extinguishers.
   b. Firefighters should understand that extinguishers can save lives.
   c. Different types of extinguishers are effective on various kinds of fires.
   d. Electrical fires require a special type of extinguisher.

56. Off-duty Firefighter Roth is walking her dog behind the apartment at 4498 Cahill Avenue when she hears someone calling for help. She looks up and sees an older man at the window on the third floor. The man shouts that his wife may have had a heart attack and his phone is out of order. Roth goes into the building and calls 911 from the superintendent's phone. Which of the following statements reports the emergency most clearly and accurately?
   a. Send an ambulance to the apartment building at 4498 Cahill Avenue. A woman on the third floor may have had a heart attack.
   b. A woman may have suffered a heart attack behind 4498 Cahill Avenue and needs an ambulance.
   c. The woman's husband on the third floor of the apartment building said she had a heart attack, but his phone is out of order.
   d. An ambulance is immediately needed at 4498 Cahill Avenue. I spoke to the victim's husband in the alley behind the building where she had a heart attack.

57. Firefighter Delgado is returning to the station during a torrential rainstorm. As he is making a left turn onto Bartola Street from Unity Road, he slides on the slick pavement. He loses control of the truck, and it bounces up over the curb and hits a bus shelter. Fortunately, no one is waiting for the bus. The truck, however, is disabled. Which of the following statements reports this information most clearly and accurately?

a. At the bus shelter near Unity Road in the rain, I lost control of the truck that became disabled after hitting the curb. The bus shelter was empty.

b. During the rainstorm, my disabled truck attempted a left turn onto Bartola Street. When I got to the bus shelter, no one was waiting for the bus, which was fortunate when I lost control and ran up over the curb.

c. From Unity Road, I missed the turn onto Bartola Street after I lost control of the truck. It bounced over the curb, which hit the bus shelter. Although the truck is disabled, the shelter did not sustain injuries.

d. As I was turning left onto Bartola Street from Unity Road, the truck slid on the wet pavement. I lost control and hit the bus shelter. The shelter was empty, but my truck is disabled.

58. While taking out the trash at his home at 804 Olive Street, Firefighter Johnston slips on the icy sidewalk and twists his right ankle. Johnston is in pain and soon realizes that he cannot put weight on his ankle. His neighbor takes him to the hospital where a doctor tells him he has a severe sprain and should not go back to work for at least a week. The next day, Johnston calls his chief to tell her why he will not be reporting for work. Which of the following statements describes the situation most clearly and accurately?

a. I fell on the ice outside my home and suffered a severe ankle sprain. The doctor has advised me not to return to work for at least a week.

b. After falling on the ice, my neighbor took me to the hospital last night, so I will not be reporting for work all week.

c. I cannot put weight on my right ankle where I fell on the sidewalk at 804 Olive Street and am not coming into work as the doctor prescribed.

d. The right ankle is sprained. This occurred when the trash was taken out on the sidewalk, and a doctor at the hospital has warned me not to come to work for a week.

Answer questions 59–63 based solely on the information in the following passage.

Firefighters are often called upon to speak to school and community groups about the importance of fire safety, particularly fire prevention and detection. Because smoke detectors cut a person's risk of dying in a fire in half, firefighters often provide audiences with information on how to install these protective devices in their homes.

A smoke detector should be placed on each floor level of a home and outside each sleeping area. A good site for a detector would be a hallway that runs between living spaces and bedrooms.

Because of the "dead" air space that might be missed by turbulent hot air bouncing around above a fire, smoke detectors should be installed either on the ceiling at least four inches from the nearest wall, or high on a wall at least four but no further than twelve inches from the ceiling. Detectors should not be mounted near windows, exterior doors, or other places where drafts might direct the smoke away from the unit. Nor should they be placed in kitchens and garages, where cooking and gas fumes are likely to set off false alarms.

59. What is the main focus of this passage?
- a. how fire fighters carry out their responsibilities
- b. the detection of "dead" air space on walls and ceilings
- c. the proper installation of home smoke detectors
- d. how smoke detectors prevent fires in homes

60. The passage implies that "dead" air space is most likely to be found
- a. on a ceiling, between four and twelve inches from a wall
- b. close to where a wall meets a ceiling
- c. near an open window
- d. in kitchens and garages

61. The passage states that, when compared with people who do not have smoke detectors, persons who live in homes with smoke detectors have a
- a. 50% better chance of surviving a fire
- b. 50% better chance of preventing a fire
- c. 100% better chance of detecting a hidden fire
- d. 200% better chance of not being injured in a fire

62. A smoke detector should NOT be installed near a window because
- a. outside fumes may trigger a false alarm
- b. a wind draft may create a "dead" air space
- c. a wind draft may pull smoke away from the detector
- d. outside noises may muffle the sound of the detector

63. The passage indicates that one responsibility of a firefighter is to
- a. install smoke detectors in the homes of residents in the community
- b. check homes to see if smoke detectors have been properly installed
- c. develop fire safety programs for community leaders and school teachers to use
- d. speak to school children about the importance of preventing fires

64. Firefighter Lopez was getting into his truck after responding to a small garage fire in the middle of the 2200 block of Howard Street when a woman suddenly ran up to the vehicle. The woman, Ina Barry, explained that her gold watch had fallen into the street the previous evening and that a street sweeper had swept it up. She wanted Lopez to tell her where the city's street sweepers deposited what they picked up. Lopez carefully explained that this problem was not under his jurisdiction and told her to file a report with the Sanitation Department. When he returned to the station, Lopez reported the incident to his chief. Which of the following describes the incident most clearly and accurately?

a. Ina Barry is the name of the woman who said that her gold watch was confiscated by a street sweeper in the 2000 block of Howard Street. I told her to call the Sanitation Department because she was talking to the wrong department.

b. While I was putting out a garage fire on Howard Street, I told a woman named Ina Barry to file a report with the Sanitation Department about her gold watch.

c. A woman named Ina ran up to my truck as I was getting into it and said that the street sweeper was responsible for the loss of her gold watch and that this should be reported to the Sanitation Department.

d. As I was getting into my truck in the 2200 block of Howard Street, a woman named Ina Barry ran up and told me that her watch had been swept up by the street sweeper. I advised her to contact the Sanitation Department.

65. A job announcement states, "The application period for this position is from January 15 through March 1. Applications are available at the Fire Department at 600 Main Street. Application forms must be received at the department by 5:00 P.M. on the closing date of the application period." Which of the following statements describes this announcement most clearly and accurately?

a. Application forms for this position must be received at the Fire Department at 600 Main Street between January 15 and 5:00 P.M. on March 1.

b. Application forms should be picked up at 500 Main Street and returned to the same location by 6:00 P.M. on March 1 to be considered for the position.

c. According to the job announcement, the closing of the application is between January 15 and March 1 at the Fire Department on Main Street.

d. Pick up applications at the Fire Department at 600 Main Street. Return application forms on January 15 or March 1 at the same location.

Answer questions 66–68 based on your best judgment and common sense.

66. While on duty you see a fellow firefighter behaving in what seems to you a suspicious manner. You suspect he is sabotaging another firefighter's equipment. You should

a. tell the firefighter to stop, and threaten to report him if you see him doing it again

b. do nothing because you are not absolutely sure of the true nature of the incident

c. tell the firefighter whose equipment may have been tampered with that she should be careful

d. report the incident and your impressions to your superior officer

67. While searching a fire scene for hidden pockets of fire, you find a book of matches with a cigarette inside rolled up in newspaper. You show it to the investigating officer because you are convinced that that was how the fire was started. The investigator is able to determine who the arsonist was from that evidence. Later, a reporter comes into the firehouse to ask you about the arson suspect who was just arrested. The reporter was told that evidence found at the fire scene led to the arsonist being caught and wants to give you credit for helping in the case. How should you answer the reporter's questions?
   a. Don't answer any of the questions because the arsonist may come after you.
   b. Tell the reporter you have no comment, and call your superior officer over.
   c. Don't answer any of the questions because this is strictly a police matter.
   d. Tell the reporter everything you know because your actions were truly heroic.

68. Your company responds to a call of a car fire on the main highway. The first order your superior officer gives you is to put flares on the road. The flares serve to
   a. warn motorists that they need to use extreme caution
   b. give citizens confidence that their tax money is being put to good use
   c. educate passing motorists on just how dangerous car fires can be
   d. let the police know where the firefighters are working

69. Firefighter Yamata is responding to a report of a smoking dumpster at an apartment building in the 700 block of Norcross Road. While he is checking the dumpster, two boys run up to his truck and spray graffiti on the driver's door. Mrs. Stanley, who is walking her dog, is the only witness to the crime. She stops Yamata and tells him that one of the boys, Randy McGill, age thirteen, lives in the 800 block of Norcross. When Yamata returns to the garage, he files a report. Which of the following statements most clearly and accurately describes what occurred?
   a. On the 700 block of Norcross Road, which I was responding to, Mrs. Stanley told me about the graffiti on the truck. It appeared there after teenagers living on the next block ran down Norcross with a spray can. It was on the driver's side.
   b. Mrs. Stanley was walking her dog and said that Randy McGill lived in the next block of Norcross from the one I was doing the pickup. He was thirteen and spray painted the truck, but I did not get an eyewitness myself because I was busy with the dumpster.
   c. Mrs. Stanley and her dog told me that Randy McGill lived in the 800 block of Norcross while I was responding to a call in the 700 block. He was thirteen with another boy, and I was told that they were the ones to spray the graffiti. However, I did not witness this myself.
   d. As I was responding to a call in the 700 block of Norcross Road, Mrs. Stanley witnessed two boys spraying graffiti on the driver's side of my truck. She identified one of the boys as thirteen-year-old Randy McGill who lives in the 800 block of Norcross.

70. New county regulations for fire prevention state that all property owners must clear away dry undergrowth on or before May 15 of each year. By the same date, property owners must also trim back any tree limbs that overhang or are touching the roof of the house or any other buildings on the property. After May 15, firefighters who are making inspections may cite owners for failing to comply with the regulations. On May 1, Mr. Jacobs phones the fire station and asks Firefighter Jones to explain the new regulations. Which of the following statements is the most clear and accurate explanation?

a. During the next week, you should clear away the dry undergrowth and tree limbs that are touching the roof of your house and which overhang them.

b. By May 15, you must remove all dry undergrowth and trim back any tree limbs that overhang or are touching the roof of any building on your property.

c. Trim back all tree limbs and remove all dry undergrowth that overhangs or touches your house or any other building on your property by May 15 of each year.

d. You will be fined for any and all tree limbs that overhang your roof or for the dry undergrowth that you should have removed before May, which is the deadline.

71. Firefighter Jarvis is returning to the station after having spoken to students at an elementary school. There had been rain earlier in the day, but now the temperature has dropped below freezing. Jarvis is heading east across the Livingston Bridge when his truck hits a patch of ice and slides into a guardrail. Fortunately, he is not hurt. There is slight damage, however, to the right side of the truck. Later, Jarvis files a report on the accident. Which of the following reports describes the incident most clearly and accurately?

a. As I was driving on the Livingston Bridge, I hit some ice and slid into a guardrail, damaging the right side of the truck.

b. The guardrail damaged the right side of the truck, which was sitting on the Livingston Bridge on a patch of ice.

c. When I hit an icy patch along the Livingston Bridge, the guard rail hit the right side of the truck, causing me to slide into it.

d. Though I was not hurt, the truck was on its right side after it hit the guard rail on the bridge.

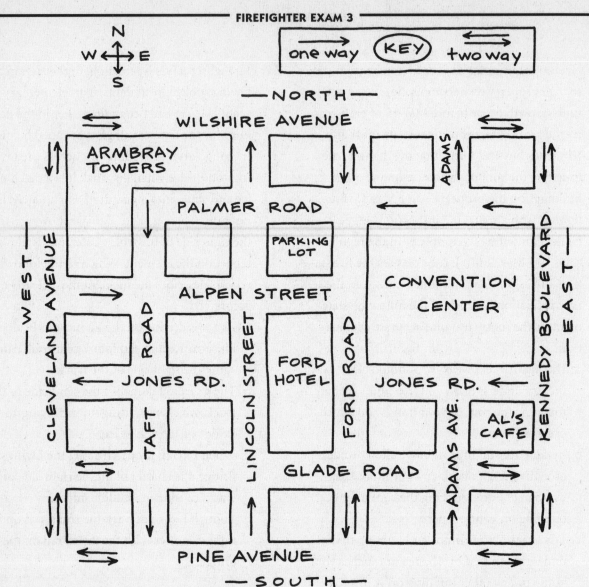

Answer questions 72–74 solely on the basis of the above map. The arrows indicate traffic flow; one arrow indicates a one-way street going in the direction of the arrow; two arrows represent a two-way street. You are not allowed to go the wrong way on a one-way street.

72. Firefighters Muldoon and Chavez have just gotten off work and are eating breakfast at Al's Cafe, which faces Jones Road. They get a call of a serious fire at the Cleveland Avenue entrance to the Armbray Towers and are asked to come and help. What is their most direct route to the Armbray Towers?

a. Go east on Jones Road, then south on Kennedy Blvd., then west on Glade Road, then north on Cleveland Avenue to the Armbray Towers.
b. Go west on Jones Road to Cleveland Avenue, then north on Cleveland to the Armbray Towers.
c. Go west on Jones Road, then south on Ford Road, then west on Glade Road, then north on Cleveland Avenue to the Armbray Towers.
d. Go west on Jones Road, then north on Glade Road, then west on Palmer Road, then south on Taft Road, then west on Jones Road, then north on Cleveland Avenue to the Armbray Towers.

73. Firefighters Chang and Parker are returning from a meeting and are northbound on Lincoln Street and have just crossed Alpen Street. They hear on the radio that a pickup truck has caught fire on Adams Avenue at Pine Avenue and is blocking traffic. They decide to go see if they can be of assistance. What is their most direct route to the truck fire scene?
   a. Continue north on Lincoln Street, then east on Wilshire Blvd., then south on Ford Road, then east on Glade Road, then south on Adam's Avenue to the accident scene.
   b. Continue north on Lincoln Street, then west on Palmer Road, then south on Taft Road, then east on Pine Avenue to the accident scene.
   c. Make a U-turn on Lincoln Street, south on Lincoln Street, east on Pine Avenue to the accident scene.
   d. Continue north on Lincoln Street, then east on Wilshire Avenue, then south on Kennedy Blvd., then west on Pine Avenue to the accident scene.

74. Firefighter Tananga is southbound on Kennedy Blvd. He makes a right turn onto Glade Road, then a left onto Taft Road, a right onto Pine Avenue and another right onto Cleveland Avenue, and then a right onto Wilshire Avenue. Which direction is he facing?
   a. west
   b. south
   c. east
   d. north

Answer questions 75–78 based on your best judgment and common sense.

75. You are a guest at dinner in a friend's home. The friend yells for help from the kitchen, and you rush in to find that grease in a frying pan has caught fire. The first thing you should do is
   a. remind everyone you are a firefighter to avoid the danger of panic
   b. turn off the stove and cover the pan with a metal covering
   c. pour water on the pan
   d. call 911

76. You receive a call at the firehouse in which a citizen reports smelling gas in her home. The first thing you should advise the citizen to do is to
   a. avoid doing anything that might cause a spark, including making any more calls
   b. turn off all gas appliances and leave the house immediately
   c. open all the doors and windows to ventilate the house
   d. call the gas company from the house next door

77. Which of the following would be the best way for the driver of a fire truck that is responding to an alarm to approach a red light at an intersection?
   a. Stop and wait for a green light.
   b. Have firefighters riding with you motion other vehicles away.
   c. Drive straight through because a fire truck always has the right of way.
   d. Stop and proceed as soon as the traffic is clear.

78. You are at an elementary school with your lieutenant, doing an inspection of the school. While walking through the halls, you are approached by a six-year-old boy who asks why he should bother to learn fire safety rules. You should tell him that
   a. learning fire safety rules will help him and his family know what to do in case of emergency
   b. he needn't memorize the rules as he might get them wrong; he should let his parents or school officials advise him what to do in case of an emergency
   c. knowing fire safety rules can show who is the smartest student in the class
   d. he should write a letter to the fire commissioner for a complete answer

Answer questions 79–82 based solely on the passage below.

A knowledge of just what takes place when a fire starts and continues to burn is essential for firefighters, because methods of attack, control, and extinguishment are based on this knowledge. With knowledge and understanding comes a lessening of the natural fear of fire that is ingrained in human beings. If this fear can be dispelled or minimized, a recruit can become a proficient firefighter.

Fire is the chemical reaction of fuel and oxygen (rapid oxidation), usually accompanied by light and heat. Therefore, the foundation of fire safety and fire extinguishment knowledge is the familiar Fire Triangle with its three essential legs: fuel, oxygen, and heat.

The combination of a substance with oxygen is known as oxidation. This process may take place slowly, rapidly, or instantaneously. Slow oxidation is exemplified by the dry rotting of wood, the yellowing of paper, or the rusting of iron. An example of instantaneous oxidation is the explosion of certain substances in the form of flour dust. The emphasis in fire training is principally on rapid oxidation, which is the phenomenon known as fire.

79. According to the passage, methods of attack, control, and extinguishment of fire are based on the firefighters'
   a. sound understanding of the principles of smoke
   b. thorough knowledge of the behavior of fire
   c. willingness to abide by the legal oath they must swear to obey
   d. willingness to put themselves in danger

80. According to the passage, the fire triangle consists of all of the following EXCEPT
   a. smoke
   b. heat
   c. oxygen
   d. fuel

81. An explosion is an example of
   a. slow oxidation
   b. instantaneous oxidation
   c. high oxidation
   d. recurrent oxidation

82. Firefighters inspecting a building notice some oxidation but take no action to attack or control it. The oxidation is probably the result of
a. a chemical reaction getting out of control
b. the ignition of flour dust in the air
c. a propane-air mixture in heavy concentrations near an open flame
d. iron rusting, paper yellowing, or wood rotting

Answer questions 83–84 based on your best judgment and common sense.

83. While operating at a fire, you notice cracks developing in the walls and the ceiling starting to sag. Your best first course of action is to
a. do nothing since these are usual conditions at a fire and are to be expected
b. immediately communicate your observation to your superior officer and other firefighters
c. run out of the building immediately
d. go to the floor above to find the cause of the damage

84. Firefighters should take great care when handling flammable liquids because the vapors from these liquids can travel to sources that can ignite them easily. Which of the following would NOT be advisable when refueling fire-fighting equipment?
a. keeping as many other firefighters from entering the area as possible
b. taking pains not to overfill the equipment
c. allowing smoking in the area as long as it is done some distance away
d. opening windows and doors in the immediate area

85. Your company is responding to a multi-vehicle accident at which injured citizens are trapped. You are driving an engine and have two more

blocks to go when you see a detour sign, and the road ahead is blocked off. You were just down this same block this morning, and no construction was going on. Following the detour sign will take you four blocks out of your way. You should
a. proceed directly through the traffic barrier, knocking it out of the way
b. move the traffic barrier and call the fire commissioner when you return to the firehouse to report a detour that should not exist
c. follow the detour sign because you can't be sure that construction was not begun since you last drove by this spot
d. call your superior officer and ask that officer what you should do

Answer questions 86–88 based on the Dwelling Inspection Form on the next page. Each item on the form is numbered. The questions refer to those numbers.

86. The presence of a handicapped person should be marked under which number?
a. 12
b. 15
c. 16
d. 11

87. While inspecting a residence, a firefighter finds cans of turpentine and gasoline under the back stairs. Which number should the firefighter mark to show this?
a. 10
b. 8
c. 12
d. 15

DWELLING INSPECTION FORM

Address: _____1_____ Date:_____2_____

The firefighter doing the inspection was: _____3_____

of Station No. _____4_____ Telephone:_____5_____

If home owner is not in, check here:__6___

If home owner refuses entry, check here:__7___

    With your consent a member of the fire department has just completed an inspection of your home. By eliminating any of the conditions or hazards checked below, you will make your home a safer place in which to live.

Improper use of extension cords, check here:__8___

Overfusing, check here:__9___

Improper storage of flammable or combustible liquids, check here:__10___

Defective smoke pipe vent or chimney, check here:__11___

Housekeeping, check here:__12___

Illegal burning. Burning in barrels, portable incinerators, or on the open ground is prohibited. Check here:__13___

Other conditions, check here:__14___

Remarks:_____15_____

_____

16. Are there invalids? Yes_____ No_____ Posted? Yes_____ No_____

17. Are there any smoke detectors in the home? Yes_____ No_____

18. Are there any fire extinguishers in the home? Yes_____ No_____

19. Are there any children under age 18 in the home? Yes_____ No_____ Posted? Yes_____ No_____

20. Are there any animals in the home? Yes_____ No_____

88. Which number shows the inspecting fire-fighter's station?

a. 5

b. 7

c. 10

d. 4

Answer questions 89–90 based on your best judgment and common sense.

89. An elementary school is visiting the firehouse. Some of the students begin climbing on the truck, others ask to hear the siren and see the lights, and still others want to slide down the pole. The best way to handle this is to

a. ask the teacher to gather the class into a group for an organized tour of the firehouse

b. advise the teacher on how to give the tour so that you can return to more important duties directly related to firefighting

c. tell the teacher the class will have to leave but may come back when the children have learned proper behavior in a firehouse

d. scold the children for not behaving in the firehouse and advise the teacher to either bring them under control or leave

90. While you are walking to work, dressed in your uniform, you witness an automobile accident. Which of the following actions is the most appropriate?

a. You leave because if you stay you will be late for work.

b. You stay to offer any information about what you saw, since you are a witness.

c. You leave after giving your name to the persons involved in the accident, so you can be contacted later about what you saw.

d. You leave so that you will not involve the fire department in what may become a court case.

Answer questions 91–94 based on the following information.

Firefighters must sometimes use the aerial ladder on the fire truck in order to reach the upper levels of a building during a fire. This is the large ladder that is attached to the fire truck and can pivot and extend as high as four stories. In order to operate the aerial ladder, firefighters must take the following steps in the order shown.

1. Activate the outriggers to stabilize the truck.

2. Increase the idle speed of the truck's internal combustion engine to 2,500 RPM, because the engine is used to drive the motors that operate the ladder.

3. In order to prevent electrocution, check the locations of overhead wires prior to activating the ladder.

4. Observe the following with regard to the three control levers that operate the ladder: Lever #1 controls the angle of the ladder, which must not exceed 60 degrees. Lever #2 controls the extension of the ladder, which must not exceed 50 feet. Lever #3 controls the rotation of the ladder.

5. If the wind is blowing at more than 30 miles per hour, do not extend the ladder more than 30 feet, and do not raise the ladder to an angle of greater than 35 degrees.

91. Firefighters have determined that they require the use of the aerial ladder to investigate the third floor of a high-rise building that is on fire. What should they do next?
    a. raise the ladder to 60 degrees
    b. turn on the pumps
    c. activate the outriggers
    d. check the wind speed

92. What is the maximum allowable angle to which the aerial ladder can be raised when the wind speed is less than 30 miles per hour?
    a. 60 degrees
    b. 50 degrees
    c. 3 degrees
    d. 30 degrees

93. What is the maximum distance the ladder may be extended when the wind speed is greater than 30 miles per hour?
    a. 2500 feet
    b. 50 feet
    c. 60 feet
    d. 30 feet

94. Firefighters who are using the aerial ladder want to extend it from 40 to 45 feet. They should use
    a. Lever #1
    b. Lever #2
    c. Lever #3
    d. Lever #4

Answer questions 95 and 96 based on your best judgment and common sense.

95. While on duty, you are ordered by your superior officer to issue a summons to a car parked directly in front of a fire hydrant. A citizen is upset because of your giving a neighbor a summons. What should you do?
    a. Put the incorrect license number on the summons and tell the citizen his neighbor will not receive a summons, but that the neighbor should not do it again.
    b. Tell your superior officer you do not feel it is your place to write a summons.
    c. Tell the citizen he must leave the scene or you will give him a summons as well.
    d. Explain to the citizen what a serious problem blocked fire hydrants are at fires.

96. A writer from *Firefighters Weekly* walks into the firehouse. She is doing a story about alcoholism in the workplace and wants you to give a statement. A source has told her that a firefighter in your firehouse has had a problem with alcohol. What should you tell her?
    a. that you know the firefighter she is referring to and will find out if that firefighter is willing to talk with her
    b. that you personally know of no one in this firehouse who has an alcohol problem but that you will report the rumor to your superior officer
    c. that you do not wish to comment but will get your superior officer for her
    d. that as a good citizen you will tell her what she wants to know as long as your name does not appear in the article

Answer questions 97–100 based on the following information.

The maintenance required on the fire truck is quite extensive. It is critical that all equipment be in proper working order at all times. A few of the major maintenance activities for the truck are shown below.

1. The internal combustion engine must be regularly maintained, which includes changing the oil, changing the air filter, checking the fluids, and changing the spark plugs.

2. The pumps must be lubricated and have their seals checked.

3. The hoses and fittings must be regularly inspected for wear.

4. All hand tools, such as axes, the Jaws of Life, halligans, and saws, must be inspected and stored in the proper location on the truck for quick access.

5. All valves and gauges must be checked and calibrated on a regular basis.

6. The extension ladders must be checked for possible structural problems.

97. When performing fire truck maintenance, firefighters must regularly replace the air filter on the
    a. breathing apparatus
    b. internal combustion engine
    c. pumps
    d. hoses

98. Which of the following is NOT typical fire truck maintenance?
    a. inspecting the gauges
    b. inspecting the valves
    c. inspecting the fire hydrants
    d. inspecting the ladders

99. During fire truck maintenance, structural problems must be checked for on the
    a. gauges
    b. ladders
    c. electric motors
    d. tires

100. Regular fire truck maintenance includes changing the spark plugs on the
    a. pumps
    b. electric motors
    c. internal combustion engine
    d. valves

ANSWERS

1. c. A fire escape is visible on the right side of the diagram; there are no stairs shown in the diagram.

2. a. Fire can be seen in two windows of building #935.

3. d. The people can be seen on the third and fifth floors and on the fire escape.

4. b. The fire hydrant is located in the front of the fire building.

5. d. The sign *B & G Candy Store* can be seen on the first floor of the apartment building.

6. c. A TV antenna, a smoke stack, and an air shaft can be seen on the roof.

7. a. No people can be seen in the hair salon.

8. b. No basement is represented in the diagram.

9. a. The dining room is adjacent to the kitchen.

10. c. There are two smoke detectors in the hall of the apartment.

11. b. The kitchen opens onto a terrace.

12. d. These rooms have windows that can be seen from the street.

13. a. Eight doors can be counted when standing in the hallway. There are also three doorways, but the question specifically asks about doors.

14. b. Raising a ladder to the bedroom window would be the best way for you to get in and for any occupants to get out.

15. a. The dining room may be entered from the living room or the kitchen.

16. c. See the paragraph that comes just before the list of procedures.

17. b. See step 2 of the procedure.

18. c. The cylinder is turned on after completion of step 2, which is checking the cylinder gauge.

19. a. The inspection of the face piece is step 5. Checking the hoses (step 4) is the only step that is done *before* the face piece is inspected.

20. b. All firefighting equipment is maintained so that it is available for maximum use in case of a fire. Choice **d** is minor by comparison. The truck won't go faster just because the tank is full, and it will not necessarily stall if it is less than half full (choices **a** and **c**).

21. d. The possibility that there is no one to rescue is not a problem for the firefighters; it is simply one less thing to worry about. The other choices are all hazards when fighting a fire in a vacant building.

22. a. Firefighters must report suspicious happenings to their superior officers. There is no reason to think this would interfere with police procedure (choice **c**). Choices **b** and **d** are illegal.

23. d. The first two sentences of the passage indicate that a backdraft is dangerous because it is an explosion. The other choices may be potential dangers, but they do not define a backdraft.

24. b. The second paragraph indicates that there is little or no visible flame with a potential backdraft. The other choices are listed at the end of the second paragraph.

25. c. This is clearly stated in the last paragraph. Choice **a** is not mentioned in the passage. The other choices would be useless or harmful.

26. a. The passage indicates that hot, smoldering fires have little or no visible flame and insufficient oxygen. It can be reasonably inferred, then, that more oxygen would produce more visible flames.

27. c. Choice **a** will take the man to the park, not to the Senior Citizens Center. Telling the man to ask a police officer (choice **b**) would be unnecessary and discourteous. Choice **d** will take him to the Senior Citizens Center, but not to the entrance.

28. d. Choice **a** will take the librarian the wrong way on Avenue C. Choice **b** shows the wrong directions for the streets—Brooklyn Street runs north-south and Avenue B runs east-west. Choice **c** will leave the librarian one block east of the gas station.

29. b. The other choices will bring you to the high school legally but are not as direct.

30. d. Route **a** is less direct. Route **b** does not start from the hospital and at any rate will involve going the wrong way on Avenue B. Route **c** will be less direct and will involve going the wrong way on Avenue D.

31. a. Choice **b** is less direct and will involve going the wrong way on 1st Avenue. Choice **c** will lead away from 1st Avenue, not toward it. Choice **d** will be less direct and will involve going the wrong way on Avenue C and 1st Avenue.

32. d. This is clearly stated in the last paragraph (*first aid measures should be directed at cooling the body quickly*). The other responses are first aid for heat exhaustion victims.

33. b. This is clearly stated in the first sentence of the second paragraph. Choices **a** and **c** are symptoms of heat stroke. Choice **d** is not mentioned.

34. c. Heat stroke victims have a *blocked sweating mechanism*, as stated in the third paragraph.

35. b. This is an inference from the information given in the second paragraph: If the victim still suffers from the symptoms listed in the first sentence of the paragraph, the victim needs more water and salt to help with the *inadequate intake of water and the loss of fluids* that caused those symptoms.

36. b. This is the only clearly written sentence. Choice **a** makes no sense. Choices **c** and **d** are unclear

because they are poorly worded and have misplaced modifiers.

37. c. This is the only clear statement. In choice **a**, it is not clear who has not been found. Choice **b** sounds like the underbrush has not been found. Choice **d** sounds like the teenagers are both lost and searching.

38. c. See the second bulleted section. Choices **a** and **b** deal with residents, not fire companies. Regarding choice **d**, water sources were clearly located, although overall water supply posed a problem.

39. d. See the last sentence of the first bulleted section. All the other choices are fair assumptions but are not included in passage.

40. a. See the first sentence of the last bulleted section.

41. d. Choice **a** appears in the fourth bulleted section. Choice **b** appears in introduction. Choice **c** appears in last bulleted section.

42. a. This is the most direct route to the Hillary Mansion, requiring the fewest changes in direction. Choice **b** requires the firefighter to drive through the Rossmore Hospital. Route **c** takes the firefighter the wrong way up West Broadway. Choice **d** takes the firefighter the wrong way on North Avenue.

43. c. This route requires the fewest number of turns. Choice **a** is wrong because Martin Road is a one-way street. Choice **b** requires a number of turns and goes the wrong way on Arthur Way. Choice **d** would mean traveling the wrong way on a one-way street.

44. b. The answer is clearly stated in paragraph 2.

45. c. See the third paragraph.

46. a. This can be surmised based on next to last sentence.

47. d. See the third paragraph.

48. c. Choice **a** is mentioned in the fourth paragraph (*a check must be made near all gas appliances* implies that they are potential sources of contamination). Choice **b** is mentioned in the third paragraph (*CO poisoning symptoms* are listed). Choice **d** is mentioned in the second paragraph (*calibrated meters* should be taken onto the premises).

49. d. Firefighters must not neglect their responsibilities. People's lives depend on firefighters reporting for duty as scheduled. A baseball game has much lower priority.

50. b. If an unforeseen occurrence will hinder your arrival at the fire station, you must inform your superior officer. The other choices involve leaving the scene, which would be illegal.

51. a. The fire department is in the best position to assist the family in this type of emergency. Choice **b** might put the child in further danger. Choice **c** is an overreaction to a somewhat common occurrence. The child's safety is more important than taking the easy way (choice **d**).

52. a. See the second and fourth paragraphs.

53. b. See the second paragraph. Sheets are made of cloth (Class A). This is proper procedure for extinguishing Class A fires.

54. a. See the fourth paragraph, relevant to power being shut off.

55. c. See the first paragraph. The other choices are too narrow.

56. a. Choice **b** is incorrect because it implies that the woman is in the alley. Choice **c** leaves out important information. Choice **d** is inaccurate.

57. d. This is the only clear and accurate statement. Choice **a** implies that Delgado has been disabled; choice **b** leaves out important information; choice **c** is both inaccurate and unclear.

58. a. This is the only clear and accurate statement of the event. Choice **b** sounds as though the neigh-

bor may have fallen on the ice. Choice **c** is unclear. Choice **d** doesn't say whose ankle was sprained.

59. c. Although the passage mentions firefighters' responsibilities (choice **a**), the main focus of the passage is the installation of smoke detectors. Choice **b** is only a detail. Choice **d** is not mentioned.

60. b. The answer can be inferred from the first sentence of the third paragraph.

61. a. The answer is found in the first paragraph (*smoke detectors cut a person's risk of dying in a fire in half*).

62. c. The answer can be found in the next to last sentence of the passage.

63. d. The answer is implied by the first sentence of the passage. There is no information in the passage to indicate that the other choices are a firefighter's responsibility.

64. d. This is the only clear and accurate account of what happened. Choice **a** implies that the watch was stolen. Choice **b** implies that the event occurred while Lopez was putting out a fire. Choice **c** is inaccurate and unclear.

65. a. This is the only clear and accurate statement. Choice **b** gives the wrong address and time. In choice **c**, the phrase "the closing of the application" is unclear. Choice **d** gives incorrect information.

66. d. Sabotaging another firefighter's equipment is a serious matter. If your impression is correct, both the firefighter whose equipment has been sabotaged and the civilians who are counting on her would be in great danger. You must therefore report the incident.

67. b. In matters dealing with the public or press, the best course of action is to refer them to your superior officer.

68. a. Working on a main highway is hazardous, and for this reason flares are standard emergency equipment. They will alert motorists to firefighters' presence.

69. d. This is the only clear report. Choice **a** is unclear and distorts the facts; choices **b** and **c** provide most of the information but are unclear.

70. b. This is the only clear and accurate explanation. Choice **a** gives a wrong deadline date; choices **c** and **d** are poorly worded and unclear.

71. a. This is the only clear and accurate statement. None of the other choices even indicate that Jarvis was driving the truck. Choice **d** is inaccurate and does not say where the accident took place.

72. c. This is the quickest way around the Ford Hotel and then to Cleveland Avenue. Choice **a** is not correct because it requires the officers to go the wrong way on Jones, a one-way street. Choice **b** would require the firefighters to drive through the Ford Hotel and then to Cleveland Avenue. Choice **d** has too many turns to be the most direct.

73. b. This is correct because it is the quickest and most direct route. Choice **a** has too many turns to be the most direct. Choice **c** is a one-way street going north and wouldn't be the right choice. Choice **d** takes the firefighters several blocks out of their way and is not the most direct.

74. c. A right turn onto Glade Road turns Firefighter Tananga west. The left onto Taft Road turns him south; the right onto Pine Avenue turns him west and the right onto Cleveland Avenue turns him back north, and the right onto Wilshire Avenue turns him east.

75. b. Covering the pan is the quickest way to extinguish the flame, which is the most important thing. Grease that is very hot will explode if water is poured on it (choice **c**). Choices **a** and **d** take time, during which the fire may spread.

76. a. The most dangerous thing in this situation would be an explosion, which could be set off by a spark.

77. d. Caution is always used while driving through the streets. While the fire engine does have the right of way and need not wait for a green light (choices **a** and **c**), getting into an accident en route to the fire scene would delay firefighters at best and cause damage and injury at worst. There is no way the firefighters with you can control traffic; their gestures might not even be noticed by other drivers (choice **b**).

78. a. Fire prevention and safety is something every child should know.

79. b. The answer can be found in the first sentence of paragraph 1.

80. a. The answer can be found in the second sentence of paragraph 2.

81. b. The answer can be found in the first two sentences of paragraph 3.

82. d. The answer can be found in the third sentence of paragraph 3.

83. b. The first priority is safety, not only your own but that of the other firefighters. A natural reaction may be to run out, but firefighters must work as a team.

84. c. When firefighters refuel their equipment they should make sure the room is well ventilated from the fumes and should be careful not to spill the highly flammable liquid, so choices **b** and **d** are incorrect. The unnecessary presence of anyone else would be a needless hazard, so choice **a** is incorrect. On the other hand, smoking, even some distance from the refueling operation, could ignite the vapors from the liquid.

85. c. Driving through a closed-off area (choices **a** and **b**) could delay you longer than if you just went around, since conditions might have changed since you passed this way in the morning. Calling your superior officer (choice **d**) would likely cause more delay than taking the detour.

86. c. Refer to dwelling inspection form, item number 16.

87. a. Refer to dwelling inspection form, item number 10.

88. d. Refer to dwelling inspection form, item number 4.

89. a. A firefighter is always expected to behave in a courteous manner when dealing with civilians, especially children. Children should be taught to respect firefighters so they will turn to firefighters for help if they need it. All the other choices would be discourteous.

90. b. It is a firefighter's duty to be honest and upstanding on or off duty. Leaving for any of the reasons given would mean neglecting an important civic responsibility.

91. c. This is the first step in the procedure.

92. a. Though step 5 of the procedure states that the maximum angle is 35 degrees when the wind speed is more than 30 mph, step 4 is the one that covers limitations (60 degree maximum angle and 50 feet maximum extension) for situations when the wind speed is less than 30 mph.

93. d. See step 5 of the procedure.

94. b. See step 4.

95. d. A direct explanation is the best response to civilian complaints. Blocking a hydrant can have serious consequences, so answer **a** is not an option. Firefighters should not disobey their superior officers (choice **b**) or threaten civilians (choice **c**).

96. c. In matters dealing with the public or press, the best course of action is to refer them to your superior officer.

97. b. See step 1 of the procedure.

98. c. Inspecting fire hydrants is not mentioned in the procedure.

99. b. See step 6 of the procedure.

100. c. See step 1 of the procedure.

SCORING

In most cities you need a score of at least 70–80 percent (that is, 70–80 questions right) to pass the exam. However, since you may need a much higher score than that to be called for the next step in the process, and since your rank on the eligibility list may be partly based on your score on the written exam, you should try for the highest score you can possibly reach. You have probably seen improvement between your first practice exam score and this one. If you didn't improve as much as you would like, here are some options:

- **If you scored below 60 percent,** you should do some serious thinking about whether you're really ready to take a firefighter exam. An adult education course in reading comprehension at a high school or community college would be a very good strategy. If you don't have time for a course, you should at least try to get some private tutoring.
- **If your score is in the 60 to 70 percent range,** you need to work as hard as you can in the time you have left to boost your skills. Consider the LearningExpress book *Reading Comprehension in 20 Minutes a Day* (order information at the back of this book) or other books from your public library. Also, re-read Chapters 6, 7, 9, 11, and 12 of this book, and make sure you take *all* of the advice there for improving your score. Enlist friends and family to help you by making up mock test questions and quizzing you on them.
- **If your score is between 70 and 95 percent,** you could still benefit from additional work to help improve your score. Go back to Chapters 6, 7, 9, 11, and 12 and study them diligently between now and test day.

- **If you scored above 95 percent,** congratulations! Your score should be high enough to make you an attractive candidate to the any fire department. Be sure you don't lose your edge; keep studying this book up to the day before the exam.

If you didn't score as well as you would like, try to analyze the reasons why. Did you run out of time before you could answer all the questions? Did you go back and change your answer from the right one to a wrong one? Did you get flustered and sit staring at a hard question for what seemed like hours? If you had any of these problems, go back and review the test-taking strategies in Chapter 3 to learn how to avoid them.

You should also look at how you did on each kind of question on the test. You may have done very well on reading comprehension questions and poorly on map-reading questions, or vice versa. If you can figure out where your strengths and weaknesses lie, you'll know where to concentrate your efforts in the time you have left before the exam. Take out your completed answer sheet and compare it to the table on the next page in order to find out which kinds of questions you did well in and which kinds you had difficulty with. Then go back and spend extra time studying the chapters that cover the questions that gave you the most trouble.

Finally, one of the biggest factors in your success on the exam is your self-confidence. Remember, because you're using this book, you're better prepared than most of the other people who are taking the exam with you.

FIREFIGHTER EXAM 3

Question Type	Question Numbers	Chapter
Memory and Observation (15 questions)	1-15	7, "Memory and Observation"
Reading Comprehension (25 questions)	23–26, 32–35, 38–41, 52–55, 59–63, 79–82	6, "Reading Comprehension"
Map Reading (10 questions)	27–31, 42–43, 72–74	11, "Spatial Relations"
Following Procedures (20 questions)	16–19, 44–48, 86–88, 91–94, 97–100	9, "Judgment and Reasoning"
Judgment (20 questions)	20–22, 49–51, 66–68, 75–78, 83–85, 89–90, 95–96	9, "Judgment and Reasoning"
Verbal Expression (10 questions)	36–37, 56–58, 64–65, 69–71	12, "Verbal Expression"

C·H·A·P·T·E·R

FIREFIGHTER EXAM 4

14

CHAPTER SUMMARY

This is the last of the four practice exams in this book covering the areas most often tested on firefighter exams. Compare your score on this test with your score on the previous practice exams to see how much you have improved after working through the instructional chapters in this book.

L
ike Firefighter Exam 2 in Chapter 5, the practice exam that follows tests some of the basic skills that you need to do well as a firefighter: reading comprehension, verbal expression, logical reasoning, mathematics, and mechanical aptitude. For this final exam, simulate the actual test-taking experience as much as possible. Find a quiet place to work where you won't be interrupted. Tear out the answer sheet on the next page and find some number 2 pencils to fill in the circles with. Set a timer or stopwatch, and give yourself two and a half hours for the entire exam. When that time is up, stop, even if you haven't finished the entire test.

After the exam, use the answer key that follows it to see how you did and to find out why the correct answers are correct. The answer key is followed by a section on how to score your exam and suggestions for continued study.

1.	ⓐ	ⓑ	ⓒ	ⓓ
2.	ⓐ	ⓑ	ⓒ	ⓓ
3.	ⓐ	ⓑ	ⓒ	ⓓ
4.	ⓐ	ⓑ	ⓒ	ⓓ
5.	ⓐ	ⓑ	ⓒ	ⓓ
6.	ⓐ	ⓑ	ⓒ	ⓓ
7.	ⓐ	ⓑ	ⓒ	ⓓ
8.	ⓐ	ⓑ	ⓒ	ⓓ
9.	ⓐ	ⓑ	ⓒ	ⓓ
10.	ⓐ	ⓑ	ⓒ	ⓓ
11.	ⓐ	ⓑ	ⓒ	ⓓ
12.	ⓐ	ⓑ	ⓒ	ⓓ
13.	ⓐ	ⓑ	ⓒ	ⓓ
14.	ⓐ	ⓑ	ⓒ	ⓓ
15.	ⓐ	ⓑ	ⓒ	ⓓ
16.	ⓐ	ⓑ	ⓒ	ⓓ
17.	ⓐ	ⓑ	ⓒ	ⓓ
18.	ⓐ	ⓑ	ⓒ	ⓓ
19.	ⓐ	ⓑ	ⓒ	ⓓ
20.	ⓐ	ⓑ	ⓒ	ⓓ
21.	ⓐ	ⓑ	ⓒ	ⓓ
22.	ⓐ	ⓑ	ⓒ	ⓓ
23.	ⓐ	ⓑ	ⓒ	ⓓ
24.	ⓐ	ⓑ	ⓒ	ⓓ
25.	ⓐ	ⓑ	ⓒ	ⓓ
26.	ⓐ	ⓑ	ⓒ	ⓓ
27.	ⓐ	ⓑ	ⓒ	ⓓ
28.	ⓐ	ⓑ	ⓒ	ⓓ
29.	ⓐ	ⓑ	ⓒ	ⓓ
30.	ⓐ	ⓑ	ⓒ	ⓓ
31.	ⓐ	ⓑ	ⓒ	ⓓ
32.	ⓐ	ⓑ	ⓒ	ⓓ
33.	ⓐ	ⓑ	ⓒ	ⓓ
34.	ⓐ	ⓑ	ⓒ	ⓓ

35.	ⓐ	ⓑ	ⓒ	ⓓ
36.	ⓐ	ⓑ	ⓒ	ⓓ
37.	ⓐ	ⓑ	ⓒ	ⓓ
38.	ⓐ	ⓑ	ⓒ	ⓓ
39.	ⓐ	ⓑ	ⓒ	ⓓ
40.	ⓐ	ⓑ	ⓒ	ⓓ
41.	ⓐ	ⓑ	ⓒ	ⓓ
42.	ⓐ	ⓑ	ⓒ	ⓓ
43.	ⓐ	ⓑ	ⓒ	ⓓ
44.	ⓐ	ⓑ	ⓒ	ⓓ
45.	ⓐ	ⓑ	ⓒ	ⓓ
46.	ⓐ	ⓑ	ⓒ	ⓓ
47.	ⓐ	ⓑ	ⓒ	ⓓ
48.	ⓐ	ⓑ	ⓒ	ⓓ
49.	ⓐ	ⓑ	ⓒ	ⓓ
50.	ⓐ	ⓑ	ⓒ	ⓓ
51.	ⓐ	ⓑ	ⓒ	ⓓ
52.	ⓐ	ⓑ	ⓒ	ⓓ
53.	ⓐ	ⓑ	ⓒ	ⓓ
54.	ⓐ	ⓑ	ⓒ	ⓓ
55.	ⓐ	ⓑ	ⓒ	ⓓ
56.	ⓐ	ⓑ	ⓒ	ⓓ
57.	ⓐ	ⓑ	ⓒ	ⓓ
58.	ⓐ	ⓑ	ⓒ	ⓓ
59.	ⓐ	ⓑ	ⓒ	ⓓ
60.	ⓐ	ⓑ	ⓒ	ⓓ
61.	ⓐ	ⓑ	ⓒ	ⓓ
62.	ⓐ	ⓑ	ⓒ	ⓓ
63.	ⓐ	ⓑ	ⓒ	ⓓ
64.	ⓐ	ⓑ	ⓒ	ⓓ
65.	ⓐ	ⓑ	ⓒ	ⓓ
66.	ⓐ	ⓑ	ⓒ	ⓓ
67.	ⓐ	ⓑ	ⓒ	ⓓ
68.	ⓐ	ⓑ	ⓒ	ⓓ

69.	ⓐ	ⓑ	ⓒ	ⓓ
70.	ⓐ	ⓑ	ⓒ	ⓓ
71.	ⓐ	ⓑ	ⓒ	ⓓ
72.	ⓐ	ⓑ	ⓒ	ⓓ
73.	ⓐ	ⓑ	ⓒ	ⓓ
74.	ⓐ	ⓑ	ⓒ	ⓓ
75.	ⓐ	ⓑ	ⓒ	ⓓ
76.	ⓐ	ⓑ	ⓒ	ⓓ
77.	ⓐ	ⓑ	ⓒ	ⓓ
78.	ⓐ	ⓑ	ⓒ	ⓓ
79.	ⓐ	ⓑ	ⓒ	ⓓ
80.	ⓐ	ⓑ	ⓒ	ⓓ
81.	ⓐ	ⓑ	ⓒ	ⓓ
82.	ⓐ	ⓑ	ⓒ	ⓓ
83.	ⓐ	ⓑ	ⓒ	ⓓ
84.	ⓐ	ⓑ	ⓒ	ⓓ
85.	ⓐ	ⓑ	ⓒ	ⓓ
86.	ⓐ	ⓑ	ⓒ	ⓓ
87.	ⓐ	ⓑ	ⓒ	ⓓ
88.	ⓐ	ⓑ	ⓒ	ⓓ
89.	ⓐ	ⓑ	ⓒ	ⓓ
90.	ⓐ	ⓑ	ⓒ	ⓓ
91.	ⓐ	ⓑ	ⓒ	ⓓ
92.	ⓐ	ⓑ	ⓒ	ⓓ
93.	ⓐ	ⓑ	ⓒ	ⓓ
94.	ⓐ	ⓑ	ⓒ	ⓓ
95.	ⓐ	ⓑ	ⓒ	ⓓ

SECTION 1: READING COMPREHENSION

Answer questions 1–6 based solely on the information in the following passage.

An ecosystem is a group of animals and plants living in a specific region and interacting with one another and with their physical environment. Ecosystems include physical and chemical components, such as soils, water, and nutrients, that support the organisms living there. These organisms may range from large animals to microscopic bacteria.

Ecosystems also can be thought of as the interactions among all organisms in a given habitat; for instance, one species may serve as food for another. People are part of the ecosystems where they live and work. Human activities can harm or destroy local ecosystems unless actions such as land development for housing or businesses are carefully planned to conserve and sustain the ecology of the area. An important part of ecosystem management involves finding ways to protect and enhance economic and social well-being while protecting the physical environment.

1. The passage describes an ecosystem as
   a. a community of animals, plants, and bacteria that interact with one another
   b. any human activity that can do great damage to the environment
   c. microscopic bacteria that provide food for plants and animals
   d. a system that provides economic and social protection for a group of people

2. According to the passage, one way ecosystems can be destroyed is by
   a. tiny bacteria
   b. plants and soils
   c. land development
   d. ecosystem management

3. In the second paragraph, the author mainly argues in favor of
   a. the building of more new homes
   b. protecting local businesses
   c. stopping all land development
   d. protecting ecosystems

4. Based on the passage, which of the following is NOT an organism?
   a. a small animal
   b. water
   c. a plant
   d. microscopic bacteria

5. The statement "one species may serve as food for another" is an example of
   a. a habitat
   b. social well-being
   c. an interaction
   d. a chemical component

6. The author of this passage most likely believes that ecosystems
   a. can be harmed by people
   b. will soon die out
   c. should not include people
   d. are less important than affordable housing

Answer questions 7 and 8 by referring to the following table, which shows a lack of precipitation for certain towns in 1999.

LACK OF PRECIPITATION, 1999, IN HURST COUNTY TOWNS

Town	Days Without Precipitation*	Status**
Riderville	38	LEVEL TWO
Adams	25	LEVEL ONE
Parkston	74	LEVEL THREE
Kings Hill	28	LEVEL TWO
West Granville	50	LEVEL THREE
Braxton	23	LEVEL THREE
Chase Crossing	53	LEVEL FOUR
Livingston Center	45	LEVEL THREE

*Rainfall of less than an inch in a 48-hour period.
**The higher the level, the greater the potential for fire.

7. The status of the town with the LEAST number of days without significant precipitation is
   a. LEVEL ONE
   b. LEVEL TWO
   c. LEVEL THREE
   d. LEVEL FOUR

8. Compared to Riderville, Livingston Center
   a. is more likely to experience a fire
   b. is less likely to experience a fire
   c. is just as likely to experience a fire
   d. has gone a shorter period without significant precipitation

Answer questions 9–12 based solely on the information in the following passage.

The National Aeronautic and Space Administration (NASA) waited twenty-five years to send another craft to land on the moon. The Lunar Prospector took off in January of 1998, in the first moon shot since astronauts last walked on the moon in 1972. On this trip, the moon-traveler was only a low-cost robot, who would spend a year on the surface of the moon, collecting minerals and ice.

Unlike the moon shots of the 1960s and 1970s, Lunar Prospector did not carry a camera, so the American public did not get to see new pictures of the moon's surface. Instead, Prospector carried instruments that would map the make-up of the entire surface of the moon. Scientists were anxious for the results of one exploration in particular—that done by the neutron spectrometer. Using this instrument, Prospector examined the moon's poles, searching for signs of water ice. There has long been speculation that frozen water from comets may have accumulated in craters at one of the moon's poles and may still be there, as this pole is permanently shielded from the sun. The neutron spectrometer can detect the presence of as little as one cup of water in a cubic yard of soil.

9. Which of the following pieces of information is included in the passage?
   a. why NASA waited twenty-five years between moon landings
   b. how many astronauts walked on the moon in 1972
   c. what the purpose of the neutron spectrometer was
   d. if frozen water was detected on the moon

10. One difference between the 1998 moon landing and the 1972 moon landing is that
   a. on the 1998 landing, no astronauts walked on the moon
   b. on the 1998 landing, robots were not used
   c. on the 1972 landing, Americans did not see pictures of the moon
   d. on the 1972 landing, minerals were not collected

11. How were minerals collected during the Lunar Prospector mission?
   a. by astronauts
   b. by a robot
   c. by the neutron spectrometer
   d. by an instrument that is not named in the passage

12. Which of the following is the best meaning of the underlined word *speculation* as it is used in the second paragraph of the passage?
   a. a theory
   b. an investment
   c. a vision
   d. an image

Answer questions 13 and 14 based on the following circle graph, which shows the distribution of residential fires in a particular city.

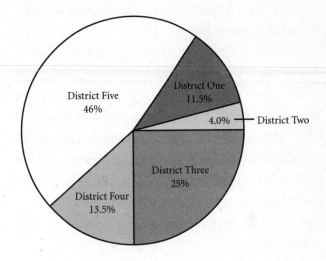

13. Which districts combined had half of the total number of fires?
   a. One, Two, and Three
   b. One, Two, and Four
   c. Three and Four
   d. Two and Five

14. If there were 200 fires throughout Centerville, how many fires were there in District Three?
   a. 4
   b. 25
   c. 50
   d. 66

Answer questions 15–18 based solely on the information in the following passage.

Due to recent national events, the Yardley City Government has introduced new bomb threat procedures for government buildings. This information is for department use only.

From this point on, all personnel must be on the highest alert. You must pay close attention to your surroundings. If a vehicle you do not recognize enters the parking lot, observe driver and passenger behavior. If an employee has been terminated recently, examine his or her performance evaluations and exit interview reports. If there are incidents involving visitors, notify your supervisor. Keep in mind, however, that we must not overreact. Part of being alert is exercising proper judgment.

If there is an actual bomb threat, carry out the following procedures: First, evacuate the premises. Do not fall into fire drill routines; remember, you are vacating in order to avoid injury stemming from premeditated violence. Leave the building immediately. Take nothing with you. Do not shut down electrical equipment. Keep movement to a minimum. If there are visitors and/or persons with special needs in the building, make certain they are evacuated.

Proceed to the area AWAY from the building designated in the fire drill policy. Do not enter vehicles parked nearby. Take attendance. Make mental notes about any missing personnel or any questionable activity in or near the building. If you received the actual threat, record as much information as possible: gender, specific language, "insider" information, type of violence threatened. Once you reach your designated safe area, identify emergency personnel and share the information with them.

15. Which of the following organizational scheme does the passage mainly follow?
    a. hierarchical order
    b. chronological order
    c. order by topic
    d. cause-and-effect

16. The passage as a whole suggests that, during an actual bomb threat incident, the most important priority is to
    a. avoid overreacting
    b. follow proper procedures
    c. notify the supervisor of suspicious activities
    d. keep the bomb threat information inside the department

17. Which of the following is NOT included in this passage?
    a. where to go in the event of a bomb threat
    b. what to do if an unknown vehicle parks near the station
    c. what to do with specific bomb threat information
    d. how to identify a potentially dangerous fired employee

18. If there is a bomb threat incident, and you have previously seen a visitor enter the building in a wheelchair, you should
    a. direct the visitor to the designated evacuation area
    b. notify your supervisor
    c. notify emergency personnel
    d. carefully observe the visitor's behavior

Answer questions 19–21 by referring to the following graph, which compares the average annual rainfall with the actual rainfall for one year in a particular city.

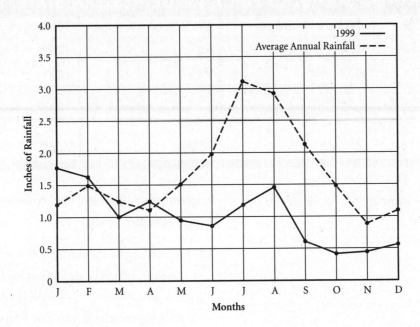

19. In which of the following months during 1999 was the rainfall nearest normal?

a. April

b. May

c. June

d. July

20. What is the average rainfall amount for the month of September?

a. 0.5 inches

b. 0.7 inches

c. 2.0 inches

d. 2.1 inches

21. During 1999, how many months had above-average rainfall amounts?

a. 2

b. 3

c. 6

d. 9

Answer question 22 by referring to the following table, which shows total wildfires in a certain state in 1999.

WILDFIRE STATISTICS FOR A LARGE WESTERN STATE				
Cause	1999	10 Year Average	1999 % of Average	1998 % of Average
Lightning	260	404	64%	149%
Human	770	819	94%	107%
Total Fires	1030	1223	84%	120%
Acreage Burned	4,616	25,096	18%	266%

22. Approximately how many fires were caused by lightning in 1998?
  a. 400
  b. 600
  c. 800
  d. 1,000

Answer questions 23–28 based solely on the information in the following passage.

Typically people think of genius, whether it manifests in Mozart's composing symphonies at age five or Einstein's discovery of relativity, as having a quality not just of the supernatural but also of the eccentric. People see genius as a "good" abnormality. They also think of genius as a completely unpredictable abnormality.

Until recently, psychologists regarded the quirks of genius as too inconsistent to describe intelligibly. However, a ground-breaking study by Anna Findley has uncovered predictable patterns in the biographies of geniuses. These patterns, however, do not dispel the common belief that there is a kind of supernatural intervention in the lives of unusually talented men and women, even though these patterns occur with regularity. For example, Findley's study shows that all geniuses experience three intensely productive periods in their lives. One of these periods always occurs shortly

before the genius's death; this is true whether the genius lives to nineteen or ninety.

23. According to the information presented in the passage, which of the following best sums up the general populace's opinion of genius?
  a. It is predictable and uncommon.
  b. It is scornful and abnormal.
  c. It is unpredictable and erratic.
  d. It is extraordinary and erratic.

24. Which of the following would be the best title for passage?
  a. "Understanding Einstein"
  b. "Predicting the Life of a Genius"
  c. "The Uncanny Patterns in the Lives of Geniuses"
  d. "Pattern and Disorder in the Lives of Geniuses"

25. Given the information in the passage, which of the following statements is true?
  a. Anna Findley is a biographer.
  b. The lives of geniuses are eccentric and unpredictable.
  c. A genius has three very productive times in his or her life.
  d. Mozart discovered relativity.

26. Findley's study is described as "ground-breaking" most likely because
   a. it was written in an intelligent way
   b. it was conducted by a genius
   c. other psychologists agreed with Findley
   d. it provides information that was not known earlier

27. The tone of this passage could best be described as
   a. gloomy

   b. informative
   c. humorous
   d. joyful

28. The passage gives all of the following pieces of information EXCEPT
   a. what Anna Findley's study discovered
   b. when Mozart began composing music
   c. the way in which many people define genius
   d. why geniuses have three productive periods

Answer questions 29 and 30 by referring to the following table, which shows fire fatalities statewide for certain ages.

FIRE FATALITIES STATEWIDE BY AGE, RACE, AND GENDER										
Ages	1-4	5-10	10-14	15-19	20-24	25-34	35-44	45-54	55-64	Totals
White Male	7	1	0	2	2	9	8	7	4	40
White Female	7	1	0	1	0	2	3	1	6	21
Non-White Male	5	3	2	0	0	5	8	3	7	33
Non-White Female	3	3	0	0	2	3	3	2	1	17
Totals	22	8	2	3	4	19	22	13	18	111

Note: For the purposes of this study, persons under 20 years of age are classified as children. Persons 20 years of age and older are classified as adults.

29. According to the table, the greatest number of fatalities among children aged 1–14 occurred in which group?
   a. white males
   b. non-white males
   c. white females
   d. non-white females

30. If the trend shown on the table continues in future years, which of the following statements is accurate?
   a. Fewer white males than white females will die.
   b. Fewer white females over age 20 than white females under 20 will die.
   c. More adults than children will die.
   d. More non-white persons than white persons will die.

SECTION 2: VERBAL EXPRESSION

For questions 31–35, choose the word that most nearly means the same as the italicized word.

31. On the witness stand, the suspected arsonist, usually a flashy dresser, appeared uncharacteristically *nondescript*.
a. lethargic
b. undistinguished
c. indisposed
d. impeccable

32. According to the code of conduct, "Every firefighter will be held *accountable* for his or her decisions."
a. applauded
b. compensated
c. responsible
d. approachable

33. Since the townspeople were so dissatisfied, various methods to *alleviate* the situation were debated.
a. ease
b. tolerate
c. clarify
d. intensify

34. The fire education officer was an *indispensable* member of the department, so they had no choice but to offer him a higher salary to stay on.
a. indulgent
b. experienced
c. essential
d. apologetic

35. After the storm caused raw sewage to seep into the ground water, the Water Department had to take measures to *decontaminate* the city's water supply.
a. refine
b. revive
c. freshen
d. purify

For questions 36–38, choose the word that best fills the blank.

36. You cannot join the fire safety team without the _____ three-week training course.
a. prerequisite
b. optional
c. preferred
d. advisable

37. The suspect gave a _____ explanation for his presence at the scene of the fire, so the police decided to look elsewhere for the arsonist.
a. plausible
b. credible
c. insufficient
d. apologetic

38. The general public didn't care about the new building code and so was _____ about the outcome.
a. enraged
b. apathetic
c. suspicious
d. saddened

For questions 39–42, replace the underlined portion with the phrase that best completes the sentence. If the sentence is correct as is, choose option **a**.

39. An American poet of the nineteenth century, <u>Walt Whitman's collection of poems, *Leaves of Grass,*</u> celebrates nature and individualism.
  a. Walt Whitman's collection of poems, *Leaves of Grass,*
  b. *Leaves of Grass,* a collection of poems by Walt Whitman,
  c. Walt Whitman published a collection of poems, *Leaves of Grass,* which
  d. Walt Whitman published poems, collected as *Leaves of Grass,* that

40. <u>When two angles have the same degree measure, it is said to be congruent.</u>
  a. When two angles have the same degree measure, it is said to be congruent.
  b. When two angles has the same degree measure, it is said to be congruent.
  c. Two angles with the same degree measure is said to be congruent.
  d. When two angles have the same degree measure, they are said to be congruent.

41. <u>The likelihood</u> of a region's experiencing an earthquake can be estimated, earthquakes cannot be accurately predicted.
  a. The likelihood
  b. Although the likelihood
  c. Since the likelihood
  d. In fact, the likelihood

42. Everyone signed the petition before <u>submitting it</u> to the city counsel.
  a. submitting it
  b. you submit it
  c. we will submit it
  d. we submitted it

43. Which of these expresses the idea most clearly?
  a. As soon she realized that the hurricane was going to strike, the mayor told the residents to evacuate the city.
  b. As soon she realized that the hurricane was going to strike, the city residents were told to evacuate by the mayor.
  c. As soon she realized that the hurricane was going to strike, the mayor tells the city residents of her decision to evacuate.
  d. As soon she realized that the hurricane was going to strike, the residents of the city were told to evacuate by the mayor.

44. Which of these expresses the idea most clearly?
  a. A sharpshooter for many years, a pea could be shot off a person's shoulder from 70 yards away by Miles Johnson.
  b. A sharpshooter for many years, Miles Johnson could shoot a pea off a person's shoulder from 70 yards away.
  c. A sharpshooter for many years, from 70 yards away off a person's shoulder Miles Johnson could have shot a pea.
  d. A sharpshooter for many years, Miles Johnson could shoot from 70 yards away off a person's shoulder a pea.

45. Which of these expresses the idea most clearly?

   a. Ultra-violet radiation levels are 60 percent higher at 8,500 feet from the sun than they are at sea level, according to researchers.

   b. Researchers have found from the sun ultra-violet radiation levels 60 percent higher, they say, at 8,500 feet than at sea level.

   c. Researchers have found that ultra-violet radiation levels from the sun are 60 percent higher at 8,500 feet than they are at sea level.

   d. At 8,500 feet researchers have found that ultra-violet radiation levels are 60 percent higher from sea level with the sun's rays.

SECTION 3: LOGICAL REASONING

46. Look at this series: 2, 5, 28, 8, __, 20, 14, 17,... What number should fill the blank?

   a. 11

   b. 17

   c. 20

   d. 28

47. Look at this series: 84, 89, 86, 91, 88, __, 90,... What number should fill the blank?

   a. 83

   b. 85

   c. 92

   d. 93

48. Look at this series: $\frac{1}{9}$, $\frac{1}{3}$, 1, __, 9,... What number should fill the blank?

   a. $\frac{2}{3}$

   b. 3

   c. 6

   d. 27

49. Look at this series: F2, __, D8, C16, B32,... What letter and numbers should fill the blank?

   a. A16

   b. G4

   c. E4

   d. E3

50. Look at this series: JAK, KBL, LCM, MDN, __,... What letters should fill the blank?

   a. OEP

   b. NEO

   c. MEN

   d. PFQ

For questions 51–53, find the pattern in the sequence.

51.

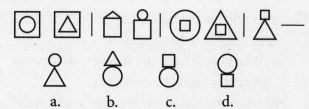

   a.   b.   c.   d.

52.

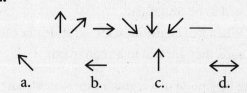

   a.   b.   c.   d.

53.

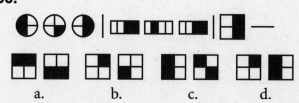

   a.   b.   c.   d.

For questions 54–57, complete the analogy.

54. Baker is to bread as congressman is to
   a. senator
   b. law
   c. state
   d. politician

55. Control is to dominate as magnify is to
   a. enlarge
   b. preserve
   c. decrease
   d. divide

56. Yard is to inch as quart is to
   a. gallon
   b. ounce
   c. milk
   d. liquid

57. Sponge is to porous as rubber is to
   a. massive
   b. solid
   c. elastic
   d. inflexible

58. The temperature on Monday was lower than on Tuesday.
   The temperature on Wednesday was lower than on Tuesday.
   The temperature on Monday was higher than on Wednesday.
   If the first two statements are true, the third statement is
   a. true
   b. false
   c. uncertain

59. Battery X lasts longer than Battery Y.
   Battery Y doesn't last as long as Battery Z.
   Battery Z lasts longer than Battery X.
   If the first two statements are true, the third statement is
   a. true
   b. false
   c. uncertain

60. Middletown is north of Centerville.
   Centerville is east of Penfield.
   Penfield is northwest of Middletown.
   If the first two statements are true, the third statement is
   a. true
   b. false
   c. uncertain

SECTION 4: MATHEMATICS

61. Firefighter Green earns $26,000 a year. If she receives a 4.5% salary increase, how much will she earn?
   a. $26,450
   b. $27,170
   c. $27,260
   c. $29,200

62. Which of the following rooms has the greatest perimeter?
   a. a square room 10 feet × 10 feet
   b. a square room 11 feet × 11 feet
   c. a rectangular room 12 feet × 8 feet
   d. a rectangular room 14 feet × 7 feet

63. If it takes four firefighters 1 hour and 45 minutes to perform a particular job, how long would it take one firefighter working at the same rate to perform the same task alone?
a. 4.5 hours
b. 5 hours
c. 7 hours
d. 7.5 hours

64. Which of the following hose diameters is the smallest?
a. $\frac{17}{20}$ inches
b. $\frac{3}{4}$ inches
c. $\frac{5}{6}$ inches
d. $\frac{7}{10}$ inches

65. When a sprinkler system is installed in a home that is under construction, the system costs about 1.5% of the total building cost. The cost of the same system installed after the home is built is about 4% of the total building cost. How much would a homeowner save by installing a sprinkler system in a $150,000 home while the home is still under construction?
a. $600
b. $2,250
c. $3,750
d. $6,000

66. If one gallon of water weighs 8.35 pounds, a 25-gallon container of water would most nearly weigh
a. 173 pounds
b. 200 pounds
c. 209 pounds
d. 215 pounds

67. A firefighter knows that the floor of a large garage has a width of 40 feet and a length of 42 feet. What is the area of that floor space?
a. 162 square feet
b. 168 square feet
c. 1608 square feet
d. 1680 square feet

68. Which of the following rope lengths is longest? (1 cm = 0.39 inches)
a. 1 meter
b. 1 yard
c. 32 inches
d. 85 centimeters

69. A safety box has three layers of metal, each with a different width. If one layer is $\frac{1}{8}$ inch thick, a second layer is $\frac{1}{6}$ inch thick, and the total thickness is $\frac{3}{4}$ inch thick, what is the width of the third layer?
a. $\frac{5}{12}$
b. $\frac{11}{24}$
c. $\frac{7}{18}$
d. $\frac{1}{2}$

70. A person can be scalded by hot water at a temperature of about 122°F. At about what temperature Centigrade could a person be scalded? $C = \frac{5}{9}(F-32)$
a. 35.5°C
b. 55°C
c. 50°C
d. 216°C

71. At 1:05 A.M. at the scene of a fire, the gauge on a fire engine's pump control panel indicated a pressure of 260 pounds per square inch (psi). By 1:20 A.M., the same gauge indicated a pressure of 110 psi. The pressure decreased, on average, about how many psi per minute?
   a. 10
   b. 11
   c. 12
   d. 20

72. Studies have shown that automatic sprinkler systems save about $5,700 in damages per fire in stores and offices. If a particular community has on average 14 store and office fires every year, about how much money is saved each year if these buildings have sprinkler systems?
   a. $28,500
   b. $77,800
   c. $79,800
   d. $87,800

73. If a firefighter weighs 168 pounds, what is the approximate weight of that firefighter in kilograms? (1 kilogram = about 2.2 pounds)
   a. 76
   b. 77
   c. 149
   d. 150

74. Tank A, when full, holds 555 gallons of water. Tank B, when full, holds 680 gallons of water. If Tank A is only $\frac{2}{3}$ full and Tank B is only $\frac{2}{5}$ full, how many more gallons of water are needed to fill both tanks to capacity?
   a. 319
   b. 593
   c. 642
   d. 658

75. Fire departments commonly use the following formula to find out how far from a wall to place the base of a ladder: (Length of ladder ÷ 5) + 2 = distance from the wall. Using this formula, if the base of a ladder is placed 10 feet from a wall, how tall is the ladder?
   a. 48 feet
   b. 72 feet
   c. 40 feet
   d. 100 feet

SECTION 5: MECHANICAL APTITUDE

Use the information provided in the question, as well as any diagrams provided, to answer the questions below.

76. Of the actions described below, which one best illustrates the principle of preventative maintenance?
   a. fixing a device after it fails
   b. making periodic adjustments on a device to keep it working smoothly
   c. purchasing a new device just before an old one wears out
   d. purchasing a new device after an old one wears out

77. A hinge is most likely to be used on which of the following?
   a. a hand rail
   b. a digital clock
   c. an electric fan
   d. a cabinet door

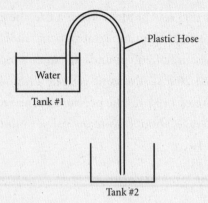

78. The hand tool shown above is a
   a. crescent wrench
   b. hammer
   c. screwdriver
   d. pair of pliers

79. Which of the following groups of items listed below consists entirely of fasteners—that is, devices that are used to connect two items together?
   a. duct tape, nails, and springs
   b. string, scissors, and glue
   c. rivets, levers, and bolts
   d. snaps, buckles, and buttons

80. Which of the following best describes the purpose of welding?
   a. joining
   b. cleaning
   c. lifting
   d. moving

81. What mechanical device could be used to transfer water from tank #1 to tank #2?
   a. a pulley
   b. a siphon
   c. a gauge
   d. a spring

82. Which of the following mechanical devices is used to open a common soft drink can?
   a. a winch
   b. a lever
   c. a wrench
   d. a piston

83. Which hand tool listed below is used to tighten a nut and bolt?
   a. a crescent wrench
   b. a screwdriver
   c. an awl
   d. a hammer

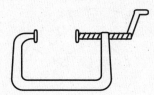

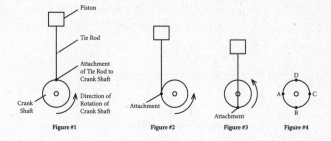

84. The C-clamp shown above would most likely be used to
   a. temporarily hold two boards together
   b. hold up a car in order to repair a flat tire
   c. secure a nut as the bolt is tightened
   d. make a straight cut on a board

85. The primary function of a wire mesh screen is to
   a. transport water on a construction project
   b. aid in reading a directional compass
   c. separate large particles from smaller ones
   d. lift heavy loads in a warehouse

86. A crane is primarily used to perform which of the following functions?
   a. pushing
   b. drilling
   c. welding
   d. lifting

87. An elevator is most similar to which of the following mechanical devices?
   a. a lever
   b. a hydraulic jack
   c. a crane
   d. a spring

88. Figure #1 above shows the initial position of a piston that is connected to a crankshaft by a tie rod. Figure #2 shows the relative positions after the crankshaft is rotated 90 degrees (one quarter of a revolution) in the direction shown. Figure #3 shows the relative positions after another 90 degrees of rotation. In Figure #4, what will be the position of the tie rod attachment to the crankshaft after yet another 90 degree rotation?
   a. position A
   b. position B
   c. position C
   d. position D

89. A bicycle wheel has a diameter of 1.9 feet and a circumference of 6 feet. A little girl rides this bicycle for two revolutions of this wheel. How far down the driveway does she travel?
   a. 20 feet
   b. 12 feet
   c. 4 feet
   d. 2 feet

90. The primary purpose of a pump is to
   a. lift heavy equipment
   b. move fluids from one point to another
   c. reduce vibration of internal combustion engines
   d. regulate the speed of an electric motor

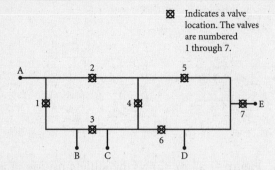

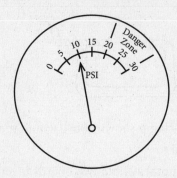

91. In the diagram shown above, all valves are initially closed. Which valves must be opened to allow water to flow from point A to points B and D but NOT to points C and E?
a. valves 2, 4, and 6
b. valves 1, 2, and 3
c. valves 1, 2, and 4
d. valves 1, 2, and 5

92. Which of the following is an electrical, as opposed to a mechanical, device?
a. a wrench
b. a clamp
c. a hydraulic jack
d. a battery

93. Newton's First Law of physics says, "A body (such as a car) that is in motion along a straight line will remain in motion, at the same speed, along the same straight line, unless acted upon by an outside force." A car is traveling down a straight, flat road at 30 miles per hour. The operation of all but one of the items listed below can help demonstrate Newton's First Law. Which item CANNOT be used to demonstrate this Law?
a. the brakes
b. the gas pedal
c. the steering wheel
d. the radiator

94. On the gauge in the diagram above, what is the maximum recommended operating pressure in psi (pounds per square inch) for the needle to remain in a safe zone?
a. 10 psi
b. 20 psi
c. 25 psi
d. 30 psi

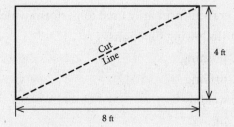

95. A four-foot by eight-foot sheet of plywood is cut into two pieces as shown above. What are the shapes of the two resulting pieces?
a. triangles
b. rectangles
c. squares
d. octagons

ANSWERS

SECTION 1: READING COMPREHENSION

1. **a.** The first paragraph clearly provides this definition of an ecosystem. There is no support for the idea that an ecosystem provides economic protection, which rules out **d.**

2. **c.** The passage states that unless land development is carefully planned, local ecosystems can be destroyed. There is no support for either **a** or **b.** Choice **d** can be ruled out because ecosystems can be saved by ecosystem management.

3. **d.** The last sentence clearly states the author's point of view. The author does imply it is important to protect economic well-being, but the main concern of the passage is the protection of ecosystems. There is no support for the other choices.

4. **b.** The passage defines organisms as living things (sentences 1 and 2). This is the only choice that is not a living thing.

5. **c.** The answer is found in the first sentence of the second paragraph. A habitat (choice **a**) is where an ecosystem occurs. There is no support for either **b** or **d.**

6. **a.** The third sentence in the second paragraph supports this choice. Choice **b** can be ruled out because the author states that ecosystems can be saved through management. There is no support for either **c** or **d.**

7. **c.** Braxton, with 23 days, is at LEVEL THREE. (Note—according to research, lack of precipitation or abundance of precipitation does not necessarily equate with greatest fire potential.)

8. **a.** Livingston Center is at LEVEL THREE; Riderville is at LEVEL TWO.

9. **c.** Read each choice and review the passage to determine whether or not the information is included. Choice **c** is correct because the purpose of the neutron spectrometer is detailed in the second paragraph. Choices, **a, b,** and **d** are NOT included in the passage.

10. **a.** This answer is clearly stated in the first paragraph. There is no support for either **b** or **d.** Choice **c** is contradicted in the first paragraph.

11. **b.** This is a specific-detail item, and the answer is clearly stated in the last sentence of the first paragraph: *a low-cost robot, who would spend a year on the surface of the moon, collecting minerals and ice.*

12. **a.** Either **a** or **b** are possible definitions of speculation, however, the passage suggests that in this case the author is referring to a theory (choice **a**). The other choices are vaguely similar, but are not accurate, based on the passage as a whole.

13. **d.** District Two has 4%; District Five has 46%. Together, these are 50% of the total fires. Districts One, Three, and Four combine to provide the other 50%, but this is not one of the choices.

14. **c.** Twenty-five percent of 200 is 50.

15. **a.** Although cause-and-effect is involved in the second paragraph, the passage mainly follows a hierarchical order, beginning with evacuating the premises and ending with sharing information with the emergency personnel.

16. **b.** This choice gets broadest coverage in the passage. All other choices are mentioned, but are too narrow to be called the most important priority.

17. **d.** Choice **a** can be found in the last paragraph. Choice **b** can be found in the second paragraph. Choice **c** is mentioned in last sentence.

18. **a.** See last sentence, third paragraph.

19. a. The correct answer is choice a. In April, the dotted line (representing the average) is closest to the solid line (representing 1999 rainfall).

20. d. To arrive at the correct answer, read the dotted line for September.

21. b. The graph shows that during January, February, and April, rainfall amounts were above average.

22. b. The 1998 figure is 149% (almost one and a half times) more than the 10-year average (404). Therefore, 404 multiplied by 1.5 is approximately 600.

23. d. The passage says that people in general consider genius *supernatural, but also . . . eccentric;* the pairing of *extraordinary* and *erratic* in choice d includes both meanings given in the passage. Choices a and c cover only one side of the passage's meaning. Choice b contains definitions that the passage does not ascribe to the common view of genius.

24. c. This title covers the main point of the passage that, while there are predictable patterns in the life of a genius, the pattern increases the sense of something supernatural touching his or her life. Choices a and b are too general. Choice d is inaccurate because the passage does not talk about disorder in the life of a genius.

25. c. The answer is found in the second to last sentence. Choices a and d are clearly false. The statement in b is wrong because Findley's study found some *predictable* patterns in the lives of geniuses.

26. d. This answer is arrived at through the context of the passage. Findley's study uncovered some new information about geniuses. Choice a may be true, but it is not stated in the passage. There is no support for b or c.

27. b. The main purpose of this passage is clearly to provide information, and the tone of the passage reflects this purpose.

28. d. Notice that this question asks for something that is NOT in the passage. Choice d is correct because the passage states that there are three very productive times in a genius's life, but it does not say why. Choice a appears in the first paragraph; choices b and c appear in the second paragraph.

29. b. Ten non-white males died. The next highest number is 8.

30. c. Seventy-six adults died, compared with 35 children.

SECTION 2: VERBAL EXPRESSION

31. b. Something that is *nondescript* is without distinction or *undistinguished.* The keys here are the words *usually a flashy dresser* and *uncharacteristically.*

32. c. To be held *accountable* is to be held answerable or *responsible.*

33. a. To *alleviate* something is to make it more bearable or *ease* it.

34. c. To be *indispensable* is to be necessary or *essential.*

35. d. To *decontaminate* and to *purify* both mean to remove impurities.

36. a. A *prerequisite* is something that is necessary or required. The fact that you can't join the team without the training course means that it is required. The other choices do not imply a hard and fast rule.

37. b. If something is *plausible,* it is believable or credible. This is the only logical choice.

38. b. To be *apathetic* is to show little or no interest or to be indifferent.

39. c. The opening phrase, *An American poet of the nineteenth century,* should modify a noun that identifies the poet. Only choice c does this. In choices a, b, and c, either *collection* or *Leaves of Grass* is illogically credited with being the poet. Choice

d is incorrect because the subject of the resulting dependent clause, *poems,* would not agree with its verb, *celebrates.*

40. d. This is the only choice to have agreement between the subject and verb and between the pronoun and its antecedent.

41. b. This is a correct choice because it makes a complete sentence that is clear and logical.

42. d. This is the correct choice. Choice **a** is unclear. Choices **b** and **c** make an illogical shift in verb tense.

43. a. This choice is clear, has no misplaced modifiers, and has no shifts in verb tense. Choices **b** and **d** have misplaced modifiers and result in unclear sentences; **c** has an unnecessary shift from past to present tense.

44. b. This is the only choice that does not have a misplaced modifier. Because Miles Johnson is the sharpshooter, his name should be placed immediately after the introductory phrase—which rules out choices **a** and **c**. Choice **d** is awkwardly constructed and unclear.

45. c. This is the only choice that makes logical sense.

SECTION 3: LOGICAL REASONING

46. a. Two series alternate here, with every third number following a different pattern. In the main series, 3 is added to each number to arrive at the next. In the alternating series, 8 is subtracted from each number to arrive at the next.

47. d. This series alternates the addition of 5 with the subtraction of 3.

48. b. This is a multiplication series; each number is 3 times the previous number.

49. c. The letters decrease by 1; the numbers are multiplied by 2.

50. b. This is an alternating series in alphabetical order. The middle letters follow the order ABCDE.

The first and third letters are alphabetical beginning with J. The third letter is repeated as a first letter in each subsequent three-letter segment.

51. c. All four segments use the same figures: two squares, one circle, and one triangle. In the first segment, the squares are on the outside of the circle and triangle. In the second segment, the squares are below the other two. In the third segment, the squares on are the inside. In the fourth segment, the squares are above the triangle and circle.

52. b. Each arrow in this continuing series moves a few degrees in a clockwise direction. Think of these arrows as the big hand on a clock. The first arrow is at noon. The last arrow before the blank would be 12:40. Choice **b**, the correct answer, is at 12:45.

53. d. In each of the segments the figures alternate between one-half and one-fourth shaded.

54. b. A baker makes bread; a congressman makes laws. The answer is not choice **a,** because a senator and a congressman both make laws. Choice **c** is incorrect because a congressman does not make a state. Politician (choice **d**) is also incorrect because a congressman is a politician.

55. a. *Control* and *dominate* are synonyms, and *magnify* and *enlarge* are synonyms. The answer is not choice **b** or **d** because neither of these means the same as *enlarge.* Choice **c** is incorrect because *decrease* is the opposite of *enlarge.*

56. b. A yard is a larger measure than an inch (a yard contains 36 inches). A quart is a larger measure than an ounce (a quart contains 32 ounces). Gallon (choice **a**) is incorrect because it is larger than a quart. Choices **c** and **d** are incorrect because they are not units of measurement.

57. c. A sponge is a porous material. Rubber is an elastic material. Choice **a** is incorrect because rubber would not generally be referred to as massive.

The answer is not choice **b** because even though rubber is a solid, its most noticeable characteristic is its elasticity. Choice **d** is incorrect because rubber has flexibility.

58. **c.** We know from the first two statements that Tuesday had the highest temperature, but we cannot know whether Monday's temperature was higher than Tuesday's.

59. **c.** The first two statements indicate that Battery Y lasts the least amount of time, but it cannot be determined if Battery Z lasts longer than Battery X.

60. **b.** Because the first two statements are true, Penfield is west of Centerville and southwest of Middletown. Therefore, the third statement is false.

SECTION 4: MATHEMATICS

61. **b.** There are three steps involved in solving this problem. First, convert 4.5% to a decimal: 0.045. Multiply that by $26,000 to find out how much the salary increases. Finally, add the result ($1,170) to the original salary of $26,000 to find out the new salary, $27,170.

62. **b.** First you have to determine the perimeters of all four rooms. This is done by using the formula for a square (P = 4S), or for a rectangle (P = 2L + 2W), as follows: $4 \times 10 = 40$ for choice **a**; $11 \times 11 = 44$ for the correct choice, **b**; $(2 \times 12) + (2 \times 8) = 40$ for choice **c**; and $(2 \times 14) + (2 \times 7) = 42$ for choice **d**.

63. **c.** To solve the problem you have to first convert the total time to minutes (105 minutes), then multiply by 4 (420 minutes), then convert the answer back to hours by dividing by 60 minutes to arrive at the final answer (7 hours). Or you can multiply $1\frac{3}{4}$ hours by 4 to arrive at the same answer.

64. **d.** To solve the problem, one must first find the common denominator, in this instance 60. Then the fractions must be converted: $\frac{17}{20} = \frac{51}{60}$ (for choice **a**); $\frac{3}{4} = \frac{45}{60}$ (for choice **b**); $\frac{5}{6} = \frac{50}{60}$ (for choice **c**); and $\frac{7}{10} = \frac{42}{60}$ (for the correct choice, **d**).

65. **c.** First you must subtract the percentage of the installation cost during construction (1.5%) from the percentage of the installation cost after construction (4%). To do this, begin by converting the percentages into decimals: 4% = 0.04; 1.5% = 0.015. Now subtract: 0.04 − 0.015 = 0.025. This is the percentage of the total cost which the homeowner will save. Multiply this by the total cost of the home to find the dollar amount: 0.025 x $150,000 = $3,750.

66. **c.** To solve the problem, take the weight of one gallon of water (8.35) and multiply it by the number of gallons (25): $8.35 \times 25 = 208.7$. Now round to the nearest unit, which is 209.

67. **d.** The area is the length times the width (A = LW). So you must multiply: $42 \times 40 = 1,680$.

68. **a.** First it is necessary to convert centimeters to inches. To do this for choice **a**, multiply 100 cm (1 meter) by 0.39 inches, yielding 39 inches. For choice **b**, 1 yard is 36 inches. For choice **d**, multiply 85 cm by 0.39 inches, yielding 33.15 inches. Choice **a**, 1 meter (or 39 inches), is the longest.

69. **b.** To solve the problem, you must first find the common denominator, in this instance, 24. Then the fractions must be converted: $\frac{1}{8} = \frac{3}{24}$; $\frac{1}{6} = \frac{4}{24}$; $\frac{3}{4} = \frac{18}{24}$. Add the values for first and second layers together: $\frac{3}{24} + \frac{4}{24} = \frac{7}{24}$, then subtract the sum from the total thickness ($\frac{18}{24}$): $\frac{18}{24} - \frac{7}{24} = \frac{11}{24}$.

70. **c.** First convert Fahrenheit to Centigrade using the formula given: $C = \frac{5}{9}(122 - 32)$; that is, $C = \frac{5}{9} \times 90$; so C = 50.

71. **a.** First, find the length of time covered by subtracting the later time from the earlier: 1:20 − 1:05 = 15 minutes. Next, find the number of psi the pressure dropped in that time: 260 − 110 = 150 psi. Now divide the number of psi the pressure dropped (150) by the length of time covered (15 minutes): 150 ÷ 15 = 10.

72. **c.** To solve this problem, multiply the amount saved per fire, $5,700, by the average number of fires: 5,700 × 14 = 79,800.

73. **a.** To solve this problem, divide the number of pounds (168) by the number of kilograms in a pound (2.2): 168 ÷ 2.2 = 76.36. Now round to the nearest unit, which is 76.

74. **b.** To solve this problem, find the number of gallons of water missing from each tank ($\frac{1}{3}$ of Tank A, $\frac{3}{5}$ of Tank B), and then multiply by the number of gallons each tank holds when full (555 for Tank A; 680 for Tank B): $\frac{1}{3} \times 555 = 185$ gal for Tank A.; $\frac{3}{5} \times 680 = 408$ gal for Tank B. Now add the number of gallons missing from both tanks to get the number of gallons needed to fill them: 185 + 408 = 593.

75. **c.** Since the distance from the wall is known, the formula would be: $(x \div 5) + 2 = 10$. To find x, start by subtracting 2 from both sides, so you have $x \div 5 = 8$. Then multiply both sides by 5, and you end up with $x = 40$.

SECTION 5: MECHANICAL APTITUDE

76. **b.** Preventive maintenance is done on a device while it is still working, to prevent its breaking down or failing. Examples of preventative maintenance include changing the oil in a car engine, adjusting the brakes on a car, lubricating the moving parts on a pump, and changing the fan belts and hoses on a truck.

77. **d.** The function of a hinge is to connect two items together and to allow rotation of one of the items relative to the other. Of the choices, a cabinet door is the most likely to use a hinge.

78. **b.** A hammer is used for driving nails and performing other general carpentry functions.

79. **d.** The items listed that are not fasteners are springs, scissors, and levers.

80. **a.** Welding is the process of connecting two pieces of material such as metal or plastic. The two pieces to be joined are positioned next to each other, and heat is used to melt a small amount of each piece along the intersection. The melted material mixes together and then cools to form a bond that holds the pieces together.

81. **b.** To use a siphon, you would first submerge the entire length of hose in tank #1 in order to completely fill it with water. You would then place one end of the hose in tank #1 and the other end in tank #2, as shown in the diagram. Since the end of the hose in tank #2 is lower than the end in tank #1, the extra weight of the water in the right side of the hose will cause the water to flow into tank #2.

82. **b.** The little tab you use to pry open the can is a lever. You lift on one end of the lever, which rotates around a pivot point and forces the other end of the lever downward, so that the can pops open.

83. **a.** A crescent wrench is used to tighten bolts. A screwdriver is used to tighten screws, an awl to start holes in wood to accommodate nails or screws, and a hammer to drive nails.

84. **a.** The C-clamp would be placed around the two boards and tightened by turning the screw with the handle.

85. **c.** Besides being used on windows and doors—where they keep large particles such as flies out of your living room—screens are typically used in industrial applications to sift granular materials such as rock, sand, and dirt in order to separate large pieces from small pieces.

86. d. A crane is used to raise and lower large items that are too heavy or awkward to lift by hand.

87. c. An elevator is simply a crane that raises and lowers people.

88. c. Figure #3 shows the attachment of the tie rod to the crankshaft at the bottom of the crankshaft. Another 90-degree counter-clockwise rotation would place the attachment point on the right side of the crankshaft at position C.

89. b. The circumference is the distance around the outer edge of the wheel. Two revolutions of a wheel 6 feet in circumference would result in a distance traveled of 12 feet.

90. b. A pump is a rotating piece of machinery normally driven by an electric motor. Fluid is pulled into the front of the pump, accelerated through the pump, and discharged through the back of the pump. Pumps are used to move fluids such as water, gasoline, milk, and waste water, as well as thick industrial slurries such as fertilizer and mine tailings.

91. d. Carefully follow the flow diagram to verify that you must open valves 1, 2, and 5. If you opened valves 4 and 6, water would flow to point C as well as to point D.

92. d. A battery is an electrical device. The other items listed are common mechanical devices.

93. d. Newton's First Law says that a vehicle will move at the same speed unless an outside force is applied. Both the brakes and the gas pedal could be used to apply such a force. Newton's First Law also says that the vehicle will travel along the same straight line unless an outside force—the action of the steering wheel, for instance—is applied. The radiator does not affect the speed or direction of the car's motion.

94. b. The gauge indicates that any pressure greater than 20 psi is in the danger zone.

95. a. The resulting shapes are three-sided closed polygons, or triangles.

SCORING

A score of 70 is usually enough to put you on the firefighter eligibility list. But you should aim to score significantly higher, particularly if you're applying to a city that uses the written exam score to help determine your *rank* on the eligibility list. Check your score carefully and calculate the percentage of questions you answered correctly in each portion of the exam. Be sure to carefully review the chapters that pertain to the sections on which you received the lowest scores and try to understand why you made the mistakes you did.

In fact, unless your score was nearly perfect, you should plan to spend as much time as you can studying and practicing so your actual test results are as close to 100 percent as possible. Remember, not all cities test all of the skills covered in this exam. So if your exam doesn't include one of the following areas, you don't have to spend much time on that section.

- If your **reading comprehension** scores could use some improvement, review Chapter 6. You should also try to fit in as much reading as possible between now and exam day. If your city offers a study guide, review it thoroughly.
- If your scores in the **verbal expression** section could be higher, review Chapter 12. You may also want to build these skills by working with a vocabulary builder and a grammar handbook.

- If your **logical reasoning** scores need improvement, review Chapter 9. You may also want to practice working analogies and logic puzzles on your own.
- If your **math** scores were low, review Chapter 8. You may also want to seek situations in your daily life where you can practice your math skills. If you normally rely on a calculator, do all of your calculations by hand.
- If you had difficulty with the **mechanical aptitude** section, review Chapter 10. You may also want to practice on your own by taking things apart and putting them back together or working on 3-D puzzles.

The more you can find everyday situations in which you can practice these skills and imagine the types of questions that may be asked, the higher you are likely to score on the exam.

Another key element to your success is self-confidence. The more comfortable you are with your ability to perform, the more likely you are to do well on the exam. You know what to expect, you know your strengths and weaknesses, and you can work to turn those weaknesses into strengths before the actual exam. Your preparedness should give you the confidence that you'll need to do well on exam day.

C·H·A·P·T·E·R 15

THE PHYSICAL ABILITY TEST

CHAPTER SUMMARY

This chapter describes the physical test that's required in the firefighter selection process. It focuses on the specific tasks involved, including tips from the experts about how to ace these tasks and how you can practice ahead of time.

Have you ever crossed a bridge and noticed someone at the side rail pulling up a rope that has a bookbag full of rocks attached at the end? There's a good chance that person wants to be a firefighter.

Ever walked to your car in a parking garage and noticed a person with a loaded-down fanny pack running up and down six flights of stairs? Probably a firefighter candidate.

Ever see someone in a harness pulling a car? Yep, another firefighter candidate.

As odd as these activities may seem, these are examples of how firefighting candidates can prepare for the Physical Ability Test (PAT). Fire departments around the country use the PAT to determine if candidates have the physical ability to be considered for the fire academy, which is where they learn firefighting tasks. Academy directors emphasize that all candidates must have high levels of strength and aerobic energy, commonly referred to as stamina.

"Fitness is a real high indicator of the ability to cope with the stress in the academy," says Al Baeta, a physical education instructor at American River College in Sacramento, California. Baeta devised a program for the Sacramento Fire Department that not only prepares academy candidates for the PAT, but also keeps firefighters fit throughout their careers. "Academy recruits have come back and told me how surprised they were at the physical activities in the fire academy. Fire departments work them hard. It's strenuous physical work, from dawn to dusk, and it's difficult emotionally—often done in a paramilitary-type environment. The base every candidate needs is an aerobic capacity and overall body strength."

Fire academies are demanding because fires are demanding. Firefighters must work quickly, efficiently and safely. Their job requires them to run, jump, bend and climb while lifting, pulling or carrying heavy weight and while wearing heavy protective gear. They carry out these tasks in a chaotic, life-threatening environment and often in extreme heat. The ability to perform and think under these conditions requires preparation, and overall physical fitness is the foundation.

STRENGTH + STAMINA = SAFETY

There is no doubt, the Physical Ability Test (also called Physical Agilities Test or Physical Performance Test) is a crucial step toward becoming a firefighter. It's also quite clear that it is something you have to prepare for. Though the type of tests may vary somewhat from state to state and city to city, academy directors insist that the PAT requires training, particularly for upper-body strength and stamina.

"The PAT tests your potential to complete a recruit academy," says Bill Wittmer, academy director of the Oakland (California) Fire Department. "If you have problems in the PAT, then you're going to have a problem in the recruit academy, which is harder and runs 10 to 16 weeks. That's where you are throwing ladders, pulling hose, doing physical work all day long. They're tough."

Fire departments have answered the request of the courts in recent years to make their PATs reflect the duties found in fighting fires. As such, more departments have moved away from PATs that included mile-and-a-half runs and pushups. More and more PATs around the country now include tasks that are directly related to firefighting, such as raising ladders, hoisting bundles of hose and dragging heavy dummies.

Departments are also quite sensitive to charges that their tests favor men. Academy directors stress that women can pass these tests—the Dallas (Texas) Fire Department, for example, has 60 female firefighters in its ranks. However, women may have to work more on certain areas, particularly their arms and shoulders, to pass the physical tests. Rancho Santiago Community College in Santa Ana, California has the largest firefighting program in the state, and instructor Terri Wann notes that women who pass this program are a definite minority "mainly due to lack of upper-body strength."

KNOW THE PROCEDURES

Because PATs aren't the same at every department, it's important to find out in advance what is involved in the test you'll be taking. One thing you should know is whether you'll have to perform the test in heavy gear, such as boots, gloves, helmet, turnout coat and Self-Contained Breathing Apparatus (SCBA). Not all fire departments require the gear but, if they do, it's best to practice for the test wearing clothing that is heavy and restrictive.

Another variation in PATs is that some tend to focus on upper-body strength, others on overall fitness. Some fire departments include climbing ladders to see if you are afraid of heights. Others want to know if you become claustrophobic in your breathing gear. Every department, however, wants to see if you have the physical abilities to perform safely and efficiently on the fire grounds. You can count on being tested for agility, balance, strength and stamina.

For details about the PAT in your municipal department, call the department or personnel office to find out how the test is conducted and under what conditions.

TIMING IS EVERYTHING

The current trend among fire departments is the "sustained activity" testing procedure. This means performing anywhere from 5 to 10 firefighting tasks and completing all of them successfully under a prescribed time. These tests are built around the combination of strength and aerobic activity. They include lifting ladders, running up bundles of hose several flights of stairs, and hoisting other bundles by rope up four floors of a building—one after another, with relatively little rest between.

Some departments time each event, with a pass/fail grade riding on a candidate's ability to accomplish the task within the deadline. Other departments are more flexible, timing each event but compiling an overall total. This allows someone who might be slow in the hose lift to make up time with a fast stair climb.

You have to be clear about the requirements and what is meant by "successfully completing the task." Academy instructors do not want to see someone race through the exercises without being able to demonstrate control. For example, being able to raise an extension ladder to the prescribed length, but then letting it crash down to beat the deadline, won't meet the requirements of the test.

Failing to complete any part of the test generally means that the entire test has to be retaken. You may have to wait anywhere from 30 days to as long as a year

to retake the test. Some departments give you two chances to complete tasks but, again, failure in any event typically means you're out.

Grading of these tests varies as well. Many departments rank candidates based on their scores in several areas, including the PAT and the written exam. Others give you credit for proficiency on the PAT, which means you can be ranked in order of how fast you completed the tasks.

The White Plains (New York) Fire Department gives candidates two shots at completing each task on its PAT, then uses the best time in each to rank candidates. "You want to be careful on the first run and make sure you get through it," advises Deputy Chief Robert Keil. "On the next run, go for time. Then you are familiar with how it feels. The first run, you tend to be nervous."

THE TASKS

Each individual task within a PAT may not seem that taxing. But when they are performed in succession and with heavy gear on, they can take a great toll on the body. Making matters worse is that fire departments often require you to complete tasks by walking to a finish line, or pushing a bell. This isn't designed to frustrate you, but rather to determine whether you have the composure to think clearly when you are fatigued and under stress. It can be quite disappointing to meet the required deadline for a task, only to find out you failed because you didn't walk to the finish line.

The key is knowing exactly what is required and then preparing for it. Some departments allow candidates to practice the test on the testing grounds in advance. This is a great opportunity to understand your weaknesses and improve on them for the PAT.

Following are descriptions of various PAT tasks, including what they test for, helpful tips and some ways to prepare yourself. These examples may not reflect the exact PAT you'll face, but it's safe to say some combination of the tasks below will be found in most fire departments around the country. Also, it should be noted that fire departments from time to time re-evaluate their testing procedures, so what is used now in your area could change in the near future. Photographs illustrating some of these tasks appear on pages 8 and 9.

Ladder carry/raise: Remove an extension ladder from a holder and either carry it around cones or through an obstacle course to a designated spot (possibly back where you began to replace the ladder on the holder). Some tests require you to set the ladder up properly and then raise and lower the extension by pulling a rope hand over hand.

Tests for: Upper body strength (arms, shoulders, wrists) and agility.

Tips: Ladders, which can weigh from 40 to 80 pounds, may be 20 feet long, but when extended they may stretch as high as 35 or 40 feet. Because they're difficult to maneuver, when you're carrying them it's best to get a wide grip on the ladder and keep your balance by flexing your legs and widening your stance. Height is an advantage here because taller people tend to have a longer reach, which helps keep the ladder stable.

Raising the extension requires pulling on a rope. The higher the ladder goes, the more weight you must control. This puts great stress on the arms. Shorter candidates can lose control because they often stretch by raising up on toes, which reduces their balance and can lead to loss of control. When you're being timed, this exercise can be tough.

Practice: Find an extension ladder, load it up with weights and carry it around. A barbell loaded with weights is another good practice item.

For the extension pull, attach a 75-pound sack of sand to a rope (or start with a lighter weight if necessary). Throw the light end of a rope over a bar, or perhaps a high tree branch. Pull the sack up with your arms. It's best to use a rope that's a half-inch wide and to wear fire gloves as well.

Hose drag/pull: Grab one end of hose—usually the thick, heavy 2.5-inch-wide variety—and drag it a prescribed distance, such as 100 to 200 feet. Some departments require you to drag a "charged" line, which means it's full of water. Most prefer a dry line. After crossing the finish line, you might be required to pull the rest of the hose, hand over hand, past the line.

Tests for: Overall body strength, particularly legs, and endurance.

Tips: Get a good grasp on the end of the hose and run with a good forward lean. Building momentum early is the key because as the hose stretches out, the heavier and thus more difficult it is to control. This task is often performed in firefighting gear (coat and SCBA), which can add 50 pounds to your body weight. The extra weight and the hose will take a big toll on your legs.

In pulling the hose, get a solid stance (feet just wider than the shoulders) with flex in your knees. Pull from the center of your body, rotating hips back and forth to help the arms pull the weight.

Practice: Run uphill "sprints" of 30 to 50 yards. Or attach a tire filled with sand or bricks to a rope and drag it across 200 feet of asphalt. One woman who was in training had her father attach a harness with straps to the front axle of a car, which she then pulled in 100-foot intervals.

Hose carry/hose hoist: Carry a bundled or rolled-up length of hose (it can weigh 55 pounds) up three to four flights of stairs. Then walk over to a ledge and use a rope to pull another bundled hose, hand over hand, to your floor. Then carry another bundled hose back down the stairs.

Tests for: Overall body strength and endurance.

Tips: Academy directors who use this task in their PAT say it is the most draining event. It's difficult to prepare for this test since it's often done in turnout coat and SCBA which, along with the bundled hose, make walking up and down stairs an excruciating chore. Then pulling up the hose is really a strain, particularly on the arms and shoulders. Because of the upper body strength this takes, many training directors note that women often need work on the hose lifting.

Like the hose pull, it's best to work from a stable base: feet just wider than the shoulders, with flex at the knees. Rotate your hips to help your arms pull up the dead weight. A steady rhythm works best.

When climbing and descending stairs, make sure you understand the requirements. Some departments demand that you take each step one by one. Others allow you to bound up (if you can!) three or four at a time.

Practice: For the stair climb, run stair steps with a large weight on your shoulders, such as a bag of sand or feed. Parking structures are good because they require you to turn up each flight in the stairwell. Again, if the test requires turnout coat and SCBA, you may want to practice it in restrictive clothing and with a loaded backpack or bookbag on your back.

For the hose hoist, suspend weights from a railing or bridge and pull up. Here, too, it's best to wear a heavy coat and a backpack to simulate the turnout gear and SCBA.

Attic crawl: Crawl, with gear on, down a chute that is 5-feet wide and 3-feet high for a distance of 12 feet. You will be required to put your weight only on the rafters of the chute. If you miss, you fall through and must start over. (This task simulates crawling above a weakened ceiling.) Some departments require you to start on the floor, climb a ladder, crawl through a window into a 30-foot chute, then maneuver out and down another ladder.

Tests: Balance, hand and leg strength.

Tips: Stay low and on your hands, elbows and knees. Keep your head up and looking forward. Speed isn't as crucial as not falling through the gaps.

Practice: Set a ladder up on saw horses and practice crawling on it. Also, stretch string above the ladder to force you to stay low.

Dummy drag: Grab a life-size dummy (weighing anywhere from 150 to 180 pounds) and drag it a prescribed distance, for example, 100 feet. Some departments require you to drag the dummy through a tunnel or chute with a height of four or five feet, but in this case generally you'd go a shorter distance, like 20 feet.

Tests: Agility, leg strength, balance.

Tips: A good grip, usually behind the shoulders with your arms wrapped around the chest, is needed. Lean backward and then use your body and legs to propel yourself backward. In a tunnel or chute, you may have to lean to keep your head under the ceiling, which puts more stress on your back and legs and requires more of a backward crawl.

Practice: Find a friend who's willing to act as the dummy and be dragged over grass. Or you can load up a sheet with bulky, heavy objects (tires, bags of sand) to simulate the awkwardness of the human body. You can drag this around as much as you want without worrying about scrapes, nicks and finding new friends.

Sledge carry/roof walk: Pick up a sledgehammer (8 to 10 pounds) and walk with it on a ladder that is suspended above the ground on sawhorses. (This simulates walking along a roof line.)

Tests: Overall balance.

Tips: Good footing can be achieved by walking on the rails of the ladder, not the rungs. Put most of your weight on the balls of your feet, with your weight spread evenly over this wide stance.

Practice: Put a ladder on the ground and practice walking, with sledgehammer in hand, on the rails without falling off.

Tool use: Some departments require you to pound a roof 20 times with a sledgehammer. Others want you to hit a weighted tire to move it 20 feet. (This tests for strength to break down doors and through walls.) Others still will require you to use what's called a pick pole, which is thrust through ceilings to bring them down during a fire. The test will have you use this or a similar tool to latch onto a spring-loaded box and pull it down. (This takes considerable force and simulates tearing down a ceiling to get to an attic.)

Tests: Coordination, strength.

Tips: Good footing creates good balance. Take a wide stance, feet just wider than the shoulders, knees slightly flexed. Grab the handle near the bottom, with your hands slightly separated. Swing the tool with a wide arc to create momentum for the heavier head. For more control, separate your hands more.

Practice: Practice pounding with a sledgehammer. A softball bat, weighted down at one end, also can be used to help practice.

Wall vault: Vault yourself over a wall of four or six feet.

Tests: Balance, coordination.

Tips: Whether from a running or standing start, it's best to get both hands atop the wall. This will enable you to pull your lower body up and then swing over the wall. After other PAT tasks and with heavy gear on, this isn't all that easy to do.

Practice: Again, running sprints up hills will help develop the leg strength needed to get a good initial boost over the wall. It takes explosive power to get over the higher walls. After building up your leg strength, you can experiment by vaulting over fences of various heights.

Hang smoke ejector: Pick up a smoke ejector (about 40 pounds), walk a prescribed distance (50 to 200 feet) and hang it on a door jamb six feet above the ground. (Note: A smoke ejector is a power-driven fan which is used to eliminate smoke.)

Tests: Strength and reach.

Tips: For shorter candidates, the smoke ejector can be difficult to manage as they raise it over their heads to hang it properly, especially when they're wearing a turnout coat and helmet. Overall upper body strength, particularly in the biceps and shoulders, is needed.

Practice: This is one exercise that might be best prepared for with weightlifting. Lat pulldowns will help develop the specific muscles.

FIT FOR FIRE

Just about every fire department in the country will use some form of the above tasks in its Physical Ability Test. Academy instructors stress that preparation is the key. Some people may be able to come in off the street and pass one or two of the tests; it takes a very special person to pass an entire PAT without any advance training. It often takes months of dedicated training for most candidates to accomplish these tasks in the prescribed times.

"If you don't live the lifestyle, you will not pass the test," instructor Terri Wann says about the Rancho Santiago firefighting program, which has students from around the world who come to participate.

Like Rancho Santiago, many community colleges offer a course geared towards passing the PAT. Students are able to assess their weaknesses and develop their skills with the tasks while improving their overall physical fitness. The final exam is passing the PAT.

Instructor Al Baeta, who was a track and cross-country coach for over two decades, points out that the physical demands of the job never stop. Achieving a high level of fitness at the onset of your career as a firefighter is just the start. Many departments around the country are instigating or already have programs for their personnel to stay fit. It's becoming more and more common to find weightlifting and aerobic equipment in firehouses.

"Firefighters are tremendously professional and they will rise to the occasion to meet the demands of the job," Baeta says. "However, those who are not in the condition they ought to be pay for it with accumulated stress over their lifetime. We say, Fit for Fire. Fit for Retire."

Physical fitness is a crucial part in becoming a firefighter. But staying fit plays a crucial role throughout this career.

Hose Drag/Pull

Hose Hoist

Sledge Carry/Roof Walk

Tool Use—Sledgehammer to Roof

C·H·A·P·T·E·R

THE ORAL INTERVIEW

16

CHAPTER SUMMARY

This chapter gives you a number of guidelines, tips and scenarios to help you imagine and prepare for your oral interview. What do you say? How do you say it? You can't know ahead of time what questions you'll be asked, but there's a lot you can do to get yourself ready and boost your odds of success.

CAUTION: You may think that the oral interview is just like any other job interview. That it's not a major part of the hiring process for firefighters. That compared to the Physical Ability Test (PAT) or the written exam, for example, it isn't all that critical.

But did you know that many departments use the oral interview to eliminate the largest percentage of applicants? Did you know that in some places, the interview is used to choose those who will be allowed to take the PAT? So the point here is: don't take any chances! It's not worth risking your future as a firefighter by not taking the interview seriously.

In most municipal or county departments, the oral interview is a very important part of the application process, so important that there may be two of them—a qualifying interview and a selection interview. Each jurisdiction will have different priorities. And each interviewing panel will ask different kinds of questions and have different standards in judging the answers, especially in a first interview. But they are all pretty much focusing on one factor: the character of the applicant, who you are as shown by what you have to say for yourself.

THE QUALIFYING INTERVIEW

The qualifying interview—also known as the screening interview—is the first, and sometimes the only, oral interview that fire departments use in their hiring process. By the time you are contacted to go through this interview, you will have completed your application form, you probably will have taken the written examination, and it's possible that you may have taken the Physical Ability Test.

In any case, just being asked to interview usually means you have been chosen from the pool of applicants to go on to the next step, that you have climbed a crucial rung up the ladder toward your career goal. You should feel encouraged and confident. Remember that feeling. Courage and confidence are two traits you will need as a firefighter—traits the interview panel will be looking for in the way you present yourself to them and the way you answer their questions.

The panel that interviews you will be made up of professionals, and not just professional firefighters, but department personnel officers and interview specialists as well. They may hold any rank; a deputy chief, chief, or even a commissioner may serve on a panel. In some communities, the panel might include a civilian or two. Be aware that most community representatives are prominent citizens with some managerial experience, and they do not take this civic responsibility lightly. It' a good idea to find out in advance the make-up of the panel in your area. And always keep in mind that their experience and their position commands your respect.

THE SELECTION INTERVIEW

Many departments will ask you back for a second round of interviewing. This is usually called the selection interview or, in some places, the Chief's interview. It can be much like the qualifying interview, only conducted by higher-level personnel. Or it can be more of a formality, where the applicant is allowed to ask questions of the panel before officially being accepted for the job. Either way, it is important to take this interview every bit as seriously as the first.

If you are meeting the Chief, treat it as an executive-level interview and be sure to dress accordingly. You will have been through the qualifying interview already so you'll have the chance to review your performance. What can you learn from it? What went well? Where could you improve? Your qualifying interview will have been evaluated by the department, and that evaluation will be among the background material the second panel refers to. For instance, there could be follow-up questions or requests for clarification of previous answers.

The selection interview is their last chance to find out about you before hiring—or disqualifying—you. But don't be intimidated. The more interviews you have, the more confidence it should give you that you have the skills and abilities they're looking for.

GETTING READY

It is most likely impossible, and a waste of time, to anticipate the exact questions you will be asked during the oral interview. But it is still possible, and important, to prepare yourself for it. You know the panel has the information you gave them on your application form. Think about that for a minute. What did you tell them about your background, your skills and abilities, your character?

For example, your history of employment—what skills did you learn in the jobs you held that could help you become part of an efficient, effective team of firefighters? Do any assignments or projects you were involved in stand out as particularly challenging or representative of your capabilities? Are there gaps in your work history that need to be explained? If you were ever fired from a job, a background check will uncover that fact, and possibly the reason for it. What's your side of the story, and what's the best way to present it?

You might not know what the panel will ask you specifically, but you can get a general idea of the areas and issues that concern them from the application and exam. Did they ask about your traffic record? Drug use? Academic background? Then you'd better ask yourself—was there a problem in any of these areas? What did you do about it? Know your strengths, too. Facing and solving problems can build character; sometimes you learn the most from the experiences you had the most trouble with.

This does not mean coming up with excuses and rationalizations. Or plotting ways to steer the conversation around to your obvious strong points. Or memorizing the best possible answer to a particular type of question. All these approaches are likely to make you sound insincere, and trying to remember them will just make you anxious. The idea is to think the issue through so that you understand what the experience means to you now as a potential firefighter. It's a way for you to identify and appreciate the preparation you received— on the job, on the street, in the classroom—for the demanding profession you are about to enter.

But don't stop there. Many colleges now offer classes and programs in fire cadet training. Investigate this opportunity to hone your skills and broaden your abilities, to gain specific, useful knowledge and make yourself a more qualified applicant. Or, since so much of a modern firefighter's job requires training in handling emergencies, look into Emergency Medical Technician (EMT) training or other certified EMT-related classes in your area. Or join a volunteer fire department in a nearby locale. Or go down to your local fire station and talk to the shift on duty; who would know better than they do what it takes to do the job—and to ace the interview? Decide what you want to do to prepare for a career in firefighting, and that will help you determine what you will want to say in your interview.

PRESENTING YOURSELF

Give this your serious attention. How you present yourself at the interview—your first face-to-face meeting with your prospective co-workers and bosses—is a sign of how important the job is to you and of your respect for the panel. Fire departments have a paramilitary command structure: orders go down the ranks to mobilize a trained, disciplined fighting force, organized in companies and battalions, whose duty it is to fight fires. Respect for authority is fundamental to the occupation, and it should show in your dress and manner at the interview.

This does not necessarily mean you must wear a business suit or a classic dress, or get a severe haircut,

Watch Your Language

Standard English is the standard language of departmental command—and of the interview. So if your English needs improvement, start studying now. College English and Communications departments offer courses that can help you, as do community centers (like YMCA's) and local learning programs. Also, some fire departments that serve jurisdictions with large ethnic populations give preference to applicants who, besides English, speak the languages of those populations. Check out the needs in your area.

or sit up straight with your hands in your lap. Though none of these, if they didn't make you uncomfortable, would hurt. Your appearance should be appropriate, but it should also express your personality. The panel's job is to get to know you, so dressing up like somebody you're not just to impress them only makes their work harder to do. They asked you to interview because they decided from the information they already had that you are a serious candidate. You should be confident that you can be yourself and succeed.

Your bearing—how you stand, sit, and carry yourself—should not be phoney or self-conscious either. Be polite, attentive, interested. If you listen carefully, make eye contact with your questioners, and answer them directly and with respect, you should be fine. It's a job interview; attend to business.

And don't be late. It's advisable to arrive fifteen to twenty minutes beforehand so you can compose yourself, relax and get the feel of the place where the interview is being held. Arriving too early gives you too much time to wait, and think, and fidget, and lose focus, and make yourself nervous. And showing up late—well, what would you think if you were on the panel, looking at the applicant's empty chair, then at your watch, then at the door, ready to do your part in the important task at hand, but forced to wait for someone who apparently doesn't think it's so important? If for some reason you are unavoidably detained, be honest, straightforward and ready to go when you get there. This is your chance to show them who you are, and how prepared you are to take advantage of the opportunity they have presented you with. Just relax and give it your best shot.

ANSWERING QUESTIONS: WHAT WORKS AND WHAT DOESN'T

Most panels will ask most applicants a standard set of questions, which will, of course, vary from department to department. Your panel may or may not ask one of the most common questions: "Why do you want to be a firefighter?" But you should ask yourself. The answer to this question covers everything from your motivation to enter the profession to the goals you ultimately hope to achieve. By thinking this through ahead of time, you'll have a better idea how to answer this and many related questions you are likely to be asked.

"I want to help people" is a good answer, but too generic. Teachers and social workers help people, too. What's different about the help firefighters provide? Well, they save property, even lives, from danger and imminent destruction. And that makes the job more exciting, and perhaps more satisfying, since you get to see the results of your labor—the saved lives, the rescued pets, the spared homes and material goods—in a more immediate and dramatic manner than most other public service workers. But then what about the work of fire prevention, and public education, and equipment maintenance, which take up much more of a firefighter's time than answering fire calls? Maybe it's the varied nature of the duties and the irregular hours that appeal to you.

You may have other reasons, of course, but the answering process is the key here. At the interview, or in preparing for it, make sure to listen carefully to the question, all the way through. This will help you to present yourself as attentive and respectful, and to understand exactly what you're being asked. Then don't just answer off the top of your head—think first. Does the question relate to any preparation you've done? Is it a complicated, two-or-more-part question? Is there a specific example that comes to mind?

You always want to give a thoughtful response. Once you get a job in a fire department, your advancement through the ranks is determined to a great extent by examinations, in everything from hydraulics to public administration, so your answers need to show the panel that you are a thinking person. Then speak clearly, directly to the panel, so they can hear and understand your answer and get to know you. And stay focused on giving the information that answers the question. This will demonstrate to the panel your intelligence, your ability to follow orders, and your efficiency at performing the task at hand.

THINK IT THROUGH

Consider the following example: One of the panel members, while looking over a copy of your application, says to you, "You only have two years of college experience." This is a sensitive area in your life, and you are defensive about it. You have good reasons for having left school before getting your degree—family responsibilities; financial hardship; an awareness that until you really understood why you were in school, the education was not going to be meaningful to you. But these reasons are difficult for you to articulate because when somebody brings up your lack of a college degree, you always feel you are being judged negatively. So though you are quick to defend yourself, your answer comes across as a hodgepodge of emotional responses that sound like excuses.

The panel member stops you. "I was going to ask," he continues, "if, despite your limited college experience, you feel you are prepared for a career in firefighting?" This is a different question entirely from the one you thought you were being asked. And if you had not been so quick to answer, if you had taken a breath after the panel member's first statement and let him finish, if you had listened carefully, you could have given him the information he wanted and not revealed a vulnerable, defensive side to your character. And if you had considered this part of your application beforehand, and thought through this issue about your educational background, you could have prepared yourself, pre-

sented your reasons in a stronger manner and overcome your vulnerability.

At least you have now been given a better question to answer, one that isn't negative and isn't asking about something you didn't do. Now you can be positive, telling them what you are doing to make yourself a qualified firefighter. Immediately you get an idea. You have just that morning gone through a strenuous physical workout, one designed to help you build up the strength and stamina necessary to excel at the Physical Ability Test. So you tell them about your workout regimen, how you have set up a program of weight training for muscle development, especially in the upper body, and rotations on the stationary bike and stairmaster, along with a 5-mile weekend jog, to increase your endurance. You enjoy working out; it makes you feel good and clears your mind. And you are proud of the progress you've made in lifting free weights, both in the amount of weight and the number of repetitions, and you fill the panel in, tracing the rise in pounds and reps over the last couple of months.

OK, fine—your physical condition is an essential qualification for the job. Your answer does show enthusiasm, thought and commitment. And it's specific, which is good. However, it's enthusiastic, thoughtful, committed and specific about working out, not about preparing for a career in a fire department. So before you ever get to the interview, ask yourself a few thought-provoking questions. For example, how did you decide what exercises to include in your workout? If you learned from talking to active duty firefighters in the area that the PAT consists of a timed hose drag, ladder lift, stair climb and tunnel crawl, all while you're wearing a turncoat, helmet, gloves and air bottle, and that firefighters need strong arms, shoulders, backs, and legs, should you tell the panel? After all, they already know this stuff. What they don't know, however, and what is key for them to understand, is your reasoning, your thinking process. Plus, it's evidence of your enthusiasm and your commitment to the profession that you did this research, that you went out and talked to working firefighters. The difference between a good answer and the best one you can think of is the thought you put into it.

SHOW YOUR STUFF

If you have a clear idea of what you want to say, you are more likely to speak clearly. If you are not comfortable with public speaking, you may be self-conscious about talking to the panel. But the basics are simple. Make sure they can hear you: if they have to listen hard to follow what you're saying, you are making them work harder than they should have to and you are more of a problem than other interviewees. Make sure they understand you: try to speak in full sentences, and don't use slang if you can help it. Also make sure they can see you: your facial expressions can help the panel understand what you're saying, and making eye contact will help them get to know you. Don't mumble or look away if you get a little lost or confused. Keep your head up and eyes front. This is the panel's chance to meet you face-to-face—don't disappoint them.

Your answers should let the questioners know not only what you think, but how you think. If you feel as if you're getting off the subject of the question you were asked, you probably are. Recall the question—which is easier if you listened carefully in the first place—and rethink your answer. Sometimes staying focused is a matter of getting back on track, and sometimes it is a matter of considering the question again and finding a better way to answer it. In the case of the above question, perhaps you also tried to prepare by enrolling in a training program for firefighters at a local college, but were unable to afford the time or expense at this point in your life. You're not sure you should tell the panel about this attempt because it didn't work out, like your other try at college. But upon a moment's reflection you may decide that they should know that you investigated the possibility and hope to take advantage of it in the future. This shows that you have a plan, a goal you're working toward. It is a positive response and speaks to your qualities of patience and perseverance, which are good traits for a firefighter to have.

If you are looking into college programs to prepare for your career, you might consider a course in public speaking (see sidebar, "Public Speaking 101"). Part of a firefighter's job is community outreach, educating the public on fire prevention, public safety issues and the role of a firefighter. You may be asked to speak to workers and management in local businesses, citizen groups and neighborhood meetings, and schoolchildren at various levels. Becoming an effective speaker will help you be an effective firefighter. The lessons you learn in a public speaking course won't hurt your interview skills, either. Let professionals help you develop better listening habits and speaking techniques, and give you a forum where you can get much-needed practice. To become a more comfortable, confident public speaker, there is no substitute for experience.

The answering process is something you can practice as part of your preparation for the interview. Remember to:

- LISTEN CAREFULLY
- THINK FIRST
- SPEAK CLEARLY
- STAY FOCUSED

Each step of the process, in and of itself, will communicate your seriousness and self-control to the panel. You will be showing your respect for them and gaining their respect at the same time.

STICK TO THE FACTS

If you are scheduled for an interview, you have already been identified as someone the department thinks they want. Chances are, then, that they have done a background check on you, based on the information in your application. They may have talked to your former bosses about your employment record. Did you leave a certain job under questionable circumstances? Then they're likely to ask questions about it. Did you quit? Were you fired? In either case, why?

When a panel asks such questions, they probably have your boss's response in front of them. But even if they specifically ask you to respond to one of your employer's comments, complaints and excuses aren't the way to go. Instead, give them an answer that shows you've looked at the situation honestly, examined your actions, and learned from the experience.

If you prepared yourself to face this type of inquiry, as was suggested above, you would be ready for it and it would be less likely to throw you off balance. In general, what did your prior work experience—good,

---

Public Speaking 101

If speaking in public makes you nervous, or if you just need to practice and get some useful feedback, take a public speaking course. This can be a great means to learn, study and polish the skills necessary to ace the interview.

As an example of what's involved in a public speaking course, the following excerpts are from the syllabus for a course in Effective Speechmaking given at the City University of New York.

Course Objectives:

- To develop a basic understanding of interpersonal communication
- To develop an understanding of standard American speech
- To develop an understanding of oral interpretation
- To develop knowledge of interview techniques

Class Activities and Areas of Focus:

- Interpersonal exercises and small group discussions
- Verbal and non-verbal exercises
- Self-concept and perception
- Defense mechanisms and fallacies
- Breathing, posture, articulation
- Listening
- Controlling nervousness
- Informing, persuading, entertaining

Course Rationale and Reminders: Lessons from this class should help you interact in the public and professional worlds outside of class. Feedback is of prime concern, so ask questions. Evaluation is based on individual improvement in voice production and speech delivery. Clearly enunciate and articulate—and relax!

bad, or otherwise—mean to you at the time? And what does it mean to you now that you are on the threshold of a new career?

With questions like these, as with all the questions you are asked on application forms or in interviews, it is critical that you answer truthfully. This certainly means don't lie. But it also means don't try to scope out the panel and tell them what you think they want to hear. To begin with, it's impossible to know what even one person wants to hear you say, much less a panel of three or more people. They may not know themselves. If they ask standard questions, they may be satisfied with standard answers, but a personal response that is out of the ordinary may capture their attention and make you stand out from the other applicants.

So should you strive for the uncommon answer that makes you different from the rest? But how would you know what "different" was without knowing how everyone else answered? As you can see, this approach can't possibly work. It's a dead end. Besides, experienced interviewers can usually recognize a false sentiment or phoney tone, even if your answer isn't technically a lie. And the more sincere you "act," the more your lack of sincerity will show through. In the end it's safest, and smartest, to give a personal response, to tell the panel the truth—as you see it.

CHARACTER COUNTS

"It appears that your driving record over the last several years has been less than perfect." The panel member is looking down at your application, and you can tell from her tone of voice that the last phrase—"less than perfect"—was meant to be a sarcastic understatement. You start to think through the violations you've gotten in the recent past, but you wait to respond until she asks a question. "Do you," she asks, "have a problem when you get behind the wheel?"

This is a question about your character, not about any specific traffic violation you committed. Your impulse may be to rise to your own defense: "No, I don't have any problems driving, none at all." But that's not the way to go—after all, the background check the department has done will provide the panel with the officers' reports and a record of the citations you've received. Again, making excuses for particular instances is not as important as the qualities of character you present to the panel.

So you're better off confronting the issue: "I like to drive and I'm confident at the wheel. But I have had a problem in the past when it comes to speed. And now I'm dealing with that. If I'm going to call myself a good driver—which in general, I believe I am—then I can't be getting speeding tickets. I don't want to endanger anybody's life, including my own, and that means obeying the speed limit." What does this answer tell the panel? That you recognized the problem and are making an effort to correct it. That you learned from the past and don't want to repeat it. If you really mean what you say, that shows character.

GETTING PERSONAL

As much as possible, fire departments want to know "the real you." They want to know something about your opinions, your habits and your personality—as it relates to the job, of course, not because they're snoops.

For example, there might be questions about how you'll cope with the lifestyle and working conditions of a firefighter: "How well do you function without sleep for a full day? Or on an irregular schedule, like four days on, 24 hours a day, then four days off?" They might ask you how you handle diversity—meaning, working and living with people from various ethnic and cultural backgrounds, and both females and males. This is an important issue in many fire departments. A curt "no problem" type of answer will not be as convincing as one that refers to specific recent instances, in the workplace or the community, where you cooperated and interacted successfully with a diverse population. Some answers call for specific examples, especially if this information is not stated in your application.

In some jurisdictions, you may have taken a psychological test and an interviewer may ask questions based on that. These questions could focus, for example, on your personal beliefs, attitudes or behavior. They may seem obscure—"How do you feel about the opposite sex?" Or probing—"How do you feel about your family?" The answers to these sorts of questions may only be significant in relation to the answers you gave during the psychological test. So there is no way to judge what a "correct" or even an "appropriate" answer might be. Therefore, as always, be honest. You have more to lose by trying to trick or please the panel than by answering frankly and directly.

SITUATIONAL QUESTIONS

Interview panels often ask questions in which they describe a firefighting situation that raises certain ethical or professional dilemmas. They want to get a sense of how you may respond in such a situation. Some departments ask these kinds of questions almost exclusively. Some don't ask them at all, feeling that it's hard to imagine a firefighting situation until you've been in one.

Situational questions might be more difficult to anticipate and to answer than general or personal questions, but the answering process and the principles of presentation and honesty still apply. It's a good idea to prepare for this type of question in case you're asked one like the following: "You are alone in a private house with another firefighter. You see him take a wristwatch from the top of a dresser and put it in his pocket. What do you do?" Good question. Like most ethical problems, it can be answered simply or lead to difficult choices among complicated options. In the end, you have to trust yourself and your common sense.

Another kind of scenario will place you in a firehouse situation. "You are playing handball against the firehouse wall with three members of your company. A member of the local block association walks by, and stops to criticize you, loudly, for playing a game while you're on the job. What do you do?" Let's look at several potential answers.

- Answer 1: "I'd tell the person that I am doing my job."
- Answer 2: "I'd tell the person that I am doing my job, that I live at the firehouse 24 hours a day, 4 days in a row. Just because I'm taking a little time out to play a game with members of my crew doesn't mean I'm not on the job. I mean, if I hear the bell, I'm ready to go. We all are. And we'll get the job done—don't worry about it. Of course, how I say this will depend on if I know the person or not. If they're on the block association, I've probably seen them around. I might even end up inviting them to play."
- Answer 3: "I'd explain to the person, in a calm and friendly manner, that firefighting is stressful work. An occasional game of handball lets off some of the pressure, and it helps keep us in shape. The exercise is good for us, but we're ready to go as soon as that alarm bell rings."

Answer 1, while based on truth, is rather abrupt. Answer 2 shows more thought, and some cleverness, but has a somewhat confrontational tone. The speaker tries to make up for that toward the end of the answer, but trying to change the tone leads the speaker to ramble a bit. Answer 3 gets to the point, shows thought and stays focused. It is the best of the three options in terms of answering the question. (Keep in mind, however, that this is only a model—your answers need to sound like you.)

Scenarios are also used to hypothesize emergency conditions. "You arrive at the site of a fire call and find a woman in hysterics, screaming and gesticulating out of control, in the street. What do you do?" If you are unfamiliar with such situations, being confronted with one, even in an interview, can be stressful. And that's the point. Stress is an occupational hazard in firefighting. Questions that produce stress let the panel see first-hand how you handle it. This is one reason why many jurisdictions give preference to candidates with EMT or military experience. The ability to perform under conditions of stress is one of the key worker traits in the firefighting profession, and it is important that you develop and be prepared to demonstrate this ability.

DO WHAT IT TAKES

The oral interview is a crucial step on your way to becoming a firefighter. You can and should prepare for it. So do some research both on the life and work of a firefighter. And do some research on yourself—your background, opinions, strengths and weaknesses. Self-awareness leads to self-confidence, especially in an interview situation. Seek experience in areas where you think you need it. Practice interviewing skills. Demand the best from yourself. The panel, and the profession, certainly will.

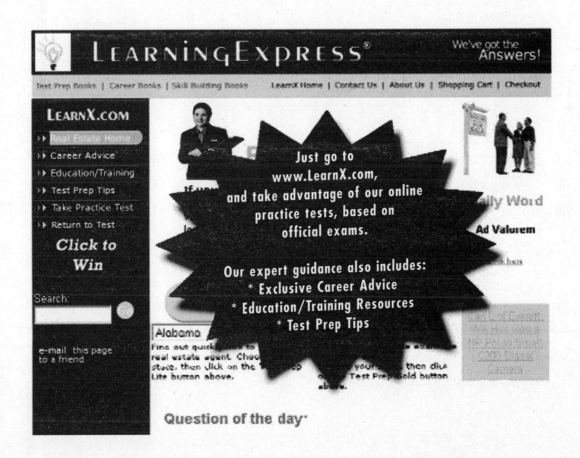